Published by Baker Academic
a division of Baker Book House Company
P.O. Box 6287, Grand Rapids, MI 49516-6287

Printed in the United States of America

Library of Congress Cataloging-in-Publication Data

Wolterstorff, Nicholas P.
    Educating for life : reflections on Christian teaching and learning / Nicholas P. Wolterstorff ; edited by Gloria Goris Stronks and Clarence W. Joldersma.
        p.   cm.
    Includes bibliographical references and index.
    ISBN 0-8010-2479-X (pbk.)
    1. Christian education—Philosophy. 2. Reformed Church—Education. 3. Church schools—United States. 4. Church schools—Canada. I. Stronks, Gloria Goris. II. Joldersma, Clarence W. III. Title.
BV1464.W65   2002
371.071—dc21   2002000685

Unless otherwise noted, Scripture is taken from the Revised Standard Version of the Bible, copyright 1946, 1952, 1971 by the Division of Christian Education of the National Council of the Churches of Christ in the USA. Used by permission.

Chapter 1 is adapted from *Curriculum: By What Standard?* (Grand Rapids: National Union of Christian Schools, 1969). Used by permission.

Chapter 3 is adapted from "Return to Basic Christian Education," *The Reformed Journal* (March/April 1978): 17–30. Used by permission of Eerdmans Publishing Company.

Chapter 4 is adapted from "Between Isolation and Accommodation," *The Banner*, 18 April 1983, 9–11. Used by permission of *The Banner*.

Chapter 10 is adapted from "Looking to the Eighties: Do Christian Schools Have a Future?" *Joy in Learning*, the newsletter of the Curriculum Development Center, fall 1979. Used by permission.

Chapter 11 is adapted from *Religion and the Schools* (Grand Rapids: Eerdmans, 1965). Used by permission of Eerdmans Publishing Company.

Chapter 12 is adapted from "Human Rights in Education: The Rights of Parents," *Whose Child Is This?* the newsletter of the Illinois Advisory Committee of Non-Public Schools, 1978.

Chapter 13 is adapted from "The Schools We Deserve," in *Schooling Christians*, ed. Stanley Hauerwas and John H. Westerhoff (Grand Rapids: Eerdmans, 1992), 3–28. Used by permission of Eerdmans Publishing Company.

For information about Baker Academic, visit our web site:
        www.bakeracademic.com

Educating for Life

Educating for Life

Reflections on Christian Teaching and Learning

Nicholas P. Wolterstorff

Edited by Gloria Goris Stronks
and Clarence W. Joldersma

 Baker Academic

A Division of Baker Book House Co
Grand Rapids, Michigan 49516

Words are for those with promises to keep.

W. H. Auden

To
Nick and Claire's grandchildren,
and to all our children's children,
who, like us, will have promises to keep
while making their own decisions
concerning Christian schooling

Contents

Part 3 Christian Education in a Pluralistic Society

Part 4 Educating for Shalom

Preface

Few people have influenced the development of Christian schools in the Reformed tradition in North America and elsewhere as much as philosopher Nicholas Wolterstorff. Christian school people who, like us, have appreciated his many appearances as keynote speaker at conferences will understand the pleasure with which we put this book together.

For thirty years, Nicholas Wolterstorff taught philosophy at Calvin College in Grand Rapids, Michigan, and during part of that time also held an appointment at the Free University of Amsterdam. Presently, he has a joint appointment in the divinity school and the philosophy and religion departments at Yale University. He has presented not only the prestigious Gifford Lectures in Scotland but also the Wilde Lectures at Oxford. In addition, he has written numerous books and articles, a selection of which can be found in the bibliography.

Throughout his illustrious career, Wolterstorff has willingly taken the time to provide needed direction for Christian schools. His work in that area has been greatly valued by teachers and administrators, many of whom have likely never read his more philosophical writings. As one high school teacher said:

I doubt that there is any reflective person who has taught in Christian schools and has not been plagued with the uncertainty that faces me in my darkest moments, that perhaps Christian schooling might not be worth all the effort and expense we are putting into it. Then Nick Wolterstorff comes to talk to us and tells us that truly *Christian* schools are enormously worthwhile, and he shows us yet one more way that we might think about them. After listening to him, I can return to my task with renewed energy and the sure confidence that what I am doing is important and worthwhile.

In 1952, while a college senior and editor of *Chimes*, the student newspaper at Calvin College, Wolterstorff reflected on the nature of Christian education. In answer to those who say that Christian education should be much like indoctrinating students into the Christian faith, he wrote an editorial telling, in part, what Christian education is *not:*

> It may seem true to you that a college is a place for people to soak up a tradition and not to learn to think, but do not suppose then that what you are proposing is Christian education. It may seem safer to you to advise your students to keep out of contact with opposing religious systems, but do not suppose then that the still-born, culture-abstracted system you present has much at all to do with Christian education. It may seem surer to you to demand of your students that they memorize a whole list of dogmatic propositions and then when questioned about their validity sneak quietly into your asylum of ignorance and say that God has not chosen to reveal the truth of what you are saying, but then never for a moment delude yourself that you are participating in Christian education. . . . A pagan educator can indoctrinate, for he has only to get the audience to assent to the principles of a man-made system. . . . Yet, to fail in the task of EDUCATION is to run the risk of placing Christian doctrine on the same level as a pagan system.[1]

What provided the foundation for this early understanding that God calls us to examine what we do with a holistic understanding of sin and its effects? In his essay "The Grace That Shaped My Life," Wolterstorff describes the people who were part of his family life in rural Minnesota, saying that they

> were and are a remarkable family: feisty, passionate, bright, loyal. Though our family lived in the village, most of the others were farmers. So after morning church they all came to our house—aunts and uncles, cousins, everybody, boisterous dozens of them. Sweets were eaten in abundance, coffee drunk; and the most dazzling intellectual experience possible for a young teenager took place. Enormous discussions and arguments erupted, no predicting about what: about the sermon, about theology, about poli-

tics, about farming practices, about music, about why there weren't as many fish in the lakes, about what building the dam in South Dakota would do to the Indians, about the local schools, about the mayor, about the village police officer, about the Dutch Festival, about Hubert Humphrey. Everyone took part who was capable of taking part—men, women, teenagers, grandparents.[2]

At the very center of the family Wolterstorff describes was a piety centered on the Bible:

> Centered not on experience, and not on the liturgy, but on the Bible; for those themselves were seen as shaped by the Bible. Christian experience was the experience of appropriating the Bible, the experience of allowing the Bible to shape one's imagination and emotion and perception and interpretation and action. . . . Here one learned what God had done and said, in creation and for our salvation. . . . The practice of the tradition taught without telling me that the Bible had to be interpreted; one could not just read it and let the meaning sink in. I was aware that I was being inducted into one among other patterns of interpretation, the pattern encapsulated in the Heidelberg Catechism.[3]

He then goes on to explain how that tradition influenced him:

> The tradition operated with a unique dialectic of affirmation, negation, and redemptive activity. . . . The tradition operated also with a holistic understanding of sin and its effects, of faith and of redemption. By no means was everything in society, culture and personal existence seen as evil; much, as I have just remarked, was apprehended as good. The holistic view of sin and its effects instead took the form of resisting all attempts to draw lines between some area of human existence where sin has an effect and some area where it does not. The intuitive impulse of the person reared in the Reformed tradition is to see sin and its effects as leaping over all such boundaries. To the medievals who suggested that sin affects our will but not our reason, the Reformed person says that it affects our reason as well. To the Romantics who assume that it affects our technology but not our art, the Reformed person says it affects art too.
>   . . . The idea is not, once again, that everything in the life of the believer is different. The idea is rather that no dimension of life is closed off to the transforming power of the Spirit—since no dimension of life is closed off to the ravages of sin. . . . The scope of divine redemption is not just the saving of lost souls but the renewal of life—and more even than that: the renewal of all creation. Redemption is for flourishing.
>   . . . The grace of God that shapes one's life came to me in the form of induction into this tradition. That induction into tradition should be an instrument of grace is a claim deeply alien to modernity. Tradition is usually seen as a burden, not grace. But so it was in my case. If you ask me

who I am, I reply: I am one who was bequeathed the Reformed tradition of Christianity.[4]

Wolterstorff describes being a student at Calvin College as entering a world of dazzling brightness and being at a place where students were as energized and instructed by each other as by teachers. He tells how important were his interactions with William Harry Jellema, Alvin Plantinga, and others:

> Here too nobody was offering evidences for the truth of Christianity, arguments for the inspiration of Scripture, proofs for the resurrection of Jesus, best explanation accounts of Christian faith. The challenge set before us was to interpret the world, culture and society in the light of Scripture— to describe how things look when seen in Christian perspective, to say how they appear when the light of the gospel is shed on them.[5]

Wolterstorff speaks with gratitude of the thirty years he spent as a faculty member at that college and says that the Calvin community was for him an "instrument of grace, supporting, encouraging, chastising, disciplining." He describes with great passion his work for the cause of suffering people, whether they were Palestinians or South Africans, and the effect of being confronted with the faces and voices of people suffering injustice.

> These experiences have evoked in me a great deal of reflection and reorientation. Justice has become for me one of the fundamental categories through which I view the world. I think of justice not so much as a virtue but as a condition of society: a society is just insofar as people enjoy what is due them—enjoy what they have a legitimate claim to. Previously the fundamental moral category for me was responsibility. Now I have come to see that the moral domain is interplay between rights and responsibilities. To the Other in my presence I have responsibilities; but also the Other in my presence comes bearing rights. The violation of moral responsibilities yields guilt; the violation of moral rights yields injury. The proper response to guilt is repentance; the proper response to moral injury is lament and outrage.[6]

And then Wolterstorff came to know pain and suffering in an even more personal way through the death of his son, Eric. His moving book about that experience, *Lament for a Son*, has found its way into the lives of thousands of people. His poignantly honest expression of his grief and confusion has helped others find ways to express their own grief and to understand that lament is also a way of living faithfully. He closes his essay on the grace that shaped his life with the following words:

God is more mysterious than I had thought—the world too. There's more to God than grace; or if it's grace to one, it's not grace to the other—grace to Israel but not grace to Jeremiah. And there's more to being human than being that point in the cosmos where God's goodness is meant to find its answer in gratitude. To be human is also this: to be that point in the cosmos where the yield of God's love is suffering.[7]

Wolterstorff's experience of personal pain and loss as well as his support of those suffering injustice have greatly shaped his outlook on life and his views of education.

In selecting essays for this book from the vast number of Wolterstorff's speeches and writings, we chose selections that speak to people today who struggle with what makes education truly Christian. Most of these selections originated as speeches, and little attempt has been made to change the rhetoric from speech to essay. Gender references reflecting language usage of an earlier time were changed to clarify meaning and to be more inclusive, but gender references to God have been kept as in the originals.

The selections as a whole are not in chronological order. However, they are in chronological order within each of the four parts. In part 1, readers will find selections that provide guidance concerning the nature of Christian education. This section includes essays concerning Christian approaches to curriculum, reminders that the goal of Christian education is Christian life and not just Christian thought, exhortations that schools must be concerned with more than the knowledge and abilities needed to live life, and explorations concerning students' tendencies to use their knowledge and abilities in living life.

The essays in part 2 depict the challenges and objections Christian schools face in a changing world, the most important of which come from within. Is it possible, without isolating students and their families from the surrounding society, to conduct genuinely alternative Christian education? Wolterstorff explains that the life for which we educate is one of responsible, worshipful, and appreciative gratitude. He then describes the conditions under which such education can flourish. This section closes with a keynote address that describes the origins of Reformed Christian schools and explains three points of crisis that these schools faced seventy-five years into their existence. Wolterstorff summarizes the Calvinistic tradition and states that it is the task of Christian schools to take the vision and give it concrete embodiment.

Part 3 contains selections concerning what Christian learning means in a pluralistic society. In these articles and speeches, Wolterstorff addresses questions such as the following: Should Christians in a pluralistic society, who insist on freedom of religion for themselves, work to protect the religious freedom of people of differing faiths, or is it their duty to work toward creating a Christian society in which the full rights of citizenship are granted only to those who affirm Christian beliefs? Must Christians isolate themselves from general culture, or is there a better way to learn and live? He describes the circumstances under which we might expect to find school systems that express alternative images for common life.

The essays in part 4 point toward the life for which we teach and the life that we exhibit in our teaching—the concepts of gratitude and justice in the theory and practice of Christian education. Wolterstorff explains that teachers can teach such concepts through discipline, modeling, and reasoning.

We are grateful to those who provided information regarding the circumstances under which the addresses were given. We are also extremely grateful to our student assistants, Carrie Pierson and Bethany Haverkamp, for their work typing manuscripts and scanning articles into the computer and for their helpful comments. We also wish to thank Robert Hosack, senior acquisitions editor at Baker Book House, for giving us the idea for the book and for encouraging us along the way. Finally, the book would not have been possible but for the generous cooperation of Nick Wolterstorff himself. At our request, he searched his files for notes and manuscripts and his memory for occasions of presentations. We praise God for the insights and direction found in these pages.

Gloria Goris Stronks
Clarence W. Joldersma

Part 1

The Nature of
Christian Education

chapter one

Curriculum

By What Standard?

Christian schools that are part of Christian Schools International (formerly the National Union of Christian Schools) existed in North America since 1852. Many of the early Dutch immigrants came to this continent in part so that they could freely educate their children in Christian schools. As a result, small Christian schools were started wherever the immigrants settled. By 1947, school leaders began to raise questions concerning Christian school philosophy and how that philosophy might shape school objectives, teaching methodology, and curriculum policies.

Christian school leaders have held differing points of view concerning curriculum. Some believe that while, intellectually, the student must come to think as God thinks, educational methods can be adopted from the public schools. Those who speak against such a view believe that separating philosophical or theological beliefs from the way teachers instruct leads to a futile endeavor. They believe that teachers should go beyond stimulating and guiding students to structuring all learning activities so that students come face to face with God's claim on their lives. Others are concerned by what they see as fundamentalist tendencies with a strong emphasis on personal commitment. Yet others warn that Christian schools are much too willing to accept parts of progressive education in the form of open classrooms, cooperative learning, multi-age approaches, and a social curriculum. Another group favors a much more rigorous academic approach with a stronger emphasis on basic skills.

In 1966, Wolterstorff was invited to speak on the topic of curriculum at the NUCS annual meeting of principals and board members. His address, "Curriculum: By What Standard?" was recognized as a new and helpful approach for the schools. In this speech, Wolterstorff says that Christians should aim to equip students for the practical business of living the Christian life. He then suggests various dimensions of the Christian life that are of special relevance when making educational decisions.

By reference to what standard, what criterion, what measuring stick should the curriculum of a school be determined? How must a school set about selecting what it will teach?

Human beings are creatures for whom education is inescapable. Their created constitution and situation in the world make learning and being taught unavoidable. Learning and being taught are ineradicable and indestructible threads in the fabric of people's existence, for people are surrounded and encompassed by change; every day brings something new under the sun that shines on human affairs. Of this change that surrounds and encompasses them, humans find that they are conscious and aware. But people are also creatures of ignorance, deeply and profoundly ignorant and unknowing of what tomorrow will bring. Thus, they learn, unavoidably and inescapably, wholly apart from whether they wish to or not, yet finding delight and satisfaction in so doing. Unlike bugs and stones, unlike God, humans learn—learn what is the case.

Humans, as well as being creatures of consciousness, are creatures of free, reasonable action. In respect to action, too, they are deeply and profoundly unknowing and ignorant. They are thrust into the world knowing how to do almost nothing. Yet in order to stay alive and reach fulfillment, they must know how to do a legion of things. Therefore, given the pressure of their situation in the world and their own inner constitution, people learn—learn how to do things. In this way, too, people are unlike bugs and stones, and unlike God.

So learning what and learning how are, for us humans, inseparable from life. Yet not all of what a person learns is inescapable, unavoidable, and determined, for we are free agents. We can set ourselves to learn; we can choose to learn. Our freedom rescues our learning from being completely inevitable and determined. But never can we merely choose to learn; always we must choose what to learn. Always we must select, for no one of us, nor all of us together, can learn everything. Omniscience is forever beyond us. If we would choose to learn at all, we must perforce prefer some knowledge to other, regret some ignorance less than other. Few of all people's responsibilities are heavier than their responsibility for their own knowledge and their own ignorance.

Not only do I decide what I shall learn, and you decide what you shall learn. Each of us also decides what the other shall learn—I what you shall learn, you, what I shall learn. We set about teaching each other. The freedom of another person, as well as my own freedom, rescues my teaching from being completely inevitable and determined. But we can also never merely choose to teach. Always we must choose what to teach. Always we must select, for no one of us can teach everything, nor can all of us together. And within what is selected, we cannot give equal emphasis to everything. Some things must be stressed and brought to the fore; others must be allowed to recede into penumbra. If we would teach at all, we must perforce prefer that our fellow human beings know certain things rather than others. Few of a person's decisions are of more consequence than the decisions as to what one shall teach to one's fellows and what one shall not. Few of a person's responsibilities are heavier than the responsibility for the knowledge and the ignorance of others.

What Is Curriculum?

A school curriculum is the outcome of decisions as to what shall be taught to our fellow human beings and what shall not be taught to them, what shall be stressed and what shall not be stressed. What we want to discuss is how, properly, to make the decisions that result in a school curriculum. From among the mass of things that can be emphasized, how is one to decide what shall be emphasized?

Of course, what often happens in schools is that nothing deserving the title "decision" is made on such matters at all. Incredible as it would surely seem to an outsider, should any discover it, teachers often have no conscious and reflective reason whatsoever for selecting one thing

to teach rather than another, no conscious and reflective reason whatsoever for emphasizing one thing rather than another. Of the actions
that human beings perform, one would surely expect teaching to be
among those done most reflectively and with the clearest perception of
goals. But what a deluded expectation, for vast numbers of teachers just
teach, teaching as they were taught, unreflectively exercising their in-
grained habits, enslaved to custom, no more deciding what to teach and
what to emphasize than the crow decides what song to sing. The thesis
that this is indefensible and irresponsible needs no defense.

Scarcely better is something else that often happens in schools: We
teachers decide to teach those things that happen to be of greatest interest to us, and we choose to emphasize those things that happen, for
whatever reason, to excite our fancy. We make of teaching a self-dis-
course—I communing with myself, permitting others to overhear. We
conduct our teaching for the sake of ourselves, giving not a fig for what
it does to students. Surely the thesis that this is indefensible and irresponsible also needs no defense.

Teaching, I suggest, must always have its face toward the students.
It must answer to their needs. It must seek an outcome, and the outcome it seeks must be an outcome with respect to the students. It must
aim for some effect, and the effect it aims for must be an effect on the
students. The curriculum of a school must be set by reference to what
one is aiming at with respect to the students. It must be determined by
reference to some conception of when one has succeeded with the students and when one has failed, when one's goals for the students have
been attained and when they have not, when the results hoped for in the
students have been secured and when they have slipped away.

Students, however, are more than students. Students are people who
happen to be spending a few of their waking hours undergoing school
education. In view of this, what I wish to suggest next is this: School
education must be of worth and significance to students in their lives
outside the school as well as inside. The needs it answers to must not
be needs confined simply to the students' hours in school. There must
be a carryover, a significant, deliberately aimed-at carryover, from life
in the classroom to life outside the classroom. The school must inculcate those excellencies that are of worth for life outside the school as
well as inside. School must not be an end in itself. Schooling must not
be undertaken just for the sake of schooling. It must be undertaken for
the sake of life as a whole. The school acts irresponsibly when the excellencies it strives to inculcate are limited in relevance to the classroom.

Perhaps this point seems utterly bland and truistic to you. Yet it seems
to me a point of immense importance for the content of school education and one repudiated in principle or practice by large numbers of

educators. It is repudiated in principle by those progressivists who insist that the school must not seek for aims outside itself but must simply provide students with an experience that in itself is of interest to them— with an engrossing slice of life no more referential in its character than any other slice out of a child's life. Equally, it is repudiated in principle by those traditionalists who contrast the world of the intellect and culture with the world of commerce and utility, insisting that the school is to concern itself solely with the former, seeking to make the student a learned and cultured person, cognizant of the best that has been thought and said, ignorant of what people must do to make a living. And it is repudiated in practice by all those of us who assume that our teaching has been successful with respect to a given student if he or she passes our test, answers our questions on the material, repeats what we have said—in short, by all those of us who slip and slide into the belief that by observing and examining a student in school we can discover whether we have been successful, by all those of us who resent the request that we show what bearing our teaching has on life outside the school. What I want to suggest is that if teaching has its proper aim, then we can never discover in school alone whether our aim has been achieved. We shall have to look at the life of the student outside the school as well.

But *which* life of the student—the future life or the present life? Is school education to be viewed as preparation or fulfillment? Should its content, its curriculum, be determined by reference to what *will be* of worth and importance to a student's future life or by reference to what *is* of worth and importance to a student's present life? Should its focus be the life and world of the adult or the life and world of the child?

It seems to me that the proper answer to this question is, "Both." School education is maimed and distorted and its effectiveness reduced when either of these is stressed to the ignoring or downplaying of the other.

It would be irresponsible, I think, for a school to provide a student with an education that did not have, as one of its aims, to prepare him or her for future, adult life. Equally, it would be futile for a school to try, for whether one likes it or not, the traits that one develops and inculcates in a student inevitably carry over beyond childhood into adult life. So the issue cannot be *whether* we should provide students with an education that is significant for their adult as well as child life. We *will* do so, unavoidably. The issue is only what *kind* of adult life we should aim to prepare students for.

But school education must also be of worth and significance for the life of the child. Children are not merely lumps of clay that we adults have the right to fashion as we please until, lo and behold, we breathe the breath of life into them when they leave our hands at commencement. School education must be of meaning and significance to the child's life as well as to the life of the adult, for in the Christian view, the child is already a person, demanding love and respect. But children's needs are not those of adults. Accordingly, love and respect must assume different forms and colors for them than they do for adults. We must, for our schools, resolutely seek for the curricula and pedagogical techniques that will make what is learned of worth and significance both to the students' present lives and to their future lives—to their lives as a whole.

At this point in our discussion, we come to an enormously important parting of the ways. What I have said so far pertains, it seems to me, to all school education—whether it be the education provided by the public school, by Reformed Christian schools, by Catholic Christian schools, or whatever. But now the road before us has many forks, and we must choose which to travel. The aim of the school, I have suggested, must be to equip the child for life—for life outside the school as well as inside, for life in the future as well as the present. But people do not agree on what human life should be. They are of different minds as to the true, the genuine, the authentic, the well-formed human life. And so they are of different minds as to what, concretely, should be aimed at in school. At this juncture in our discussion, then, we must make a choice. We cannot, any further, discuss curriculum for the schools generally. We can only discuss curriculum appropriate to this, or that, perception of authentic human existence.

You and I are interested in Reformed Christian schools. We are interested in a school educational program that aims to equip children for the Christian life, as this is understood by Reformed Christians. Thus, our question becomes, How is one to go about determining the curriculum for such a school? What considerations are relevant? What consequences for the curriculum flow from the aim of equipping children to live the Christian life?

Determining Curriculum for a Christian School

Suppose someone says that the Christian school should eliminate all teaching of sport. Is he right or wrong? Suppose he says that the Christian school should concentrate on the humane subjects, consigning the natural sciences and mathematics to a secondary position in the curriculum. Is he right or wrong? Suppose someone says that the Christian school should teach the Bible and only as much else as is necessary to preach the biblical message to others. Is she right or wrong? Suppose she says that history has no place in the Christian school. Is she right or wrong? Suppose others say that literature should be studied, but only Christian literature; art, but only Christian art. Are they right or wrong? Suppose they say that painting and sculpting and singing and playing of musical instruments have no place in the Christian school. Are they right or wrong?

I am sure that you all have views, very definite views at that, on these matters. But could you justify them by reference to the proper aim of Christian school education? Are your curricular convictions the result of a clear perception of the nature of the Christian life and a resolute, imaginative, courageous attempt to make the curriculum of the Christian school serve the end of equipping students for living that Christian life?

Let us delineate some of the principal features of the Christian life and draw out a few of their implications for the formation of a Christian school curriculum.

The Christian life, in the first place, is the life of a person, a human being. I dare say that this seems utterly obvious to you. Let me state, however, the contrast of what I have in mind; and then, perhaps, it will seem less obvious. The Christian life is not the life of a pure spiritual soul that happens, for some God-alone-known reason, to be attached to a body. It is not the life of a mind, a rational-moral principle, that happens to be imprisoned in a chunk of flesh. Rather, it is the life of creatures who are soul *and* body, inner person *and* outer person, conscious personal being *and* biological being.

It was Plato's view that what I am, and what you are, is simply a rational, moral soul. Thus, strictly speaking, I do not walk, I do not swim, I do not eat, I have no weight, no size. I am, however, attached to a body that does and has all these things. This attachment to the body is really a kind of imprisonment. It is a sentence on me, a judgment, a punishment. In addition, the body is the source of evil in human affairs. Therefore, a person's chief duty is to die away from the body, repudiate its desires, stifle and repress its drives. Death is a person's friend. The mind, on the other hand, is the source of good in human affairs. The person's duty is to cultivate the life of the mind.

The Platonic understanding of what we are has been enormously influential in Western thought and culture. It has lodged itself firmly in Christian as well as non-Christian patterns of thought. Yet it is, at almost every juncture, an antibiblical concept. There is nothing in the biblical perspective to the effect that we are really angels who have been attached to bodies. We are, on the contrary, physical and biological creatures who are at the same time conscious, personal creatures. There is nothing in the biblical perspective to the effect that this physical and biological existence of ours is a curse and a punishment and that we should long for death. On the contrary, life is a great and good gift, whereas death is a curse and a punishment, not at all a friend, but rather the last enemy to be overcome. There is nothing in the biblical perspective to the effect that a person's root sin lies in succumbing to the desires of the body. On the contrary, one's root sin lies in alienation from God and other humans, an alienation that is effected and manifested throughout one's existence, personal as well as bodily.

Accordingly, Christian education must not be conceived of as the development of the rational and intellectual capacities in a student, as the cultivation of the life of the mind. Not that it should not do this, for we are, after all, creatures capable of rational thought. But this cannot be its full character. A curriculum that operates on the assumption that students are nothing but rational, moral souls, or on the assumption that the only capacities genuinely worth cultivation in students are the rational-moral capacities, is not a curriculum for Christian education. Christian education must educate for the full life of the person.

I am sure that you are better able than I am to trace out all the concrete curricular implications of this position. But one example of what it will certainly mean, I think, is that a physical education program—conceived as a program designed to educate students in the proper use of the body throughout life—will occupy a significant place in the curriculum of a Christian school.

The Christian life is, second, the life of faith, by which I mean not that it is a life that includes *faith, but that* as a whole *it is the life of faith.* A curriculum for Christian education will aim at equipping students to live the life of faith.

Seen in the biblical perspective, the situation of every person is a confrontation between God and humans. Through his works and deeds, God speaks to people. He sends forth his Word. And people, through *their* works and deeds, answer. God asks of people that there be fellowship with him—fellowship based on an honest and humble acknowledgment of the relative positions of both. To this call, a person answers yes or no, affirmatively or negatively. The Bible calls one's affirmative answer to God's call for fellowship "faith" or "belief." One's negative answer is called "unbelief." The Bible sees the issue of belief or unbelief as the basic issue of human life. One's choice has ramifications throughout one's existence. It determines, and is exercised in, one's entire way of life.

If we are to comprehend at all how faith and life can be related in this comprehensive manner, rather than merely to accept it as a bit of pious mystification, it is imperative that we see clearly what faith is. What model—to borrow a term from the scientists and the mathematicians—shall we use in thinking about faith?

You are all aware of the fact that some things we know, whereas some things we merely believe. I know that I am now standing and talking. On the other hand, I believe, without really knowing, that my car will start when I am ready to leave here today. This familiar contrast between things that we know and things that we merely believe has played a fundamental role in the thought of Christians about the Christian life. Faith has been thought of as a belief in propositions that we do not know, belief in propositions on the basis of authority rather than evidence. Thomas Aquinas, in fact, defines faith this way: Faith is assent to divinely revealed propositions. Now I do not deny that living the Christian life entails believing various propositions. But to see the faith to which God calls us as consisting, in its essence, of assent to propositions is to commit a radical, wrenching distortion of the Christian proclamation. It is to make the gospel a philosophy, an intellectual system. It is to make utterly obscure the connection between faith and life.

How, then, ought we to think of faith? I suggest that the model we must have in mind is not that of believing propositions but rather that of believing in a person. You all know, from your own experience, what it is to believe in a person. It is to trust him, to be loyal to him, to serve him, to give one's allegiance to him, to be willing to work for him, to place one's confidence in him. And you also know, from your own experience, how pervasively one's allegiance to a person can affect one's whole life. When faith is conceived of as belief in a person, there is no problem with the connection between faith and life, for it is with one's life that one exercises such faith.

This is the model we must use in thinking of the faith that is the focus of the Christian life. The object of such faith is not propositions. It is rather a personal God. To have faith in this personal God is not to believe various propositions about God. It is rather to give God one's loyalty, one's allegiance, one's service, one's confidence, one's trust, one's obedience. The call to faith is the call to be trusting, loyal, devoted, obedient servants of God.

What is it like to be such a person? It is to be like Jesus of Nazareth. He was the completely obedient man. He was the man who gave God undiluted service. Thus, it is in him that God's Word is focused. In him, preeminently, we see what it is to reply to God's call for fellowship with the answer of faith. So it is, in this new day of the Lord, that to have faith in God is to have faith in Jesus Christ. To believe in God is to become one of Jesus' band of followers. It is to become one of his disciples. For us, now, the call to faith is the call to be disciples of Jesus in our entire lives. It is the call to be conformed to his model in the whole of our existence—in the whole framework of our beliefs, in the whole complex of our feelings and attitudes, in the whole gamut of our actions.

Insofar, then, as Christian education fails to educate for comprehensive faith, insofar as it fails to educate for life discipleship, it fails to be fully Christian education. For example, insofar as it educates for the passive contemplation of God rather than the active service of God, it fails to reach its true end. Insofar as it confines its Christian content to separate courses in the curriculum rather than seeing all courses in Christian perspective, it fails to reach its true end. It is not faith added to understanding that we are after; it is not faith seeking understanding that we are after. Rather, it is faith realized in life.

Again, you are probably better fitted than I am to see the concrete curricular implications of this position. But let me point out two things that seem to me to flow from it. In the first place, in social studies courses there must be a good deal of emphasis on the Christian approach to contemporary social issues. I remember that in my own social studies courses in a Christian high school, we studied a good deal about such phenomena as introversion and nomadism. But there was nothing at all about the racial problem seen in Christian perspective, nothing about family relations seen in Christian perspective, nothing about a Christian view of work and recreation and private property and the welfare state. In short, my fellow students and I were not very well equipped for living the life of faith.

Second, in all the courses in which the works and institutions of people are studied, there must, I think, be a persistent effort to show students how the diverse responses of humans to God become articulated in their cultural endeavors. In literature, for example, we must try to penetrate beneath the surface of rhymes and rhythms to perceive the ultimate loyalties and fundamental perspectives that are there at work.

The Christian life, in the third place, is the life of someone who is a member of the Christian community. It is not the life of an isolated self-sufficient individual. Accordingly, Christian education must aim at equipping students to be members of the community of believers.

A person, in becoming a disciple of Christ, takes her place as an organic member of the community of believers, of the household of faith. The restoration of harmony between a person and God is inseparable from the restoration of harmony between one person and another. The church, understood not as the ecclesiastical institution but rather as the fellowship of believers, is always the context and the fulfillment of the Christian life.

The bonds uniting this community of believers are not psychological bonds; the church is scarcely a group of people all of whom like each other. The bonds are not social bonds; kings and commoners, wealthy and poor, ascetics and harlots, all are present. The bonds are rather the bonds of sharing a common faith and depending on each other for the performance of a common task.

The Christian community consists of those who have made Christ their Lord. They have renounced their own pretensions to sovereignty and sworn allegiance to a common master. They have jointly confessed that it is in love and fellowship that people realize their true nature and find fulfillment. They are united in the focal point of their lives.

But they are also united by virtue of the task that they must jointly perform. Christ has departed from his earthly existence. It now remains to his followers to be a light in a darkened world, a healing balm in a diseased age—in short, to witness to the world of the renewed life available to humans in Christ. This they do by trying to live that renewed life. But St. Paul, especially, makes it clear that no one can do this fully alone. The talents and the skills of each are limited, and only in cooperative endeavor can the task of the Christian on earth, in its full scope, be fulfilled. St. Paul compared the fellowship of believers to a republic, which he called the city of God. In this city, all the citizens together, united by a common love and mutual need, strive to bring the whole realm of legitimate human activity into captivity to Christ. All together, each doing his or her particular task, they strive to make Christ the Lord in every legitimate area of human life.

Christian education, accordingly, must be viewed as a project of the Christian community, designed to train its young members to become mature citizens of the community, so that the community may perform its full-orbed task on earth. The goals of Christian education must always be pursued in reference to the multiform needs of the Christian community for the fulfillment of its program on earth.

One consequence of this position for the curriculum is, it seems to me, that we must attempt to make students aware both of Christian tradition and of contemporary Christian thought and activity, for it is imperative that the school do all it appropriately can to ensure that there be genuine understanding among the various members of the community. And in speaking of the Christian community here, I mean the Christian community as a whole, in all its ecclesiastical divisions. The Christian school must not be guilty of perpetuating or increasing the inability of Christians to understand each other.

Another consequence is that we must seek to develop that which is unique in each student. We must not try to turn out students from a common mold. Christian education has suffered immensely from the pressures of conformity. In the Christian community, where people ought to be rejoicing in their freedom, they have instead suffered under the tyranny of social conformity and then, in hostility, have brought the same pressures to bear on others. Our schools must lend every effort to the elimination of such pressures. They must develop and encourage and prize that which is unique in each student. The body of Christians is a community, an organism. It is not a collectivity of identical atoms.

Yet another consequence is that our curriculum must not exalt some professions at the expense of others—the life of the scholar and the minister, say, above all others. In the Christian community, there are no inferior and no superior occupations. Every occupation is a vocation, a calling. It is only by diverse specialization of its various members that the Christian community can carry out its full program. Thus, Christian schools must beware of becoming college prep schools. The curriculum of Christian schools must equip students for their future lives no matter what occupations they eventually choose.

The Christian life, fourth, is a life that is to be lived in the midst of ordinary human society. The body of Christians is not to take flight from the society in which it finds itself; rather, it is to exercise its common faith in the midst of that society. Accordingly, Christian education must equip students for life in contemporary society.

For one thing, flight never does any good. The world is within as well as without. "That which I would not, that I do." But also, to take flight is to fail to live fully the Christian life. We have said it is the task of the Christian community to be a witness to the world of the renewed life available to humans in Christ. To some extent the church, by sending out missionaries and evangelists, has always recognized this. But if our earlier point is correct, that in Christ we find a new life and not just a new set of dogmatic beliefs and ritual practices, then the church can never identify its witness with its sending out of missionaries and evangelists. On the contrary, Christian life and Christian witness, Christian vocation and Christian mission will have to be seen as opposite sides of the very same coin. And since our witness must be in the world, so must be our life. The community of believers lives not for its own sake; it lives for the sake of the world. As Christ was a servant to us, so we are to be a community of servants to those around us. We are called to follow Christ on all the concrete roads and into all the grimy houses of our civilization, being of loving service to others—giving clothes where clothes are needed, giving water to the thirsty, healing the sick, giving comfort to those of troubled spirit, aiding those who are victims of the law, freeing people from false gods, shedding the light of truth on the world around us, teaching the ignorant, proclaiming that there is freedom. We are called, in short, to seek the welfare of others. We are called to serve others. This is our life, and in being our life, it is our witness. When the Christian life is lived in isolation, so that it is no longer a witness, then it is no longer the Christian life. It is no longer the life of service to God and others.

Christian education, accordingly, must not be based on those with-drawal tendencies that have so often invaded the church. Equally, it must not be based on accommodation tendencies. Rather, the aim of Christian education must be to prepare students to live the Christian life in contemporary society. This means that they must understand this society: its sources and roots, its values, its aims and ideals, its alle-giances. Hemingway must be read; Stravinsky and jazz must be heard; Picasso and Dubuffet must be viewed. This is not to say, of course, that students must be dropped into this forest without a guide. But the Chris-tian school, without flinching, must acquaint students with the world in which they will have to live out their lives. There can be no denying that this is a dangerous business. To acquaint students with the ulti-mate loyalties and allegiances of contemporary people in their cultural manifestations is to run the risk of their succumbing to the beckoning attractiveness of such things. But Christians know their business.

The Christian life, finally, is a life engaged in helping to carry out the task of cultural dominion. The legitimate tasks of the Christian com-munity are not just those of preaching the gospel, relieving suffering, and doing whatever may be necessary to stay alive. The Christian school must take the whole realm of human culture for its domain.

Philosophers, since the time of the Greeks, have sought for what is most important and significant about human beings. They have sought to find in people the capacity that distinguishes them from the creatures surrounding them and the exercise of which gives to human life its chief meaning and significance. Some have seen the capacity for reason as being this; others, the capacity for art; yet others, the capacity for lan-guage. What is striking about the biblical concept of human beings, from the opening chapter of Genesis onward, is that it shuns this quest altogether, for, according to it, what is distinct about humans, gives to human life worth and meaning, is not some capacity in humans. Rather, it is a task assigned to humans—assigned to humans by God. Of course, what is thereby presupposed is the presence in people of various capac-ities that make possible the carrying out of this task. Yet according to the biblical perspective, what is unique and significant about human beings is that to them and to them alone is assigned the task of putting all creation at their service in living a life of fellowship with God and neighbor. People are not to worship and fear their surroundings. They are to make use of them. The writer of the first chapter of Genesis puts it this way: "God said, 'Let us make man in our image, after our like-ness; and let them have dominion over the fish of the sea, and over the birds of the air, and over the cattle, and over all the earth, and over creep-ing things that creep upon the earth'" (v. 26). And the psalmist expresses the same line of thought in these words: "Thou hast given him dominion over the works of thy hands; thou hast put all things under his feet" (8:6).

There have been those in the Christian community, almost from the beginning, who thought they perceived an antithesis between Christ and culture. They thought that the sole tasks permitted a Christian beyond those necessary for continued existence are the proclamation of the gospel and the performance of simple acts of mercy. They thought they had to choose between Christ and culture. Even the great Augustine, for example, insisted that humans ought to turn their eyes away from this changing, mutable world and, insofar as possible, focus their gaze solely on the eternal and immutable God revealed in Christ. And Tertullian was so impressed with the way in which culture had been laid at the altar of false gods that, rather than saying it ought to be rededicated to Christ, he said we ought to keep ourselves separate from all but the most rudimentary cultural endeavors. I think it is clear, however, that this is a distortion of biblical thought. Christ did not abrogate the God-given task of having dominion. The redemption of people in Christ is the restoration of God's creation to its intended ends. The life of the redeemed is a life of serving God in the whole range of cultural tasks. Not Christ or culture. Not even Christ and culture. Christ *through* culture is what we must seek.

Thus, any curriculum founded on a dichotomy and disjunction between Christ and culture, between serving God and having dominion, is not a Christian curriculum. Any curriculum that teaches the Bible and only as much else as is necessary to stay alive and proclaim the gospel is not a Christian curriculum. Mathematics and natural science belong in the curriculum of the Christian school as surely as do theology and moral instruction, for the task of the Christian community in this world is to build a Christian culture, different members of the community specializing in the performance of different aspects of this whole task.

An important consequence of this for the curriculum and the pedagogy of schools is, it seems to me, that we must lay a heavy stress on creativity. By this I do not mean that we must seek to make every student an artist. Rather, I mean that instead of merely lecturing and drilling our students, we must encourage them to discuss; instead of giving them pat answers to every social problem that the Christian faces, we must encourage them to think matters through; instead of asking them to color paper plates for their mothers in art classes, we must get them to express their feelings and ideas about the gospel and life with the media of the artist. In science we must encourage them to compose experiments; in biblical studies we must get them to think through the biblical message for themselves; and throughout the curriculum we must avoid merely acquainting our students with what has been thought and said and done by others and get them to think and speak and act for themselves, as Christians. It is nothing but a pious wish and a grossly unwarranted hope that students trained to be passive and noncreative in school will suddenly, upon graduation, actively contribute to the formation of Christian culture.

Today, I have made but one point. It is this: The curriculum of a Christian education is for Christian life. It is not for the training of theological sophisticates, not for the continuation of the evangelical churches, not for the preservation of Christian enclaves, not for getting to heaven, not for service to the state, not for defeating the communists, not for preserving the United States or Canada, not for life adjustment, not for cultivating the life of the mind, not for producing learned and cultured people. Christian education is for Christian life.

chapter two

Crucial Curriculum Concerns

Remembering the impact of the address "Curriculum: By What Standard?" the Association of Christian School Administrators asked Wolterstorff to speak to them at their conference held in Philadelphia in 1969. Specifically, they requested that he address the topic "Crucial Curriculum Concerns." He began his address by reminding his listeners that parents have the right and responsibility before God to see to the education of their children. But when that authority to educate has been delegated to the school, the teacher, because of educational competence, has the duty before God to make decisions on the basis of that competence. Wolterstorff described how this might be played out in three crucial areas of the school: (1) the so-called extracurricular program, (2) the literature selected for the curriculum, and (3) instruction concerning creation and evolution.

One of the most pervasive features of our human existence is the breach between our actions and our stated aims. Sometimes this breach arises because we never intend that the aims we profess should guide our actions. Just as often it arises not out of any such lack of integrity but out of the fact that our aims are such that it is impossible even for the person of best will to guide his actions by them. Often this happens because our aims are designed for purposes other than that of guiding our actions.

This latter sort of breach between aims and practice, prominent in human affairs generally, is also found in the Christian day-school movement. In my judgment, its presence in the movement constitutes one of the most important reasons why the movement has not been more effective than it has been. Repeatedly, the aims of the movement have been stated in heavily pious or theological language. Then, when educators have gotten around to making the curricular and pedagogical decisions that go into the operation of a school, they have discovered that these statements of aim give no practical guidance for the making of decisions.

I understand, I think, why the aims of the movement have been thus stated. Sometimes it was because the outlook being expressed was actually a pietistic or theologistic outlook. But often it was because the only language available to the people for expressing their religious outlook was the language of simple devotion or of theological discourse. The people who founded and supported these schools understood such language. It was, for them, language that expressed their fundamental religious motivations for founding these schools, motivations that were not themselves either narrowly pietistic or narrowly theologistic. It was, for them, language expressive of a comprehensive religious vision. Most of them never supposed that it was anything more than this. Most of them did not suppose that it was enough to give concrete guidance to educators in the making of curricular and pedagogical decisions.

So it is primarily the fault of us educators that we have, all these years, been limping along with statements of aims that give no guidance in the making of practical decisions. It is primarily the fault of us educators that the curricular and pedagogical decisions we have had to make were not made by reference to any coherent and applicable policy. Unless aims are aims for curriculum and pedagogy, they are not educational aims. What we badly need are formulations of educational aims. Unless we have these, our aims and our curriculum and pedagogy simply fall apart from each other.

It was convictions along these lines that underlay the address I gave to your body a few years ago on the topic "Curriculum: By What Standard?" I suggested there that curricular decisions have to be made by reference to what it is that we are aiming at for our students. Then I went on to propose some aims for Christian education that I hoped were broad enough to be comprehensive and yet concrete enough to enable us to make decisions thereby. My fundamental thought was that the Christian school should aim to equip students for the practical business of living the Christian life. I suggested various dimensions of the Christian life that seemed to me of special relevance to the making of educational decisions.

Curriculum and Controversy

Today you have asked me to address you on the topic "Crucial Curriculum Concerns." Now, I know that not all crucial curriculum concerns are *controversial* curriculum concerns. Yet in thinking about the topic, I began to reflect on the matter of controversy and curriculum. These reflections led me to the conclusion that there is at least one crucial dimension of curricular decision to which I failed to call your attention in that earlier address. I now think that a school's program cannot be settled *solely* by a consideration of educational aims. That is, I am still convinced, the basic and most important consideration. But it is not, I am now convinced, the exclusive one. If a Christian school, or any school for that matter, has a magnificent educational program finely attuned to its stated aims, but it cannot get its constituency to support it in implementing that program, then obviously the school is going to have to make some changes in its program. A profitable discussion of crucial curricular concerns, therefore, demands some understanding of the complex factors introduced into the making of curricular decisions by the fact that the school is a social institution whose continued existence depends on the support of its constituents.

It is the conviction of the Christian day-school movement that parents have the right and the responsibility, before God and humans, to see to it that their children are educated and to determine the fundamental direction of this education. If parents do not carry out their obligations in this area, then the state has the right and the duty to intervene, for then the public welfare as well as the welfare of the individual child is threatened. Still, the basic right and responsibility for a child's education inhere in the parents.

But parents find, for many reasons, that they cannot themselves fully educate their children. Accordingly, schools are established for the purpose of doing so. In the case of the Christian day-school, these schools are established by men and women who have a common religious vision that they want articulated in the education of their children.

Seen from this side, the school is clearly a service institution with authority delegated to it on account of its educational competence. Its purpose is to be of service to society, or in the case of the Christian day-school, to a religiously unified segment of society. Its purpose is to carry out, for parents, their God-given task of educating the young. If the school fails in that purpose, then the ground for delegating authority to it can be rescinded. Then the responsible parent must look elsewhere.

But there is another side to the matter as well. What justifies the delegation of authority to the school is the educational competence of its staff. And what goes with competence is rightful authority. Teachers, because of their educational competence, have the right to be heard on educational matters. Not only that, they have the duty to speak. I know that these are unpopular sentiments in our populist society. But the educational decisions that a school makes ought to be made on the basis of the competence of its personnel, not on the basis of the likes and dislikes of its constituents. The constituents have the duty to respect such a decision, because of the competence underlying it. The teacher has a vocation, in society and before God. No one has the right to abuse that vocation. Everyone has the duty to respect it.

It is easy to see that, in our world of perversion and frailty, such a situation is filled with potential for conflict. Average parents lack educational competence. That is why they send their child off to school. Yet they cannot relinquish the duty to see to it that their child is educated competently and, if they are Christians, that the overall perspective of the child's education is patterned by Christian commitment and vision. This demands some judgment on the part of parents concerning competence, for not all education that goes on in schools is competent. And not all education that goes on in schools called "Christian" is patterned by the Christian faith.

On the other hand, the school has the duty, given the educational competence of its staff, to educate the students as *it* thinks best, not as the public thinks best. Yet it has to bear in mind that it must not only merit the loyalty but actually secure the loyalty of the parents, or there will be no school at all. In the case of a Christian school, it must bear in mind that it must educate in accord with the fundamental religious vision of the parents.

I am convinced that there can be a healthy relationship between a Christian school and its constituency only if there is a fundamental mutual understanding of and respect for this relationship. A community will not have a loyal and responsible Christian school unless it relentlessly demands educational competence in the implementing of the Christian vision, and unless it gives to those who are competent the freedom to act on their decisions. And a Christian school will not have a loyal and responsible constituency unless it relentlessly strives to serve its constituency by providing as competent an education within the Christian vision as it can and by constantly listening for the word of suggestion or criticism that will bring mistakes to light. Only when these conditions exist will there be a mutual loyalty. And mutual loyalty there must be. The community may not ask that the school be loyal to it unless it reciprocates. The school may not ask that the community be loyal to it unless it reciprocates.

But even when mutual loyalty exists, there will be controversies. Often these arise from the failure of parents to understand what the school is doing. The best way to handle and even avoid these controversies is for the school to conduct a systematic program of adult education, explaining to the parents what it is doing and why. I know all too many school systems that tell the parents as little as possible and then complain bitterly when some parents venture criticisms. One of the most important things I have to say to you today is this: Every school must explain itself to the parents. There must be no program of education for children without a corresponding educational program for parents. Especially in our day, when educational concepts change with great rapidity, this is absolutely imperative. The school cannot maintain itself as a vital social institution unless it understands its constituents and is understood by them.

But sometimes controversies between the school and its constituency arise not from misunderstandings but from disagreements, such disagreements usually being reflected within the community and not merely between the community and the school. What is to be done when the source of controversy surrounding the Christian day-school is really the presence of religious tensions and disagreements between the school and some part of its community, and within the community sponsoring the school? This, I think, is really the case with respect to two of the three crucial curricular areas that I will analyze shortly. To this problem I am sure that you have no cure-all. Neither have I. We would be seriously deluded if we thought that the school could be free of such tensions. When religious disagreements are the source of controversy, the school must not try to ignore this fact, nor must it act as if it has the final right to decide such issues. Rather, together we must try to understand each other, not riding roughshod over each other's convictions, working for agreement, and in the meanwhile searching for compromises with which both parties can live.

Remember, though, that controversy is not always bad. There is constructive as well as destructive controversy. The school that engenders no controversy is dead. The successful school administrator is not the one who prevents all controversy but the one who keeps the controversies surrounding the school from crossing that fine line that separates the constructive from the destructive.

The So-called Extracurricular Program

With these comments, along with that earlier address of mine, as background, I turn to an analysis of three crucial areas of the school program, beginning with the so-called extracurricular program of the school. Usually, this program does not generate controversies that threaten to be destructive. Yet I suspect that it is especially over this area that administrators have guilty consciences. They are often at a loss to discern any real principles to help them make decisions here, while at the same time they are under constant pressure to make decisions, usually in the direction of expanding this part of the school program. But it does not take much discernment to see that if one goes far in the direction of expanding the extracurricular program, the time and the interests of all will be distracted from more central parts of the school's program.

Some distinctions are in order here. Different parts of a school's extracurricular program have different purposes, and it will be essential, for a clear discussion, to make some grouping.

In the first place, schools sponsor various activities in which their students take part in some sort of public performance. They may be competitive performances: debate or speech contests, essay contests, athletic contests, musical contests, art contests, science contests, and so on. Or they may be noncompetitive in nature, intended for the appreciation of the public: plays, concerts, art displays, and so on.

I think a number of principles can be brought to bear in deciding whether to include such activities in the program of a Christian school. I begin with the observation that such activities can be and usually are tremendous builders of spirit, interest, and loyalty among all those connected with the school—students, teachers, and constituents. I am aware that academic people are often immensely scornful of them on that account. They seem to me, however, to be of great importance to a school, simply because the school, as a social institution, depends for its continuation and its success on its ability to attract the interest and the loyalty of all parties concerned. When institutions no longer attract interest and loyalty, they die. One can respond by saying that students, teachers, and constituents ought to be interested in and loyal to a school just because it teaches reading and arithmetic competently. Indeed, they ought to be. And one can respond by saying that students, teachers, and constituents ought to be interested in and loyal to a Christian school just because it does a competent job of implementing the Christian vision in the classroom. Indeed, they ought to be. But such responses strike me as singularly unresponsive to the psychology of human beings.

Some additional, qualifying comments are in order, however. For one thing, I think a school should do what it can to make these public performance activities reflective of its own sense of educational priorities. It is after all *school* spirit that needs building, not athletic club spirit. It is loyalty to a school that we want, not to a gymnastic organization. Distortion is inevitably produced, up and down the line, if the public performances that chiefly engender enthusiasm for a school are in areas that constitute only minor parts of the school's educational program. I am wistfully aware that mathematics contests are never going to engender the enthusiasm that athletic contests do. Yet I think administrators should do whatever they can to redress the imbalance and to make the public performances on the part of their students somewhat reflective of the school's sense of educational priorities.

Another principle I want to suggest is this: Every student performance, in whatever area, should be only a capstone on a school-wide program in that area. It is unfair to the student body generally when the school's entire concern with athletics and physical education is concentrated on its interscholastic athletic contests. It is unfair to the student body generally when the school's entire concern with music is concentrated on public performances by its choir and bands. It is unfair to the student body generally when the school's entire concern with speech is concentrated on interscholastic debate and forensic contests. Every student in the Christian school deserves instruction in athletics, in music, in speech. If, having such school-wide programs, one then finds that spirit is built up by having the best students in these various programs give public performances—fine. But all too often the lure of public performance is so great that the school concentrates all its attention on the elite and ignores the others. Such elitism has no place in a Christian school.

Third, whenever possible, student performances should themselves be educational for the participants. Suppose such performances really are, as I have suggested, capstones on a school-wide educational program. Surely the capstone ought not to be wholly noneducational, aimed only at the plaudits of the crowd. Choir directors should have an educational program in mind for their choir members. Directors should not merely use music they think the public will like and then train students like automata to sing the notes. It is ironic but true that in some schools the choir members receive the poorest education in music.

Often another phase of a school's extracurricular program consists of making available to limited groups of students an educational experience that is not required of all. Students with special interests, students of high ability, students from deprived backgrounds, students of low academic ability—it is for these that many parts of a school's extracurricular programs are planned. Surely this is all to the good. The Christian school must *individualize* its education in so far as it is possible. Extracurricular programs offer splendid opportunities for efforts along these lines.

Finally, one finds in the extracurricular program of most schools such activities as working on school newspapers, working on school annuals, participating in student government, and putting on student parties. I know it has been argued for every one of these that those who participate learn something worthwhile. But only an educator who has lost a sense of balance would seriously argue that the main reasons for having a school party is that it is an educational experience. School parties arise out of the fact that people who have worked closely together want some occasion on which they can simply enjoy each other's company. As such, a party can and often does make a significant contribution to the spirit of all those involved. I think parties ought to be appreciated and encouraged just on that account: because they are an expression and encouragement of the intimacy that working together in a school involves. It is, of course, true that working on a school newspaper or participating in the student government is educationally significant. But once again, this does not strike me as the *main* purpose of such ventures. One has a school newspaper and student government just because the school as an institution works better with them, and this is justification enough.

You may think that I, by appealing repeatedly to the importance of activities designed to secure the continuation of the school as a vital social institution, have given a rather freewheeling justification for extracurricular activities. Perhaps I have. I see nothing especially alarming in that. Not every one of a school's activities needs or should have a direct educational point, any more than every one of a legislature's activities needs to have a direct legislative point. Some of them have their rationale just in the continuation and the vigor of the institution. I know there is enormous suspicion in our land today as to the value of institutions and of loyalty to institutions. But I find it impossible to imagine that we could carry on our human tasks without institutions and without loyalties to them. The existence of social institutions is not a mark of disobedience but of obedience to God. The relevant questions to ask of institutions are whether they satisfy or frustrate the fulfillment of our tasks and whether they merit or merely capture our loyalty.

Perhaps one last point should be added, however: The school exists to educate children. It does not exist to perpetuate itself. When so much of a school's time and energy go into activities whose main purpose is to keep the school alive and vigorous as an institution that its strictly educational program suffers, then we are being victimized by our own institution. At that point, an institution has turned into an establishment. It then must either be reformed or put out of its misery.

Controversy Concerning Selection of Literature

When we consider literature in the curriculum, we come upon complex issues that engender controversy between almost every Christian school and some part of its constituency. Let us see if we can arrive at some understanding of the typical roots of such controversies and how they ought to be handled.

Why have literature in the curriculum of a Christian school at all? What contribution does it make to the program of equipping students for living the Christian life?

Literature is multifaceted. It can be read and taught for many purposes. One can read a work of literature to understand the character of the author. One can read a work of literature to understand the age in which the work was produced. One can read a work of literature to understand some religion or some philosophy. One can read a work of literature to understand some segment of the history of the language in which it was written. One can read a work of literature out of the expectation that it will give one a moral or psychological lift. All of these are reasons why people read literary works. None of them is bad. And literature is rich enough to reward, in some measure, all these different expectations.

But all of them are ulterior reasons for reading literature. All of them subordinate one's interest in literature to some other interest. There is, then, at least one other reason for reading a literary work, namely, to understand and appreciate it as a work of literature, as a work of literary art. One can read literature simply to understand and appreciate its aesthetic dimension.

It seems to me that the principal function of a literature course in a Christian school should be to acquaint students with the aesthetic dimension of literature. Literature, in a literature course, ought to be treated as one of the arts. Students in such a class should be taught to understand and appreciate and evaluate the aesthetic dimension of literary works. No doubt literature can be read to get at the character of the artist, but if it is biographies of artists one wants, one ought to institute a course in biographies of artists. No doubt literature can be read to gain insight into some period of human history, but if it is history one wants, one ought to institute a course in history.

We Calvinists, with our tremendous moral and theological concerns, are always apt simply to overlook the aesthetic dimension of reality. By doing so, we slight an important human-fulfilling dimension of the world in whose midst we live. The world of sounds and colors and textures is not something we ought to close our senses to or from which we should long to escape. God did not place us in the world to spite us, to frustrate us, to tempt us, to cause us grief. We are here in this garden to enjoy it and to develop it, to realize its yet unrealized possibilities, to use it for our fulfillment and for our praise to God. It is the vocation of the musician to praise God and serve people by giving us combinations of sounds that, though always possible, were never yet actualized. It is the calling of the painter to praise God and serve people by giving us hitherto unrealized but realizable color combinations. Calvinists betray a lurking scorn for the sensory world when they fail to acknowledge the aesthetic as a genuine and important dimension of reality.

In the area of the arts, I think, the first thing a Christian school must get straight, if it is to have a coherent curriculum, is that the aesthetic is a distinct and important dimension of reality that demands attention. However, a school is only begging for trouble if it tries to resolve the issue by itself. Rather, it must discuss it with its constituency. And *that* is to broach a religious issue with them, for the issue involves, as I hinted, one's whole religious attitude toward the sensory world. Did God put us in this sensory world as a fit and proper home for us? Or did God intend that we should never be anything but homesick here?

Now, suppose we resolve that in our literature courses we will attend principally to the aesthetic dimension of literature. What, more specifically, will we then be attending to?

A rough distinction to be made here is that between the *surface qualities* of a literary work and the *significance* that the work bears. Accordingly, one can choose between attending to the patterned texture of sound and meaning in a literary work and attending to what is said and expressed and symbolized in the work. Both choices have, of course, their proponents. When I think back on my own education in literature, I realize the emphasis was almost entirely on what I have called the *significance* of literary works. We were taught to look right past or through the surface qualities to the philosophical and religious message. On the other hand, there is rampant in the contemporary world the notion that one ought to ignore whatever a work of literature may say or express or symbolize and concentrate all one's attention on the surface qualities, the patterned texture of sound and meaning.

I am convinced that neither of these choices should ever be made. Literature in its aesthetic dimension has both surface qualities and significance. Both of these belong to the work. Accordingly, neither should be ignored at the expense of the other. We should not ignore the delightful patterned textures of sound and meaning, nor should we ignore literature's signifying of reality and human experience down to their most profound depths. Christians must resist reductionism in either direction. Only some sort of Platonism could lead them to ignore the surface qualities. Only some sort of positivism could lead them to ignore the significance.

Here, too, I think that a Christian school, if it is to be at all successful in educating its students, must initiate discussions with the parents. There is so much aesthetic reductionism abroad today—both in the direction of ignoring the surface qualities of literature and in the direction of ignoring the significance of literature—that a Christian school, if its program is not to be seriously misunderstood, will repeatedly have to make clear what it is doing. Such discussion can of course stand the benefit of educational competence. But once again, there are fundamental issues of religious attitude at stake. And insofar as this is true, the school should not so much think of itself as talking to the people but as coming with them to a deeper and better understanding of the Christian attitude toward the sensory world.

You might think that it follows directly from what I have said that when it comes to the issue of which works of literature to select for study in a Christian school, the only factors that ought to count are the aesthetic excellence of the works under consideration and the ability of the students to appreciate the works in their aesthetic dimension. If you have drawn this conclusion, you are probably getting alarmed, for you are well aware that it is on the issue of selection that most controversies arise. If the only consideration, apart from student ability, is aesthetic merit, what, you are thinking, are you in for? You can already visualize teachers picking aesthetically excellent but morally scurrilous works, and the resultant controversies are for you already almost palpable.

I don't think it follows that the only relevant criterion for selection is the aesthetic merit of a work. Of course, this is one essential criterion. But as I have been concerned to emphasize, literature is a multidimensional, multifaceted phenomenon. It *does* have moral and psychological effects on people. And when considering whether to put an actual concrete piece of literature into the hands of a child, one cannot merely consider the aesthetic dimension of the piece. One has to consider the whole.

It is at this point especially that people make different judgments. The literature teacher decides to require his students to read *Catcher in the Rye*. Parents protest their children being required, or even allowed, to read *Catcher in the Rye*.

What typically underlies such disagreements?

Sometimes the trouble stems from the fact that one of the parties pays no attention to the aesthetic dimension. The parent, let us say, thinks of literature wholly in moral terms; he or she thinks of reading literature only for beneficial moral effects. The teacher, however, has in mind the aesthetic dimension as well.

In other cases, both parties may acknowledge the aesthetic merit of the work, but while the teacher thinks that any danger the work may have on the moral or religious life of the student is slight, the parent thinks it is serious. Usually, I think, disputes of this sort involve divergent convictions as to wherein lie the great dangers to the Christian's moral and religious life, and perhaps even divergent convictions as to the fundamental nature of evil. There is rampant in our Reformed community, as I guess there is in most Christian communities, the belief that the great dangers in literature are obscenity and profanity. Thus, we wage strong campaigns to keep the eyes and ears of our children from "filth" as we call it. We have not the slightest compunction in allowing our children to read gross paeans of praise to nationalism, to financial success, to humanism, to militarism—just provided that they are "clean." *The Diary of Anne Frank* has enjoyed considerable success as a dramatic production in several of our Christian day-schools, and at least one of our schools has produced the musical *Lost in the Stars*. Both of these are profoundly humanistic works, the latter nauseatingly so. Yet I have heard Christian school parents speak about both in glowing terms; they were "clean" and "uplifting." Indeed, they are. But they are also religiously insidious, far more so, in my judgment, than a bit of profanity or obscenity.

What the Christian school absolutely must do is educate its constituency to these issues. It must teach them to be discerning as to the message of literary works. And *with* them—not *against* them—it must face up to the issue as to wherein lie the really serious threats to the moral and religious life of young children, and adults as well. *With* them, I say, for this latter issue is not really an issue of educational competence but of moral and religious discernment. On this, teachers have nothing even close to a monopoly.

I suggested that the drama *The Diary of Anne Frank* is religiously insidious. Does that mean that, in spite of its considerable literary merit, I would abolish it from the Christian school? Here we touch yet a third ground of disagreement. Two Christians may agree on the literary merits of a piece and the nature of its moral and religious dangers, yet one may decide to give it to students, the other to withhold it. The issue, then, is how we cope with evil. Do we, as God's children, look it square in the face? Or do we avert our gaze? How do we keep ourselves pure? By living only in pure surroundings? Or by, with God's help, warding off the impurities in our impure world? This is sometimes the real issue at stake in controversies concerning the literary works to be given to students. But should this ever be the source of controversy? For where are those pure surroundings? Is it not the case that the things in this world that look pure to me look so because I am looking for only certain kinds of impurity? Of course, immaturity is a factor here. The mature are better able to withstand some kinds of impurity than others. But only if one looks toward God can one avert one's gaze from evil. One has no choice, if one is to live in this world, but to look evil in the face, since its face is all about. Here again we are touching on fundamental religious issues. A Christian school must recognize them as such, and when controversies arise that have these issues as their origin and basis, the school must not try to sweep them under the rug nor act patronizingly sure of itself. Rather, together with its community it should work through them.

Controversy Concerning Instruction about Creation and Evolution

I turn now to the last of the curricular concerns to be analyzed: creation and evolution. How should Christian schools handle these matters of considerable controversy in the various communities that support these schools?

The first step, of course, is to understand what the issue really is.

The concept of evolution, as I understand it, is the concept of change through time in the characteristics of plant and animal species, in some cases the change being of such an order as to amount to the origin of a new species. The claim that there is in fact such a phenomenon as evolution has been made on the basis of evidence collected by various of the sciences. Some scientists have made the claim only with respect to particular species, on the basis of their detailed study of those species. But many have gone on to claim, speculatively, that all plant and animal species are caught up in an evolutionary process, whereby all present forms of life are the outcome of evolutionary changes that took place in the past. Most scientists, however, are not willing merely to claim, with more or less generality, that evolution takes place. They have tried to discern some pattern in the evolutionary process and to discover the conditions under which evolutionary change takes place. One pattern they have claimed to discern is the pattern of more complex species evolving ultimately from more rudimentary species, and, in some cases, of a variety of different species evolving ultimately from one single species.

In summary, evolution, as I understand it, is change in the characteristics of species throughout time, and the home use of this concept is in the biological sciences.

By no means, however, has the concept been confined to its home use. In typical fashion, the speculators have tried to see everything whatsoever as caught up in evolutionary change, even though, when one leaves the world of plant and animal species, the strict concept of evolution has no application. Typically, the speculators have fastened on one of the supposed patterns of biological evolution, the pattern of simpler to more complex. They have then interpreted all history—natural or human—as caught up in this pattern, simpler societies changing into more complex, and so on. In this fashion, people have made an *absolute* out of evolution. Out of it, the fabric of a new religion has been woven.

To make a religion out of evolution is, of course, to act in conflict with the Christian faith. But in the claim that the characteristics of species have changed throughout time, I, at least, find nothing whatsoever hostile to Christianity. On the contrary, there is something about it that is profoundly in the spirit of Christianity. Traditionally, before the use of this concept, scientists ignored the factor of time in their search for structure in plant and animal species. But fundamental to Christianity is an insistence on the radical importance of time. What has been called to our attention, by those who claim that biological evolution takes place, is that we can not only discern pattern in the species of the plant and animal world when we consider them *at a given time* but that we can also discern patterned change in species when we consider them *across* time. The claim that there is patterned change of species throughout time, as well as pattern in species at a given time, is not threatening to faith and is as much in accord with faith as the claim that there is patterned change in individuals. There is nothing at all in it that forces us to "leave God out."

But whether you agree with me on this point or not, surely the concept of evolutionary processes—change in the characteristics of species throughout time—has played so vast a role in contemporary thought that a Christian school cannot ignore it, no matter what its judgment as to whether evolution takes place. And in teaching this concept, a school ought to make a serious attempt to show students the many different ways—from the legitimate to the totally illegitimate—in which this concept has been used.

When we turn from evolution to belief in creation, as the Christian holds it, we enter a different dimension of human life. When Christians speak of creation, they refer, of course, to the fact that all contingent beings depend for their existence on the will of God, on God's creative resolution, on God's originating word. But here, far more even than in the case of evolution, it is important to discern the context in which this belief functions. It functions in a religious, existential context. When the biblical writers confess their belief in creation, they invariably do so in the context of a religious concern of theirs. They never do so as the conclusion of some speculation on their part. They are, for example, convinced that all humans owe to Jehovah God obedience and praise, and their belief in creation functions as the ground for this conviction. It is because God is our Maker that we must give to God praise and obedience. Allow me to cite Psalm 33 in this regard:

> Praise the LORD with the lyre,
>   make melody to him with the harp of ten strings! . . .
> By the word of the LORD the heavens were made,
>   and all their host by the breath of his mouth. . . .
> Let all the earth fear the LORD,
>   let all the inhabitants of the world stand in awe of him!
> For he spoke, and it came to be;
>   he commanded, and it stood forth.
>
> verses 2, 6, 8–9

Or again, the biblical writers are convinced that we can trust in God for what will happen; there is nothing capable of frustrating God's purposes. The ground for this conviction, too, is their belief in God as Creator. Isaiah 51 puts it this way:

> I, I am he that comforts you;
>   who are you that you are afraid of man who dies,
>   of the son of man who is made like grass,
> and have forgotten the LORD, your Maker,
>   who stretched out the heavens
>   and laid the foundations of the earth,
> and fear continually all the day
>   because of the fury of the oppressor,
> when he sets himself to destroy?
>
> verses 12–13

So you see, for the biblical writers, the belief in creation does not function as an abstract speculative idea; it functions as an essential part of their religion. Not part of their religion in the sense that they give religious devotion to the dogmatic proposition that God created. Rather, in the sense that it undergirds those fundamental human activities of ultimate trust, obedience, and worship.

When creation and evolution are understood in the sense explained—and I am firmly convinced that that is how they ought to be understood—then it is difficult to see how they could possibly conflict with each other. But if that is so, why then is this matter such a source of controversy?

Of course, you do not expect me here to give you anything near a full answer to this question. Such a process would be enormously complex. Allow me to single out but one factor from the whole.

People often think there is a conflict between evolution and creation because they read the Bible in mistaken fashion. We Christians often forget that the Bible is a *religious* book, in the double sense that it is the record of the religion of an ancient people and that it issues a call to our own religious life. We have, for example, failed to keep firmly in mind the religious thrust of the biblical passages concerning creation, and we have fixed all our attention on the proposition that God created. That proposition has become the focus of our religion. Or, in reading the opening chapters of Genesis, we have blinked our eyes to the tremendous religious proclamation made there—a proclamation as to how we should live before the face of God and in the midst of nature—and we have fixed all our attention on the details of the story. We have bothered our heads with the question as to how long it took God to create. But what could possibly be the religious significance of an answer to that question? Do the biblical writers anywhere attach any religious significance to any such answer?

Christian schools are seriously to blame for the failure of so many in our community to read the Bible as a *religious* document. It would be too embarrassing for all concerned for me to take one of the Bible manuals used in Christian schools and show how it treats the Bible as a complicated, memory-straining collection of marvels, systematically failing, because never even trying, to get across the point that the biblical writers were trying to make. You see, in the case of Genesis, it is not a matter of some believing and some not believing what it says. It is a matter of deciding *what* it says. Too many people fail to perceive that it was meant to proclaim the Word of God for the lives of the ancient Israelites and that, in so doing, it proclaims the Word of God for the lives of us today.

I am convinced that there will be no final way out of our controversies concerning creation and evolution until Christian schools begin to teach the Bible aright. But that cannot happen until our entire community begins to read it aright or has the willingness to try to read it aright. How one reads the Bible, though, is again a religious issue. We have again touched on an issue in which educational competence, though indeed relevant, is not the decisive factor. We have once again touched on an issue in which a Christian school *with* rather than *against* its community must search for deeper and better understanding.

It strikes me, upon looking back over my remarks to you today, that running throughout has been this theme: A Christian school must be involved with its community and its community with it, not in superficial, gong-beating, public-relations fashion but in an earnest attempt on the part of the school to explain its educational practices and to talk through fundamental religious issues. The school must explain to its community its educational decisions. And on the fundamental religious issues that touch the curriculum at so many points, it must, *with* its community, engage in significant discussion. A successful curriculum can exist only in the context of mutual school and community involvement.

chapter three

A Return to Basic
Christian Education

At the root of many curriculum discussions is a recurrent question: What are the basics in Christian education? Some school leaders understand "basics" as what is required to do well on standardized tests. Others believe that basic skills are meaningful only when taught within an integrated curriculum. In this article published in 1978, Wolterstorff says that basic to curriculum planning in Christian education are the three dimensions of the calling of God's people: (1) They are called to proclaim the gospel; (2) they are called to work for shalom and for liberation from all that oppresses and depresses; and (3) they are called to evidence shalom in their lives. He then goes on to describe what that means for a Christian school.

What's the point of having an alternative school that is a *Christian* school? Why not be content with the system provided free to all in our society, namely, the public school system?

I think there is no better way to get at what is basic to the Christian school system than to ask and answer this question, for, of course, the *reasons* for establishing an alternative school that is a Christian school are interlocked with the *goals* of such a school. The goals determine the reasons and the reasons determine the goals. In turn, the goals of such a school determine what goes on within it. And whether Christian schools are worth the enormous amounts of time, energy, and money that they require is determined ultimately by what goes on *within* them. It is not determined by all our talk *about* them.

For many generations, by now, Christian parents have had reasons for establishing alternative schools that are Christian schools. We could, therefore, simply look back at some of the old formulations. Yet it is worthwhile for each new generation to think through and to formulate for itself its reasons for supporting these schools. If it does not do so, then increasingly parents and teachers alike will fall into unreflective routines and submission to fads. Parents will send their children because that's the thing to do. Teachers will teach their students the way students in Christian schools have always been taught, or worse, will teach them the way everybody else is teaching students today.

There is another reason why each generation should think through and formulate for itself its reasons for supporting alternative Christian schools. There will, of course, be deep continuities from generation to generation regarding such reasons. Yet each generation differs in its self-understanding of its Christian identity, and each generation differs in the social circumstances in which it finds itself. It is of benefit, then, for each generation to formulate its reasons so that they fit *its* self-understanding and *its* situation. Otherwise, the reasons for supporting Christian schools become abstract, more and more removed from concrete experience and life, and unpersuasive.

The Task of the People of God

We must begin with the reality and task of the church in the world—meaning by "the church" not that ecclesiastical institution that we call the church but rather "the people of God." Fifteen years ago, perhaps even ten years ago, I would not have started there. I would have started with what it means for an individual to have faith, and then I would have argued for the comprehensive character of Christian faith. Today it seems to me that such an approach, though correct in stressing the comprehensive character of Christian faith, still reflects an individualism foreign to the biblical vision of life and reality. The fundamental fact confronting us all is that God has called out and chosen a people—the church.

Of course, God called out a people before he called out the church. God called out old Israel. But the significance of Pentecost was that Israel is no longer God's called and chosen people. Neither is any other natural grouping of human beings. God's called and chosen people is now the band of those who are Christ's followers and disciples.

This band of Christ's followers constitutes what is called, in the first letter of Peter, a chosen *race*, a dedicated *nation*, a *people* claimed by God for his own, the *people* of God. Thus, at Pentecost a new people was given birth. This people transcends all natural nations. It is transnational. Yet by now it is found within each. Alien to all, yet resident within each. "Elect from every nation, yet one o'er all the earth."

This people of God, the church, the band of Christ's followers, constitutes the fundamental identity of the Christian. The Christian remains an American, or a Dutchman, or a Kikuyu, and that is by no means an unimportant fact about him or her. Yet more fundamental than such national identity is his or her identity as a member of the transnational people of God. For us Christians who are Americans, when American bombs fell on the Catholic cathedral in Hanoi and the Lutheran church in Dresden, the fundamental reality was not that our (American) people were attacking *those* Vietnamese and German foreigners. The fundamental reality was that American bombs were falling on *our* people, on *your* people and *my* people, on fellow members of Christ's body.

To understand the roots of why it is that the church is an *alien* presence in all nations, we must talk about God's *purpose* for the church in the world.

Characteristically, our vision of the role of the church in the world has been terribly and tragically reduced. Characteristically, we think of the church simply as those people who have faith, who live morally and devoutly, who are charged to conduct evangelism, and who one day will be rewarded with bliss in heaven. And that, to say it again, is a terrible and tragic reduction of God's purpose for the church in the world.

God's good creation fell. It fell by virtue of humankind in its freedom revolting against God and refusing to live in trustful obedience, preferring instead to act as if it were autonomous. Thereby a dark cloud fell over the entire creation, so that the whole of it "groans" for deliverance. The incredible fact is that God resolved not to leave his creation in the grip of its misery, resolved instead to act for its renewal—to act so that God's kingdom would be established, to act so that people could live in shalom, in peace, in joyful fulfillment with themselves, their neighbor, nature, and God. Central to God's manner of working for renewal is the calling and choosing of a people to act as God's agent—first Israel, then the church, and between the two at the axis of history, God's own Son. Thus, the church is in the world for the sake of the coming of God's kingdom. The church is in the world for the sake of the coming of shalom.

The church is, in fact, God's called and chosen agent of renewal. Someday when the book of history is read in its entirety, we will see that not America, not Holland, not Canada but rather the church played the decisive role in the coming of God's kingdom—in spite of all the terrible bloody blotches on her garment. But the church is also *called* to be God's agent of renewal, for always and again she falls short of being an agent of renewal. By no means is she inevitably that on every occasion.

Three Dimensions of the Calling of the People of God

It seems to me that we can distinguish three dimensions of the church's calling to be God's agent in the world for the coming of God's shalom.

The church, in the first place, is called to proclaim the gospel of the kingdom. She is called to speak to all people everywhere of God's action in history, calling on all people everywhere to repent and believe.

Second, the church is called to act in loving service to all people everywhere. She is called to work for shalom—to seek to bring it about that people live in joyful harmony with themselves, with each other, with nature, and with God. And in order that shalom may be established, the church is called to work for liberation from all that oppresses and depresses.

But third, the church is called to give evidence, in her own style of life, of the new life to be found in Jesus Christ. She is called, in her own lifestyle, to give evidence of shalom. She is called to be an exemplary, a paradigmatic, community. In her own life we are to see the firstfruits of the full harvest, the signposts of the kingdom. She is not merely with grim patience to wait for the new age, when the Spirit will fully renew all existence. She is, here and now, to manifest signs of that renewing Spirit.

This is, all too briefly expressed, the biblical vision of the church. The church is the band of Christ's followers. She is an alien presence within every nation and is called and committed to be God's agent for the coming of God's kingdom and for the institution of shalom. The church is, and is called to be, the revolutionary vanguard in society, serving the cause of ushering in a new order, consequently finding herself continually in tension with those who want to hang on to the present order. It is in this new community that Christians find their fundamental identity.

Basic Christian Education

And now we can move on to education. The church, like any other community with a cause and a lifestyle of its own, finds it necessary to *educate*. It finds it necessary to educate its new recruits. It also finds it necessary to educate its longtime members. Thus, education by and for the community comes into existence. And that, at its most basic, is Christian education: Christian education is education *by* the Christian community *for* the Christian community. To say that Christian education is education *for* the Christian community makes such education sound inward-looking. And so, in a certain way, it is. But what we have seen above is that the church does not exist for its own sake. It exists for the sake of God's cause in the world. And that cause is the liberation of all people from oppression and depression so as to live in God's shalom. In being education for the Christian community, Christian education is education for the sake of all.

But here we come to a crux that has divided Christians throughout the ages. Do the children of believers, children who have not yet reached the state of full commitment, also belong to the Christian community, to God's people? Or are they to be counted as outside the community until such time as they make a full commitment? The educational implications of one's answer are, of course, enormous. Some who hold that the children of believers are outside the church believe that such children, like all children, should receive an education in which all life options are simply presented to them impartially, for their choice. Others who hold that the children of believers are outside the church believe that such children, like all children, should be treated as fledgling subjects for evangelism. In neither case will children be treated as members of the Christian community and educated with the goal of equipping them so that they can make their own unique contribution to the life and work of the community.

The issues here are deep and complex, and I cannot begin to address them all. Let it simply be said that the Calvinist tradition, within which I am writing, has always held that God's promise to the church, to remain ever faithful to her and to grant her members a share in the shalom of God's kingdom, includes the children of believers. "The promise is to us and to our children." Accordingly, when it is said that Christian education is education *by* and *for* the church, the children of believers are to be understood as belonging to that community which is the church. They should not merely be lumped together with all children and impartially presented a smorgasbord of life options. Neither should they be lumped together with all children and treated as fledgling subjects for evangelism. Rather, they should be grouped with all the other members of the church and equipped to make their own unique contribution to the work of God's people on earth.

That, as I see it today, is the fundamental case for Christian education. And as everyone will surely recognize, the case is rich with implications for the goals, and thus the character, of that education.

Christian Day-Schools

What must be clearly recognized, though, is that so far I have said nothing directly about the institutions within which such education should be carried on. And so I have said nothing directly about the institution known as the Christian day-school. I have talked about Christian education. I have said that it is a project *by* and *for* the Christian community. And I have said that young children of believers are to be counted as members of the community. But the arrangements and institutions required by and appropriate for conducting such education will surely differ from one historical and social circumstance to another. They will be different in first-century Corinth from what they are in twentieth-century Pella, Iowa. And they will be different in twentieth-century Netherlands from what they are in twentieth-century Ceylon. It is with the concrete situation in mind of twentieth-century North America that we must ask whether Christian education requires, or is best carried out in, alternative Christian day-schools.

For us, of course, that question takes the form of whether the American and Canadian public school systems, supplemented with a bit of church-school education, are adequate for providing a basic Christian education for our children—adequate for equipping our children to make their unique contribution to the cause of God's people in the world. The answer depends, of course, on the goals and character of education in the public schools.

The traditional vision of public school education, at least in the United States, was that it should and could be neutral with respect to all the religions in American society, while at the same time it should be religiously oriented education, indeed, *Christianly* oriented education. It was believed that public school education should be conducted on the basis of what all Americans held in common. Further, it was thought that we all held in common certain religious, even certain Christian, beliefs, to which we then added whatever "sectarian" peculiarities we wished.

Obviously, that traditional vision has collapsed in our century. It has collapsed partly under the pressure of the increasing diversity of Amer-

ican society with respect to religion and irreligion, coupled with the
Supreme Court's insistence that public schools be neutral with respect
to *all* religions and irreligions found in our society. But more fundamentally, it has collapsed because the intellectual and cultural elite in
our society, an elite that ultimately determines what goes on within our
schools, has become increasingly secularist and antireligious in its orientation. The result is that today nobody can any longer seriously believe
that there is harmony between the goals and character of education in
American public schools and the goals and character of authentically
Christian education.

People who hold to the vision of the church sketched out above will,
of course, find nothing surprising in this situation, for they see the
church as an alien presence in American society, as it is in any other
society. If then the public school system bases its education on the dominant shared beliefs of the American people, such people will expect to
find conflict between the goals and character of such education and that
of Christian education. What tended to conceal this conflict from American Christians in the past was that they did not see the church as an
alien presence in American society. On the contrary, they thought and
spoke of America as a Christian nation. They were even so bold as to
speak of America as the "New Israel," thereby giving to America the
place in God's plan reserved for the church. However, the increasingly
secular, sensate, and indulgent character of the American people is making clear to more and more Christians that this understanding of the
relationship between the church and American society is untenable.
America is not committed to serving the cause of God's new order.

But the presence of substantial conflict between the goals and character of public school education and the goals and character of Christian education does not, by itself, yield the conclusion that Christian
education should be conducted in alternative Christian day-schools.
Some suggest that the goals of Christian education are best served by
parents sending their children to the public school and then supplementing and correcting the education there received in the home. In
some places, perhaps this is what must or should be done. But in general this strikes me as a wildly idealistic suggestion. For one thing, the
suggestion is almost always made by intellectuals, who are perhaps capable of carrying it off. But in our complex society, with the results of
scholarship deeply interwoven into the fabric of the society, it is simply
impossible for most Christian parents by themselves adequately to supplement and correct the education of their children. They lack the ability and/or the training. Second, when I observe those intellectuals who
do have the ability and training to carry out such a project, I find them
all much too busy with their own occupations to have the time required.

If supplementing and correcting public education is the best strategy, there is no realistic alternative in our society but for Christian parents to hire *teachers* to conduct such training.

But is that really the best strategy, simply to supplement and correct public school education? In some circumstances, perhaps it is. But in general it seems to me it is not, for what is deficient in secular education is not that here and there it neglects saying what should be said, nor that here and there it makes some error. What is deficient is rather the *perspective* within which the education is structured and the *perspective* within which the disciplines taught have been constructed. What is deficient is what, in my book *Reason within the Bounds of Religion,* I call the "control beliefs" that have governed the construction of the theories taught. The aim of Christian education must be to conduct education and scholarship within Christian *perspective.* But to construct literary or political theory in accord with the control beliefs of the Christian and to teach students about literature and political institutions from a Christian perspective is not merely to supplement and correct the work of others. It is to construct *alternative* theories on the same subject matter and to teach the same subject matter from an *alternative* perspective. For that to be accomplished, one needs day-schools.

The conclusion seems to me irresistible: The Christian community will seek to establish Christian *schools* in which to conduct its program of Christian *education.* Sometimes, indeed, it will have to settle for something less than that ideal. But even when it does so, its goal remains the same: to equip its children to make their own unique contribution to the cause of God's people in the world.

Challenges Facing the Christian School Today

Let me close with what I see as three of the great challenges facing the Christian day-school system today.

First, the Christian community is called to be a paradigmatic, exemplary community—giving evidence in its own lifestyle of that new life to which God calls his children. An implication of this is that the Christian school must serve as a paradigmatic, exemplary community of teachers and learners. It must show, in its style of teaching and learning, what education should be like. Need I stress how far short the Christian school often comes from meeting that goal. All too often one finds aesthetic grimness in place of beauty and delight, authoritarianism in place of an authority that serves, rigidity in place of a flexible concern for a child's individuality. Obviously, there is here a great challenge confronting us.

Second, I said that a school cannot simply supplement and correct secular perspectives on art, literature, physical creation, social issues. It must communicate *alternative* perspectives, perspectives faithful to the biblical vision of reality and God's purpose for the church in the world. Yet when one scrutinizes Christian schools, all too often one does not find such alternative perspectives. Rather, one finds secular perspectives to which are attached piecemeal supplements and correctives. Here then is a second great challenge confronting the Christian school. Of course, if the Christian school is indeed to communicate alternative perspectives, there must *be* such perspectives. This challenge, therefore, is as much a challenge to scholars as to educators. There can be no Christian education in the absence of Christian scholarship.

Third, the goal of the Christian school is the formation of an alternative lifestyle, not just the formation of an alternative set of thoughts. The vision of the church as a transnational community that is an alien presence in every society remains a wholly abstract vision unless it becomes *concretized* in a way of living. Unless there is such a thing as a Christian lifestyle that transcends nations, there will be little chance that many of us will see our fundamental identity as Christians. We will see it instead as Americans, as Canadians, and so on. So the third great challenge to the Christian school is to make concrete, in our day and place, the Christian gospel—to work toward the formation of a style of life.

But there are limitations as to what a school can do. If the community supporting the school has little sense of "over-againstness," if the concrete texture of its own life hardly differs from that of those around it, if it has little sense of being an alien presence, little sense of serving God's cause in the world, little sense of being God's revolutionary vanguard in society, then the Christian school will have little chance of success. Then almost inevitably it will never advance beyond, or almost inevitably it will slide back into, making piecemeal supplements and piecemeal corrections to secular education. Insofar as it does so, the time, money, and effort spent in supporting it will be in vain—a vanity of vanities. The Christian community requires Christian schools for the success of its cause in the world. But equally, the Christian school requires a supporting Christian community for the success of its programs.

chapter four

Between Isolation and Accommodation

If it is true that Christian schools ought to do some things differently than public schools, what are some of those differences? In this article, Wolterstorff addresses that question, specifically as it applies to whether Christians should isolate themselves from culture or accommodate themselves to it.

I was talking with one of my relatives last summer, someone whom I see much less often than I would like to. For years now he has worked hard for the local Christian school, so after we had chatted for a while, I asked him how things were going at the school. Well, he said, they'd been having a bit of trouble this past year. Some of the young English teachers had assigned books for the kids to read that he and some of the other parents didn't like. He had looked into one or two of them, and they seemed like trash to him. "If they want to read trash like that, they can go over to the public school." But still, he wanted to know what I thought about it, because sometimes when he listened to the teachers, he thought he could see how they were thinking. Only, he sure didn't like those books.

My relative was assuming that the Christian school ought to do things differently than the public school—*some* things, anyway. And on this he was absolutely right. Throughout Canada and the United States, there is a vast system of public education. A local public school is available free to everyone in these two countries. So if parents send their child to a Christian school, it's because they expect the Christian school to do something *different* from what they understand the local public school to be doing, and because they *want* that difference for their child. Why else bother?

What Differences Do You Want in the Christian School?

But different parents want different differences. And so different kinds of Christian schools emerge, as well as different demands for the same school. If you have a child in a Christian school, or if you are considering sending your child to a Christian school, I recommend that you perform this exercise: Take a piece of paper and a pencil and write down the differences *you* want in the Christian school; then order them, from the most important to the least important. It would be instructive to compare your list with someone else's. The differences we want, and stress, reveal the different understandings we have of Christian education.

Recently, a rather lengthy article appeared in my local newspaper about some of the new Christian schools popping up in the United States. From the article, I gathered that the supporters of these particular schools would have written something like the following as their list of desired differences:

- I want prayers in the school.
- I want Bible study in the school.
- I want my kids to learn to respect authority.
- I want my kids to love America.
- I want my kids to learn the importance of the family.
- I want firm discipline for my kids.
- I don't want my kids learning about evolution.
- I don't want my kids reading bad novels.
- I don't want sex education in the school.

You'll agree, I'm sure, that this list gives a rather clear idea of what such parents want out of the Christian school and how they understand Christian education.

As my relative and I talked a bit further, it became evident that he and the teachers disagreed, in this case anyway, on where the differences should be. He thought the kids should not be reading those novels at all. The teachers, as I gathered from what he said, thought they should read them, but that the novels should be analyzed and critiqued from a Christian point of view. The teachers apparently saw the difference between Christian and public education not in *whether* the novels were read but in *how* they were read.

What did I say to my relative when he asked me what *I* thought about it all? Well, I began by agreeing that certain books and films are dangerous, at least for children at certain levels of immaturity—dangerous in that they threaten to turn the child into a less faithful servant of Jesus Christ. I went on to add that I think Christians often misperceive the true dangers. I myself think that swearing is less dangerous in a book than, say, the glorification of militarism. But I heartily agreed that books and films have an influence on people and that we have to be sensitive to what that influence is.

The Purpose of the Christian School

I went on to say, though, that I thought disputes such as this could not be settled without reminding ourselves of the very purpose of the Christian school—and I expressed my distress that so often that purpose seems lost from view. Schools are designed, I said, to prepare students for living a certain kind of life. The only way to get at disputes such as the one over required reading is to ask what sort of life the school is trying to prepare the students to lead.

Let me explain, I said, how I see it. I see the development of science and art, the flowering of technology, the conquering of disease, the expansion of means of communication—I see all these as good things. I see them as carrying the potential of human fulfillment. I think God wants such things as these for his human creatures. What has to be added at once, though, is that all these things participate in our fallenness. We use them for bad purposes, and we develop them in ways that have bad consequences.

How does the disciple of Jesus Christ live in the midst of such a world? That question is important to me here. Indeed, for me it is the all-important question, for I see the Christian school as a discipleship-training school.

It seems to me that disciples are not called to turn their backs on cultural developments. As members of the church, they are called indeed to preach the gospel. But they remain human beings, legitimately finding fulfillment in art, in science, in technology. At the same time, though, they will be vividly aware of the fallenness of all cultural developments. So they work for restoration, for redemption, in the name of their Lord. They do what they can to bend technology to better uses. They do what they can to change those social arrangements that result in some people starving while others wallow in superabundance. They do what they can to turn literature and the study of literature in healthier directions.

Take farming, I said. (The relative to whom I was speaking is a farmer.) Christians, disciples of Jesus, are not called to leave farming. Maybe some are, but not all. And neither am I automatically called to leave philosophy. Farming is obviously necessary to the sustenance of human life, and though I can't say that philosophy is necessary in the same way, I think it does enrich and direct our lives. So the issue is *how* we farm and *how* we do philosophy. Christian farmers are going to ask how they can cherish God's earth while also developing it, and how they can use it to serve human well-being. But farming, as we actually know it, is a fallen enterprise. It has been shaped by people who couldn't care less about cherishing God's earth. All they want is money.

I knew that the relative to whom I was speaking is different. It's true that he uses all sorts of modern technology; in fact, he loves farm implements and loves to figure out how their designers were thinking when they designed them. And it's true that he makes money. But what gives him his greatest satisfaction is that his land is now vastly richer than it was when he bought it a good many years ago and that its yield is now much higher. He has cherished and developed the piece of God's earth that he owns. That, I said, was discipleship farming. He hadn't turned his back on farming, but neither did he do his farming just like everyone else. Instead, he consistently asked how he could be a faithful disciple of Jesus Christ in this vocation of farming.

What about Those Bad Books?

And that, I said, is how I see the Christian life in general—neither *isolation* from general culture and society nor *accommodation* to it. Instead, *participation* in the use and formation of culture and society, but asking through it all how to live as a disciple.

The Christian school, as I see it, aims at preparing for such a life. It steers between isolation and accommodation. It doesn't teach us to stay out of politics and out of modern farming and out of literature and out of philosophy—except in extreme cases. But neither does it teach us to participate in these just like everyone else. It teaches us to participate in these as dedicated disciples, working for their restoration.

So what about those bad books? Well, some books should not be read in Christian schools. But I don't think we should start our thinking there, anymore than we should start our thinking by saying that some of the new farm technology is not for Christians. Probably some of it is. But we have to start our thinking by asking how one can be faithful in farming while continuing to live in a society in which farming is corrupted by sin. So, too, we have to start by asking how one can be faithful in literature while continuing to live in a society in which literature is corrupted by sin. Some technology we discard; some we adapt; some we use pretty much the way it is offered to us; perhaps some we have to invent for ourselves. But all of it we evaluate. We participate, but always our participation has a critical dimension. So, too, some literature we discard; some we adapt; some we use pretty much the way it is offered to us; some we write for ourselves. But all of it we evaluate. Our participation always has a critical dimension.

This is how our conversation went while we were leaning over the fence on that warm summer day. It may have been a bit "heavier" than most farmyard conversations! But I think we understood each other.

My own prediction is that we will continue to see new Christian schools pop up in Canada and the United States in the next several years. The reason is clear: More and more Christians are beginning to sense that the North American way of life is not the Christian way of life. So they want a different education for their children from that offered by the public school. What sort of differences do they want? Often the differences they want amount to trying to isolate their children from the influences of the surrounding culture.

The project of a school in the Calvinist tradition is different. It, too, sees the discrepancy between the North American way of life and the Christian way of life. So it, too, resists accommodation. But it doesn't go for isolation. It tries to provide discipleship training in a non-isolationist setting. To do this, successfully steering between isolation and accommodation, is the great challenge to the Christian school in the Calvinist tradition. It always has been the great challenge. But today the temptation to go for isolation is stronger than in the past and the lure of accommodation more powerful.

chapter five

Beyond 1984 in Philosophy of Christian Education

Throughout the 1970s and early 1980s, discussions continued concerning the focus of curriculum in Christian schools. In no place was that discussion more lively than in Ontario, Canada. There the discussion centered around the questions, Should curriculum in Christian schools focus on subjects that discipline the mind? Or should the curriculum be planned in a more integrated way, recognizing the holistic nature of knowledge and of God's world? The Ontario Christian School Teachers Association invited Wolterstorff to give the keynote address at their fall conference in 1984. Wolterstorff explained the roots of different sides of the debate, emphasizing that in all our discussions on curriculum, we have failed to understand that we must teach justice, delight, and gratitude.

You and I assembled here today are teachers and administrators of Christian schools in the Reformed tradition of Christendom. Of course, we are also citizens of Canada and the United States, and I trust that one manifestation of that citizenship is concern for the public schools of our lands. We may regard the dilemmas facing those schools as insoluble and the difficulties confronting them as intractable, yet those schools educate the vast bulk of those with whom we live together as citizens. So too we are members of the church ecumenical, and I trust that among the manifestations of that citizenship is concern for the welfare of the Catholic school system, the Lutheran, and so on. Perhaps indeed it is time that we find better forums for the expression of this shared concern. But today our attention is focused on the education offered in schools of the Reformed tradition.

This particular movement of nonpublic schools is now about one hundred years old on our continent. In recognition of that fact, I have decided to reflect with you today on what these schools are all about. The education we undertake to offer—toward what way of being in the world is it pointed? What is it that we would like our students to be and to do as the result of their engagement with us? Of course, more goes into the shaping of an educational program and an educational system than a perception of educational purpose. What also contributes are convictions as to how to achieve those purposes, and that involves, among other things, assumptions about how people learn. So clarity of purpose is not all-sufficient. It is, though, indispensable, and among all the issues facing the educator, no doubt it is the purposes of education that a philosopher such as myself is most competent to discuss.

It is my firm impression that the philosophy of educational purpose dominant in these schools has remained remarkably consistent over these past one hundred years. I do not say that only one such philosophy has enjoyed currency, merely that one has been dominant. Neither do I claim that those who have embraced that dominant philosophy have all done so wholly and in depth; many have grasped it only partially and superficially. Further, I think a good many things have taken place in these schools that are inconsistent with this dominant philosophy. Yet unless I am sadly mistaken, over and over when we have stood back and tried to say what our education was all about, our dominant speech has displayed remarkable uniformity. I am well aware of the fact that members of the family have often spoken as if their differences with each other were far more significant than their agreements. But you and I, at some distance now from the most intense of those disputes, can see that many of them were really family quarrels.

How can we get at that underlying philosophy—that abiding "folk wisdom"? One strategy would be for me to try to put into words my own sense of it. But I myself have some critical questions I want to put to this philosophy, questions that I will be posing later in the discussion.

And the danger of critics putting into words a shared philosophy is that, even with the best of will, they will distort it for their own purposes. So on this occasion I have decided to look at how it was put into words by one of those who expressed it most profoundly. I have in mind William Harry Jellema, one of my own teachers—a *master* teacher, I might add.

Let me first say a word about Jellema himself, since his name and work are no longer well known among us—due in good measure to the fact that he wrote very little. Jellema taught for thirty years in the philosophy department of Calvin College and for some twelve years in the philosophy department of Indiana University. Spiritually, he always located himself in that version of the Reformed tradition that took shape in the Netherlands around the last turn of the century and was centered around Abraham Kuyper. Kuyper's neo-Calvinism took root especially in the Netherlands, in North America, and in South Africa. Jellema was a central figure in the North American branch. At least some of you are aware of the intense debates that took place between members of the North American and Dutch branches. Because of those debates, important members of the two branches were scarcely on speaking terms with each other, not to mention listening terms. That, in my judgment, was profoundly lamentable. Each of the two branches had something important to say that the other would have found worth listening to. But in any case, both branches were representative of neo-Calvinism, and the dominant articulate philosophy of the Christian school movement has been a neo-Calvinism derived from Abraham Kuyper. Though the American version of that neo-Calvinism has naturally been dominant in these schools, articulate members of the Dutch branch have also had a strong voice. Let us, then, look at Jellema's version of the neo-Calvinist philosophy of education, taking note here and there where his version resembles and differs from that of others.

That which is most fundamental in the society in which we find ourselves, said Jellema, is the presence of diverse faith communities. "Faith communities" is my phrase; Jellema himself was fond of calling them *kingdoms* and *civitates*—this latter the Latin word for "cities." If we would understand the fundamental dynamics of society and culture, then what is most fundamental are not individuals—though there are, of course, individuals. And what is most fundamental are not social institutions—though there are, of course, institutions. What is most fundamental are the spiritual kingdoms of which persons are members. Jellema always made clear that on this point he was standing in the lineage of Augustine, who, you remember, saw history as fundamentally the interaction between the city of God and the city of the world—*civitas dei* and *civitas mundi*.

Jellema always saw these spiritual kingdoms as objective realities. The city of God, for example, is not the totality of Christians at some particular time nor at all times; it is rather an objective spiritual reality of which individual Christians are members. Neither is a particular kingdom a certain totality of cultural products; it is that of which the cultural products are an expression. He says that a *civitas* "cannot be identified with cultural product, not with the will to culture, not with cultural activity," yet nonetheless

> the *civitas* lives and is realized therein. It is realized in and by eating and drinking, cobbling and carpentry, work and play, science and education, law and government, love and worship; nothing human but enters into the city. The *civitas* is not one, or some, nor even all the objects tangible and intangible, which man produces or assimilates, but is the city that is objectified in the producing and assimilating of the cultural object.[1]

Something more must be said about Jellema's understanding of the structure of these kingdoms. But already we can say that education, as he understood it, is ultimately always by and for such a kingdom. Let me quote a bit of what he says:

> Formal education in the schools . . . articulates the meaning and structure of a chosen *civitas* also when it professes neutrality; and inseparably in the same process forms, molds, educates the citizen in the meaning and structure of (whichever) *civitas*. . . . Education is by a kingdom and for citizenship in that kingdom.[2]

In short, education, for Jellema, was ultimately always both a manifestation of the life of a kingdom and initiation into that life.

Various things are remarkable about this view of the nature and purpose of education. I will be calling your attention to some of them later. But right here at the beginning we should take note of Jellema's extraordinary refusal to set limits to the scope of formal education in general and, thereby, to the scope of formal Christian education. The goal of Christian education is not just the formation of a way of thinking. Nor is it that plus the development of moral character. Nor is it that plus the cultivation of a mode of piety. Nor is it that plus the transmission of one and another part of humanity's knowledge. Education is for the totality of life in a kingdom. What we find here, from one of the most profound articulators of the dominant philosophy of education in Christian schools, is an extraordinary holistic understanding of the goal of school education.

But let us look a bit more closely at the structure of those kingdoms that play so central a role in Jellema's thought, for only then will we have the materials for understanding the rest of what he says about Christian education. Determinative of every *civitas* is a mentality, or a *mind*, as Jellema customarily called it. Others in the Christian school movement, referring to the same thing, spoke of a world-and-life view; recently, some have taken to speaking simply of a worldview. Of course, Jellema didn't claim that every citizen of a kingdom had its formative mind as a whole clearly before his or her consciousness. His claim was rather that if we inquire into what it is that makes sense of a people's way of life, we always discover that this people is operating on certain fundamental assumptions about reality and life, even though few members of the community bring these assumptions as a whole to consciousness. Indeed, it may be that significant elements of the mind of a *civitas* escape the consciousness of all members. A kingdom is an expression of mind, and a kingdom *comes to* expression in the cultural activities of its members.

In turn, the objective mind or worldview of a *civitas* also has a structure. It is not just an assemblage of answers to a variety of fundamental questions. It has a determinative center. Every human being, thought Jellema, is forced to answer the question of who God is. His or her answer may be so far mistaken as to go beyond misidentifying or misdescribing God to the identification of something other than God as God; nonetheless, he and she cannot avoid giving an answer. And how one answers this question determines the mind with which one thinks, of which in turn, as we have seen, one's way of being in the world is an expression. Only, that is to put it a bit too individualistically. Better is this: The mind of a *civitas* is shaped by an answer to who God is, and an individual adopts the mind of a *civitas*, and thereby becomes a member of the *civitas*, by accepting its idea of God. Thus, Jellema remarks that "the essence of all choices, the essence of moral choice, is religious decision. The *civitas* chosen is the continuous living expression of a man's religious faith; it is his answer, writ in large letters, to the question who God is."[3]

And how does a person actually acquire the mind of a certain *civitas?* How does a person's identification of who God is actually take place? The mind of a kingdom is formed in a person by interaction with the social and cultural expression of that mind. "The *civitas*," says Jellema, "patterns the man. It shapes man as he engages in assimilating and shaping cultural products; it shapes man as he engages in living."[4] Such patterning should not be understood deterministically, however. Jellema was deeply convinced that a person is capable of choosing the *civitas* in which he or she will live as a citizen and by which, accordingly, he or she will be patterned.[5] Indeed, he sometimes said, unguardedly in my judgment, that "the only voice man has in his shaping is in choosing which *civitas* will shape him."[6]

It should be clear from what has been said that Jellema did not think that a kingdom's answer to the question of who God is consisted in the verbal enunciation of some proposition on the matter. That might indeed be an *element* in its answer. But

> man answers the question by the whole life of the kingdom of which he is a citizen. To say who God is, is with man's whole world, including also nature and culture to choose for that God's kingdom; is with man's whole world to serve in the *civitas* dedicated to praise of that God. . . . Such concrete articulation in human life of a definition of God is a *civitas*, is a kingdom.[7]

Earlier we saw that, for Jellema, education at its deepest is always by and for some kingdom—always both an expression of the life of some kingdom and initiation into its life. Now we have seen that what most decisively shapes the life of a kingdom is what it takes God to be or what it takes *as* God. It follows that education is always religious in its import.

> All formal education, then, even such as professes to be neutral, reflects some *civitas*. That it cannot escape doing so is but a phase of the fact that man cannot escape answering the question of who God is, and articulating the answer in life; that is to say, cannot escape religious decision and allegiance to some kingdom. . . . The difference between Christian and non-Christian education, is therefore, not that religious faith is present in the one and not in the other; the difference is between the Christian definition of God and a non-Christian definition; and is thus a difference and opposition between kingdoms.[8]

Education for Citizenship in the Kingdom of God: Four Themes

We must go on to see, in a general way, how Jellema thought education for *civitas dei* was to be conducted. But let me first take just a moment to call your attention to some of the characteristically neo-Calvinist themes in Jellema's thought as we have followed it thus far. One of those themes is surely Jellema's insistence on the communality of Christian existence and, thereby, of Christian education. Christian existence does not consist of solitary individuals struggling to find his or her own way through life with the option of entering into association with other Christians. It consists in living as a citizen of the city of God.[9]

To accept God's self-definition is to become a citizen in a city, the *civi-tas dei*. And Christian education is education for such citizenship.

Another characteristically neo-Calvinist theme is the assumption that human existence, both personal and social, has the fundamental char-acter of *expression:* Citizen and city alike give social and cultural expres-sion (Jellema usually called it "articulation") to their inward mind, and that in turn is the expression of an identification of God. Thus, in see-ing human existence as fundamentally *expression,* the neo-Calvinist allied himself with the Romantics, for whom this picture of human exis-tence was as deep as anything in their thought. Of course, Jellema also contended that the social and cultural activities and products in which a given kingdom expresses its mind serve in turn to implant in those entering the kingdom the mind of the kingdom.[10] There was thus a sort of circular process operative. The forming, though, was not understood deterministically. Ultimately, the forming of one's mind by some king-dom's society and culture is something one *lets happen.* One's partici-pation in the life of a kingdom rests on choice, and ultimately that choice is choice of God or idol. One's life is the expression of that choice.

We may single out this last note as a third characteristically neo-Calvinist theme: What is ultimately determinative of that inner self, which seeks outer expression, is one's identification of God. There is nothing deeper in life than religion.

It follows straightforwardly, as yet a fourth neo-Calvinist theme, that culture is not pitted against religion but is seen as the expression, the manifestation, the articulation, the embodiment of religion. The *civitas dei*, like each other city, is engaged in the cultural and social embodi-ment of its identification of God. Many of those who participated in the neo-Calvinist tradition were fond of speaking of cultural mandate: God at creation enjoined culture on humanity. Though Jellema never denied the existence of such a mandate, he always found it superfluous to appeal to it. God has created humanity with a "will to culture," as he put it; that, in his judgment, was enough to justify it. But whether humanity is to be seen as engaged in the implementation of a mandate to culture or as engaged in the exercise of a will to culture, the neo-Calvinist always insisted that culture is religion embodied. Cultural and social activities are neither alien nor indifferent to the Christian. They beckon as faith's realization.

Let me call attention to just two more characteristically neo-Calvin-ist themes in Jellema's thought—implicit in what I have been saying, yet worth highlighting. Human beings do not agree in their identifica-tion of God. Thus, there are in the world diverse kingdoms—or better, rival kingdoms, kingdoms in conflict. Indeed, Jellema, in characteristi-cally neo-Calvinist fashion, believed the essence of sin lay in humanity's turning away from the true God to establish an alien kingdom in the service of a strange God. "Sin meant that man denied his Creator; that he was unwilling to accept God's self-definition. It means that man chose to glorify a strange God; that he chose to share in the perfections of, and to be patterned after, another than the God who deserves all praise and reverence."[11]

A consequence of this fundamental conflict in society—so the neo-Calvinist characteristically insists—is that there is ultimately no such thing as religiously neutral education. For *education*, remember, "is always education by some kingdom and for citizenship in some kingdom, whether of the world or of God." But "between these kingdoms there is opposition, conflict, antithesis." Accordingly, "in this sense . . . no education is neutral."[12] It followed, as Jellema saw it, that "as citizens of the *civitas dei* Christians can be well served only by education deliberately intended for such citizens and continuously patterned by the aim to 'lay Christ in the bottom' of all life."[13]

And what did Jellema recommend as the means and content of education?

> All formal education will systematically acquaint the pupil with what is. All formal education will develop certain skills. All formal education will educate the pupil on his level in a major body of given subject matter (arithmetic, history, geography, etc.). All formal education will make an appeal to and stimulate the pupil's will to culture. But in the process of formal education, taken in its totality at any moment, the pupil will also inevitably be expressing and learning to express the pattern of some *civitas*.[14]

Jellema never wavered in saying that the teacher's primary contribution to guiding students toward expressing the pattern of the *civitas dei* is to form *the Christian mind* in the students—to induce in the students a grasp of and a commitment to the mind of *the civitas dei*. It seems to have been Jellema's conviction that it could reasonably be expected that the students who *thought* with the Christian mind would then *express* that mind in their own specific cultural and social situation.

Furthermore, the teacher, in seeking to form the Christian mind in students, will not address what Christianity has to say about all the particularities that the students are likely to face in life but will rather concentrate on Christianity's answer to those abiding questions that no kingdom can avoid addressing. "Far more important than *what* the individual happens to think about this or that is the mind with which he thinks, the mind to which he is religiously committed."[15] The formation of a Christian mind good for all citizens of the *civitas dei* and in all seasons was the core of the strategy for achieving the goal.[16]

How, in turn, did one go about forming such a mind? To the best of my knowledge, Jellema never considered in print how this should be done at the elementary level. But when it came to the secondary, and even more, to the college level, his answer was firm and unwavering: The teacher reads books with the students. For one thing, of course, books in which the Christian mind comes to expression. But not only such books; also books in which alien minds come to expression. Jellema believed that one could learn something about reality from the reading of such books as the latter; he never supposed that the non-Christian mind was entirely closed off from reality. But that was not usually the reason he highlighted. He was profoundly convinced that the *mind of modernity*, as he was fond of calling it, was deeply alien to the Christian mind. In his judgment, there was no better way to make that clear to students than to read books in which the mind of modernity came to articulate expression. Jellema was not sure that even this, however, was sufficient to loosen the grip of the modern mind on the students; it would not be uncommon for them to continue assuming that the mind of modernity is simply the right way to think about reality and to add that the Christian will, of course, want to make some revisions here and there in how people express that mind. To break this parochialism, Jellema thought it important to introduce students to the classical mind. (Of course, that too had to be judged!)

There was yet another reason why Jellema thought students should read books in which alien minds come to expression: The cultural product as it actually confronts us is the synthesized or amalgamated expression of several different minds (plus that which is inescapable for all minds).[17] Not only then did students have to grasp the mind of modernity and be loosened from its grip so that they would *think* with the Christian mind, but they also had to learn to *discriminate* in the cultural products confronting them between that which was expressive of the Christian mind and that which was expressive of some alien mind. In short, "For intelligent commitment and articulation" of the Christian mind, "the individual needs acquaintance *from the inside* with what are by this time three or four objective, well-articulated major minds."[18]

Thus, the core of Christian education, at least in its upper levels, should consist of the teacher reading books with the students, submitting those books to what can well be called *religious depth analysis*, having chosen those books with the fruitfulness of such analysis in mind. Confronting students with Plato, with Dante, with Newton—whoever—the teacher will try to get students to discern the mind or minds at work, this as a means of forming in the students a Christian mind good for all citizens in all seasons, along with the ability to discern where this mind is at work and where some other is. Formed in this way, students can then be expected to go forth and labor with the other contemporary citizens of the *civitas dei* as they seek to embody in the *polis* their identification of God.

I think there can be no doubt that Jellema's own impulse was to select books mainly from the past for this program of religious depth analysis. What contributed to that impulse was, among other things, his conviction that students didn't need very much additional acquaintance with the modern mind—they knew it all too well—and his conviction that contemporary Christian writing was generally too synthetic to give a good representation of the Christian mind. Yet he was not simply an antiquarian, as is evident from the fact that on many occasions he pleaded for the formation of a Christian university on this continent, in which the Christian mind could find fresh intellectual expression. In fact, he felt that without a Christian university, Christian education could have only limited success. "If the *civitas dei* engages in any formal education at all," he said, "it cannot do without a university in the stricter sense of the term."[19]

In my judgment, what we have here is a profound philosophy of Christian education. Perhaps I should say once again, though, that Jellema was not starting from scratch in his reflections. In good measure, he was deepening a widely shared consensus, though as always in such cases his formulation served in turn to modify and advance that consensus. His formulation powerfully shaped my own thoughts about Christian education; where I now differ, I do so in the full knowledge of being in opposition to something of stature. I myself, when I teach philosophy, set it as my goal to get students to discern, behind the clutter of "problems" a philosopher addresses, the vision or worldview or mind that led him to raise those problems and to answer them as he did—which of course is exactly what Jellema recommended. And it is clearer to me now than it was at the time that the curriculum revision at Calvin College in which I participated during the mid-1960s was based on a mere variant of Jellema's vision—a change in emphasis. For Jellema, Christian education was to be conducted by interweaving a presentation of the positive results of Christian reflection about reality with a religious depth analysis of the cultural and social products from humanity's history. What we at Calvin proposed and implemented was a curriculum in which rather more of the former occurred than Jellema would have liked and rather less of the latter. Indeed, I think that on this point few people in the Christian school movement ever did follow Jellema. Few were willing to devote as much time as Jellema desired to conducting a religious depth analysis of the cultural products of the past—of the classical mind, of the medieval Christian mind, etc. Most wanted to get on with the business of developing in students the knowledge and

skills necessary for life in the *civitas* today, taking care to do so, however, in Christian perspective, believing that in this way students would
catch the Christian mind. Jellema's own classicist, or traditionalist, bent
never really caught on. But this is clearly more a matter of emphasis
than of dogma.

There was another emphasis in Jellema's thought that never really
caught on. Jellema was much more reluctant than most of us have been
to introduce what, for want of a better word, I shall call "practical"
courses and programs: such things as professional programs at the college level and shop and home economics courses at the high school level.
He regarded the pressure for such programs and courses as a reflection
of the pragmatism so prominent in the mind of modernity, and, as you
will have gathered, his attitude toward that mind was mainly one of
abhorrence. Those who resisted such courses and programs would,
admittedly, regularly invoke Jellema's name. Yet it is clear to me that
here, too, we are dealing with a matter of emphasis rather than of
dogma—though once again none the less important for that.

In a paper he wrote on high school curriculum, Jellema not only did
not oppose commercial, industrial, and domestic programs (as he called
them) in the high schools; he *recommended* them—though only for those
not destined for college, and only on the proviso that the "practical"
component in such programs not constitute the bulk of the students'
education. I think it is clear both why he recommended these and why
he did not think college bound students should take them. Always in
Jellema's mind were two fundamental considerations that determined
the curriculum (setting off to the side now the consideration of the learning level of the students). The Christian school had to develop in students whatever knowledge and skill could best be taught in formal education and was important for citizenship in the *civitas dei;* second, the
school had to develop in students as articulate a grasp of and as firm a
commitment to the Christian mind as possible. Now, Jellema thought
that commercial and industrial and domestic courses were not very good
instruments for enabling students to grasp in depth the Christian mind.
But on the other hand, he recognized that not all students have the capacities required for grasping that mind in depth. For such students, then,
inclusion of some such courses may be just what is called for, the resultant program preparing them well for their particular citizenship. (There
is, to my mind, an unsatisfactory elitism in the way this argument is
conducted.)

From this it is also clear that the current emphasis among some of
us on *individualized* education is not something to which Jellema was
in principle opposed—though admittedly it was not something he customarily stressed. It is true that he was in principle opposed to allow-

ing the particular, more or less momentary, *interests* of students to determine the curriculum. For him, a curriculum was a disciplinary and patterning device; there had to be requirements. But he recognized that
students come with different abilities, find their fulfillment in different
activities, and will be taking up different callings in the *civitas*. He recognized that to respect these factors there had to be points at which the
education was individualized. What he emphasized, though, was the
fact that there are some fundamental issues that face all humanity at all
times—and beyond these, some that face all Christians at all times. He
was intensely concerned that these not be neglected under the impact
of slogans about the importance of being relevant, about the importance
of individual interests, and so on. He wanted education to be an instrument in the formation of a genuine community. He thought this required
a large component of commonality running throughout the curriculum.
Sheer individualism was abhorrent to him. He was deeply concerned
about the fracturing of education.

On such matters of emphasis, then, we have had our disagreements
with each other. Yet apart from these, I think that Jellema came as close
as anyone ever has to expressing the philosophy of education that has
been dominant among us.

I have slowly over the years, however, come to think that there are
some significant points that you and I must begin to reconsider. Indeed,
we have already begun such reconsideration of several of these. The
points I am referring to are not points peculiar to Jellema but are points
characteristic of the neo-Calvinist philosophy of education in general.
In the context of gratitude for the immense contribution of this philosophy, we must begin some serious rethinking.

Perhaps, before we set out, it will help to summarize Jellema's position in four connected theses:

1. The goal of Christian schooling is to equip students for active citizenship in the kingdom of God.
2. To accomplish that goal, the school must, for one thing, teach students whatever knowledge and skills are necessary for such citizenship and can best be taught in formal education; and second,
   by way of that and beyond that, it must seek to develop in students
   a grasp of and commitment to the Christian worldview—good for
   all citizens in all seasons.
3. To accomplish those goals, the school must communicate to students a knowledge of reality in Christian perspective and must
   engage in a religious depth analysis of human social and cultural
   products.

4. The chief instrument of accomplishing this, the more so as the education gets more advanced, is to read with students great texts from (especially) the Western tradition.

My own reconsiderations have tended to focus around two centers: The nature of the life for which we educate and the nature of the learning process. Let me develop them in that order.

I myself ardently embrace the first of Jellema's theses: that the goal of Christian schooling is to equip students for active citizenship in the city of God. It is my impression that some of us are a bit unnerved by the assignment of so comprehensive a goal to Christian schooling. It appears to some that this threatens too many controversies, or that it makes it too difficult to set curricular priorities, or that it threatens to violate the sovereignty of some sphere or other, or that it fails to give priority to the rational moral capacities of the human person. Some of us then are inclined to introduce one and another limit on the goal of school education. It is my impression, to be specific, that another of my teachers, Henry Zylstra, was inclined to do so. But as for me, I'm glad to be in good company. My difficulties come when I look at how the neo-Calvinist in general, and Jellema in particular, understand the *content* of citizenship in the city of God. Naturally, disagreements here will have an impact on the education we offer.

When Jellema and the other neo-Calvinists speak about life in the kingdom, little is said about injustice—I mean, about actual concrete injustices. Little recognition is given to the oppression and deprivation under which so much of humanity suffers. Little notice is taken of the sorrows and tears of our existence. Little attention is given to the significance of the Lament in the Bible. Jellema speaks of the "will to culture," and Herman Dooyeweerd speaks of the "cultural mandate." But neither speaks much of the call to bring good tidings to the afflicted, to bind up the brokenhearted, to proclaim liberty to the captives, to liberate those who are bound, to comfort all those who mourn.

Why is that?

I don't know. I have never felt that I fully understood it. So I can only speculate. Is it perhaps because those who have embraced neo-Calvinism have been near the top of the social hierarchy? Is it because they have been in power or closely connected to people in power? Is it because for them suffering was not a very prominent part of their experience? Is the basic explanation, in short, psychosocial? Has neo-Calvinism functioned as an ideology of the Christian bourgeoisie? I don't know. But I judge that this explanation cannot be dismissed out of hand.

Or is it perhaps because the neo-Calvinists have given insufficient recognition to the *fallenness* of our world? Strange indeed if that were true of those who identify themselves as Calvinists, given the reputation Calvinists have of being fixated on sin. But is it possibly true nonetheless? Has the undevelopedness of the world so struck the neo-Calvinists that its *fallenness* is insufficiently recognized? Have they focused so much on creation orders that they have neglected the rebellious and painful disorder of sin? Could it be that this is why liberation theology raises such alarm among many of us? At one point in his Stone lectures, Abraham Kuyper said that "verily Christ has swept away the dust with which man's sinful limitations had covered up this world-order, and has made it glitter again in its original brilliancy."[20] "Has swept away the dust." "Has made it glitter again in its original brilliancy." Tell that to a South African black! But no, answer for yourself: Do you think that description fits this fallen world of ours? Have you ever noticed how much time we neo-Calvinists devote to such abstract questions as, "Is politics legitimate?" "Is art legitimate?" "Is business legitimate?" and never do our listeners sit on the edge of their chairs wondering what the answer will be this time. For always the answer is, "Yes, of course, these are all legitimate." So then our students, with this legitimization ringing in their ears, plunge into politics or art or business, perhaps coming back to us later to remark on the compromises they have had to make, adding that a course in professional ethics would sure be a nice thing to take sometime. But the truth is that there is no such thing as politics in the abstract. There is only Canadian politics, and Ontario politics, etc. And all those politics are *fallen* politics. Oh yes, I know that they still reflect something of God's order, and I am thankful for that. But nonetheless they are fallen politics. And before we enter them we had better assess the compromises that we will make so as to judge whether we can enter at all. A leading Anabaptist thinker once remarked to me that "you Calvinists are always leaping over the fact of sin." I think I now know what he meant; at the time I did not.

Or is our ignoring of the injustices and the suffering of the world due perhaps to the fact that we have too easily identified sin with idolatry? If the only form of human fallenness that we recognize in our theories is idolatry, then it is easy to see all of us as consigned together to the same boat of living in a society that idolizes economic growth, or national security, or aggrandizement of nation, or whatever, and not to hear the cries of those in the bottom of the boat whose necks are being trampled on. This remark applies, as I see it, to my friend Bob Goudzwaard's work, which in so many other ways I find admirable. In very creative ways he has analyzed the idolatries of our age. Yet something about his discussions leaves me feeling uneasy. I think it is that the cries of the people are given too little voice. I have come to think that this is bound to happen if one reduces sin, in its social manifestations, to idolatry. Then one will be inclined to focus on our *joint* predicament of being enslaved to social idols. Sin yields greed and meanness and hostility and jealousy and exploitation and domination and sloth and self-loathing. Can those all be reduced to idolatry? I doubt it. Is idolatry, rather, just one of the many modes of that more pervasive and variegated thing that is sin?

Or is the fault in the neo-Calvinist vision to be traced back to that Romantic view of human existence as basically *expression?* Perhaps if one sees the call to Christian existence as fundamentally the call to express one's faith with integrity and thoroughness—the call to form and shape reality into the contours of faith—then one is unlikely to hear the cries of those outside of one. If one thinks of life as expression, then perhaps one is more inclined to talk than to listen, to make sure that one's philosophy and poetry are expressive of Christian truth than to plant trees with the Palestinians in violation of Israeli regulations, to be more concerned about the welfare of one's Christian political party than about the suffering and hopes of the Indonesians.

I don't know which of these speculations is closest to the truth; perhaps each has some truth in it. What I do know is that the life for which we educate must be a life of seeking justice and showing mercy as well as a life of wresting Christian culture from nature. I say I *do* know this. I didn't know it eighteen years ago. In preparation for this speech, I undertook to reread for the first time in many years a speech I gave in 1966 entitled "Curriculum: By What Standard?" In that speech, the miseries and injustices of the world went unnoticed and unmentioned. So the speculations through which I just took you are speculations about my own prior self. But try the experiment for yourself. Pick one of your favorite speeches or writings from our tradition and look to see whether injustices are ever mentioned—not whether the abstract thing of *injustice* is ever mentioned but whether *injustices* are mentioned.

Once I did not know, but now I do know, that a program of Christian education that grounds itself only on the command to have dominion and not also on the command to free people cannot be an acceptable program of Christian education. Once I did not know, but now I do know, that a program of Christian learning that seeks only to develop abstract science in Christian perspective and not also to develop praxis-oriented science of service to Christian social action can be of only limited use in Christian education.

Teaching for Justice, Delight, and Gratitude

I'm sure I don't have to emphasize that acceptance of the point I have been making will have many educational consequences. But before I

call your attention to a few of these educational consequences, I want
to point to what I see as a second deficiency in the standard neo-Calvinist way of understanding our citizenship in the city of God. This deficiency seems to me primarily due to that habit, along the lines of the
Romantics, of seeing our fundamental calling as giving form to nature
as the expression of faith. What gets lost in this way of looking at things
is delight and gratitude and worship: delight in God's creation, delight
in humanity's works of art, grateful worship of God. Of course, nobody
in the tradition ever explicitly opposed standing back in delight and gratitude. Yet emphasis on such receptive attitudes as these too seldom had
a place in the thought of our forebears; at best it came in as an *after-
thought*. Is it not for this reason that our worship has been so impoverished—so *non-worshipful?* Is it not for this reason that we have found
art so awkward, regularly trying to justify it by reference to what it
teaches us, apparently not finding delight noble enough? And is it not
for this reason that especially in the Dutch branch of neo-Calvinism the
image of God is so overwhelmingly that of lawgiver and the image of
our appropriate response to God so overwhelmingly that of obedience?
In the Bible, and yes, in John Calvin too, there is something deeper than
obedience to God, the lawgiver. What is deeper is gratitude to God, our
benefactor. Obedience emerges from gratitude, and one of the things
for which we are grateful is God's law. In Calvin, says the Reformation
scholar Brian Gerrish, the human being "is defined as the point of creation at which the sheer goodness of God is reflected or imaged in an
act of filial piety or thankful love."[21] To be human is to be the grateful
mirror of God's goodness.

In summary, I suggest that in the classical neo-Calvinist way of
understanding the life of the kingdom for which we educate there is
too little recognition of the importance of the struggle for justice and too
little recognition of the importance of delight and worship. In Jellema's
own scheme for education, these deficiencies show up, for one thing,
in the fact that he proposes conducting his religious depth analysis
exclusively on products of intellectual and literary culture. Though he
did not deny that art and worship and social structure express the mind
of a *civitas*, he himself never proposed conducting religious depth analysis of society in the manner of Goudzwaard nor religious depth analysis
of art in the manner of Calvin Seerveld. I suppose he thought—and of
course he was not peculiar in this—that books were the most articulate expression of the mind of a *civitas*. Yet he never, to my knowledge,
argued this. And in any case, it is clear to me that over the past ten to
twenty years we have come to see that he was a bit myopic on this score.
We have expanded the application of his own practice of religious depth
analysis to artifacts that he himself did not much bother with, even

though he firmly held that they, too, were in principle susceptible to such analysis.

But what do we do once we are persuaded that we must expand our view of life in the city of God to include the struggle against injustice and to include celebrative delight in all that is good? Do we just add these new emphases to the old ones, thereby producing an unblended stew? Do we start with a bit of cultural development, add some struggle for justice and liberation, and spice it with a bit of delight in God and world and art? No, we can do better than that. We can bring things together. I have come to think that the most promising concept for capturing God's and our mission in the world is the biblical concept of shalom. Shalom is the content of that kingdom that Jesus said was breaking in and whose ultimate presence his death and resurrection have secured. We now are to delight in the shalom we experience and to share in God's cause of advancing its presence. There is no shalom without justice. But beyond that, shalom is delight in all one's relationships: with God, neighbor, nature, and self. Shalom unites the fulfillment of culture with the liberation of justice. Life in the city of God is a life committed to struggling for shalom and to appreciating the flickers of shalom that already brighten our existence. Christian education is education for shalom.

And how do we teach for shalom? How do we teach for life in the kingdom? Jellema was clear on the matter: In and through and beyond giving students the skills and knowledge necessary for such life (making sure that the skills and knowledge are both an expression of the Christian mind), one seeks to induct students into the Christian *mind*, into the Christian way of thinking. Jellema's assumption was that once students had been imbued with the Christian mind, then they could reasonably be expected to *act on* that mind—to express it, to articulate it— in their social and cultural existence. Behind this was, of course, his assumption that Christian existence fundamentally has the structure of expression. As he saw it, the Christian way of *thinking about* the world will just naturally express itself in the Christian way of *being in* the world.

I think Jellema's philosophy on this point has been generally shared among us. Our practice has been to cultivate a Christian mind in students on the assumption that students who think with that mind will act on that mind. In recent years, Harro van Brummelen, Geraldine Steensma, and Donald Oppewal have argued for a more holistic arrangement of the knowledge we attempt to communicate, basing their argument on word studies of the biblical words regularly translated with our English word *knowledge*. But this constitutes no revision in our basic assumption that the school's contribution to the shaping of a Christian way of being in the world is the formation of a Christian way of thinking.

I suppose it was especially Cornelius Jaarsma, from among all those who contributed to the philosophy of these schools, who felt uncomfortable with the assumption that to teach for a Christian way of being in the world, one teaches a Christian way of thinking. Jaarsma found this too intellectualistic and believed it did not respect the integrated totality of a person's psyche. Beginning from this insight, he tried to compose a comprehensive philosophy of education. However, he seemed to many people to fall along the way into a constricted view of life in the *civitas dei;* some perceived him as "pietist" and "individualist." As I read the history, this prevented him from ever having much influence.

But I have come to think that we must raise the issue anew. Suppose we see clearly that we teach for a certain way of being in the world and not just for a certain way of thinking about the world. Is it correct to assume that the best strategy for achieving that comprehensive goal is to teach students to *think* in a certain way? How do we bring up children in the way they should go—not just in the way they should think but in the way they should go?

If we genuinely wish a person to act in a certain way, customarily we will regard some knowledge as relevant, and if the person does not already have that knowledge, we will do what we can to ensure that he or she acquires it. Customarily, also various skills and abilities are relevant, and if the person does not already have those, we will also do what we can to ensure that he or she acquires them. But knowledge and ability don't yet yield action. To cultivate action one must cultivate the tendency or disposition or inclination—call it what you will—on the part of the person to act in the manner desired in the relevant circumstances. So I have myself been led to ask how we can effectively and responsibly inculcate in students the tendency to act in certain ways. Specifically, is teaching them to *think* in a certain way an effective means of getting them to *act on* what they think?

It seems to me that sometimes it helps. Sometimes it really is the case that when people perceive the practical implications of the general principles they hold, they proceed to act thereon. But on the basis of the evidence, as I read it, we must at once add that usually this is not how it goes. And let me here state that when I say this, I am again raising questions about my own former self. When I helped revise the Calvin College curriculum in the mid-1960s, I assumed that the best strategy for initiating students into the life of the city of God was to ask them to study the academic disciplines—of course, the disciplines in Christian perspective. I and my colleagues argued that this would give students the knowledge relevant and necessary to live in the world in a Christian way. We never asked, though, whether there was good reason to think that this would also *tend* to make them live this way. That slip, I fear, is common among us: We raise the question of relevance but ignore the question of tendency.

The truth is that there isn't any good reason to think that, for the most part, putting the abstract academic disciplines in front of students will make them tend to adopt the Christian way of being in the world. All of us are well aware of some of the reasons why that is so. Let me mention just one: People all too often don't bother to explore the practical applications of the general principles they hold; they keep their thought and action in separate compartments. And don't think that this defect is mainly to be found among non-teachers. Repeatedly, I have heard speeches given at Christian school conventions that, so far as I could see, gave no guidance whatsoever to teachers for their activities in the classroom, or if they did give guidance, the guidance they gave went in quite different directions from those that I knew the speaker himself accepted. The talk was radical; the practice, conservative. Often these speeches are filled with truths so abstractly expressed that no guidance is forthcoming. Accordingly, over the years I have reflected on why it is that people nonetheless like such speeches, as often they do. I suspect that sometimes the very reason such speeches are given, and the very reason they are admired, is that people don't *want* their actions guided into change. They want their emotions stirred, their loyalties enhanced, their minds filled with glittering thoughts, but actions changed? No.

How *do* we shape action? I myself have come to the conclusion that the wisdom of the ages tells us, and contemporary psychology confirms it, that there are three fundamental processes for the formation of action. One such process is *discipline*. Other things being equal, we can increase the tendency of persons to act in certain ways by inducing in them the expectation that if they act that way, consequences desirable to them will ensue, or if they do not act that way, consequences undesirable to them will ensue.

A second such process is *modeling*, as it is called by psychologists. Other things being equal, the tendency of persons to act in certain ways is increased when someone who is loved or admired by that person regularly acts that way in the presence of the person.

Yet a third such fundamental process is that of *giving reasons*. Other things being equal, one can increase the tendency of persons to act in certain ways by giving them reasons for acting that way—reasons that appeal, of course, to principles that the person in question accepts.

Here I have stated these processes, or strategies, in extremely crude and unqualified fashion. In my book *Educating for Responsible Action*, I introduced a good many of the needed qualifications. The main point to notice here is that just initiating students into the Christian mind—especially when that is understood as a mind good for all citizens in all seasons—is not likely to have much effect on their actions unless the initiation actually incorporates reasons for acting in certain quite specific ways and unless it makes appropriate use of discipline and modeling. If the schooling of our children focuses just on mind formation, then we must expect that when they emerge from school and take up their adult lives, they will *talk* the Christian mind and *live* the mind of the world.

I have on various occasions reflected on the educational implications of these truths—if truths they be. I have suggested that we must begin to see the entire school situation as the educative agent and not just the curriculum. I have raised the question of how Christian schooling can possibly be effective when it occurs in an environment in which so much counter-discipline, counter-modeling, and counter-reasoning take place. I have stressed the importance of praxis-oriented scholarship in the Christian community. Here let me just observe that as we try to put together a new philosophy of Christian education that pays attention to these truths, we shall in effect have to develop a new anthropology. No longer can we think of human existence as fundamentally giving outward expression to inward thoughts, those inward thoughts shaped in turn by whom or what we name as God. Sometimes that happens, indeed. But we are also creatures of habit and disposition, creatures prone to imitation. These all shape our flow of action. We can by thought and will *intervene* in the flow of action, but it is quite mistaken to suppose that action as a whole is the expression of thought and will. Our actions emerge from our *interaction* with reality. We are *interactive* creatures: We have a structure, and reality has a structure, and we interact. I fear that you and I have fallen into the habit, characteristic of the modern philosophers, of thinking of the self as some sort of imperial entity, defined by thought and volition, floating unencumbered above the world of body and history. That view will have to go. We are creatures of dust into whom life has been breathed, to whom a mandate has been given along with the freedom to carry out that mandate, in whom openness to God has been implanted. We shall have to learn how to take *all* these ancient revealed truths seriously together.

So there is our agenda: In the light of rethinking the life for which we educate and the nature of the person educated, in the context of appropriating and building on the traditions we have inherited, we must rethink and restructure the education we offer so that it does indeed become education effective for life in that kingdom whose content is shalom and whose Lord is Jesus Christ.

I have spoken of our past and our future. But let us remember that ultimately our past and our future is in him who is the first and the last, the beginning and the end, the Alpha and the Omega, the a and the z, the sowing and the harvest, the morning star and the evening star, the one who came and the one who comes, the one behind us and the one ahead of us, our source and our end, the glow before our present dark age and the radiance after, the joy before our suffering and the rejoicing that awaits its end, the one who saw our tears coming and the one who wipes away our tears, the one who sang with the stars at their creation and the one who sings with the saints at their re-creation, the one who daily gives us loaves and fish and the one who invites us to his victory banquet, our servant and our king. It is for life   and yes, for death as well—in his embrace that we educate.

chapter six

The School
as Educative Agent

Not long after the publication of Wolterstorff's book *Educating for Responsible Action*, he addressed an audience concerning ways in which the school, itself, teaches. He explained that Christian school leaders have seriously concerned themselves with *curricular content*, and that is important. But if the goal of Christian education is Christian life and not just Christian thought, then schools must be concerned not only with the knowledge and abilities to live that life but also with the students' *tendencies* to use that knowledge and those abilities in living that life.

The school is a community. And if it is to be a Christian school, that community must be a *Christian* community. Of course, it remains a school. So the thing to say is that the Christian school must be a Christian *educational* community. That is its defining character.

84

If the school is to be a Christian educational community, then you and I, as responsible for that community, must reflect seriously on its *curricular structure,* doing our best to make sure that that structure is both reflective of the Christian gospel and responsive to the needs of the students. Second, we must reflect seriously on its *curricular content,* doing our best to make sure that this too is reflective of the gospel and responsive to the needs of the students. Third, we must reflect seriously on its *pedagogy,* making sure that this is faithful and relevant. And fourth, we must reflect seriously on the *structure of the community as community*—on the rules it lays down and the operational practices it follows, on the way authority and responsibility are distributed, and so forth, doing our best to see to it that these too are faithful to the gospel and responsive to the needs of the students. Curricular structure, curricular content, pedagogy, and community structure and operation are the things we need to reflect on in the light of fidelity and relevance.

It appears to me that we in the Christian school movement have pretty much ignored the latter two of these; our serious reflections have been focused almost entirely on the first two, curricular structure and content. Part of the reason for that is pretty clear: We believe it's primarily through curriculum that education takes place. Decisions on those other matters, particularly decisions on community structure and operation, are regarded as decisions concerning what will and what will not support the education we offer; we don't think of community structure and operation as having to do with education. Our reason, in turn, for thinking this is that in good measure we regard the goal of the school as the development of Christian *thought* on the part of the students. We want to develop in students a Christian *perspective.* It may be that the ultimate outcome we hope for in the students is a Christian way of being in the world. But we assume that the means to that outcome is developing in the students a Christian world-and-life view.

The Need for Tendency Goals

Now, as some of you know, I have for some years been working on and have just recently completed a book on the topic of effective and responsible strategies for shaping how children tend to act. I call it *Educating for Responsible Action.* What lay behind the book was my increasingly strong conviction that it's psychologically naive to suppose that shaping students' thoughts will shape their way of being in the world— that as a result of inculcating in students a Christian world-and-life view, they will exhibit a Christian way of being in the world. Knowledge does not just automatically flow into action. Of course, it's true that action *requires* knowledge. And it's also true that there's nothing one can do by way of education that *guarantees* that students will act a certain way; students remain free agents. Nonetheless, the question that motivated the inquiry that led to the book was this: What can educators do to *cultivate* in students the tendency or disposition to act a certain way? Though action of a certain sort cannot be guaranteed, perhaps there are things teachers can do that will increase its likelihood. If so, then assuming that the goal of Christian education is Christian *life* and not just Christian *thought*, the school will have to aim at developing not only the *knowledge* and the *abilities* of students but the *tendencies* of students to *use* their knowledge and abilities in certain ways. Our education will have to have *tendency* goals in addition to cognitive and ability goals.

Let me pause here for a moment. It's been my experience that some teachers in Christian schools get nervous when I say that Christian education may have to include tendency goals. Many would clearly prefer that we confine ourselves to teaching for knowledge and abilities and let the students decide what they will do with the knowledge and abilities acquired. Since such teachers are usually not opposed to trying to develop in students a Christian world-and-life view, what this objection presupposes is the conviction that developing Christian thinking in students does not by itself develop in students a disposition or tendency to act a certain way. And that's exactly the conclusion to which I've come: Knowledge and ability don't amount to disposition. But if you agree with me that the ultimate goal of Christian education is Christian life and not just Christian thought, and if you also agree with me that knowledge and ability are not tendency or disposition, then I don't see how you can avoid agreeing that the goals of Christian education have to include tendency goals. And in any case, as will become clear shortly, we who are teachers unavoidably have an influence on how our students tend to act. The question is not *whether* we will have such an influence but whether we will become reflectively aware of the influence we have and whether we will aim at having an appropriate influence.

The question whose answer I pursued then was this: How, in the light of the wisdom of the ages and the best recent psychological studies, can we responsibly shape how students tend to act? I concluded that traditional wisdom and contemporary studies together point to the conclusion that there are three grand strategies for shaping how people tend to act. There are others in addition, but these three are basic.

Three Ways to Shape Actions

The wisdom of the ages tells us, and contemporary psychological studies elaborately confirm, that if we want to influence how someone acts, it helps to attach rewards to the positive behavior and unpleasant consequences to the negative behavior. We can call this *discipline*, provided we remember that it includes the positive as well as the negative. Many important and interesting questions can be raised about using discipline as a strategy for influencing how a person will tend to act. What psychological mechanisms are at work? What sorts of rewards and punishments work best for whom and when? Do rewards work better than punishments? And so forth. But let me move on.

Second, the wisdom of the ages tells us, and contemporary psychological studies confirm, that if we want to influence how someone acts, it helps if we act that way. This is the phenomenon that psychologists call *modeling*. Children in particular, but adults as well, tend to model their actions on the actions of others. The incidence of yielding to a certain temptation can be increased in a child by putting the child in the presence of an adult who yields to that temptation. The incidence of aggressive behavior can be increased by putting a child in the presence of a model who acts aggressively. The incidence of altruistic action can be increased by putting a child in the presence of a model who acts altruistically. A child can be induced to set higher or lower standards of performance by putting him or her in the presence of a model who sets higher or lower standards. And so forth.

Before I mention a third strategy for influencing how people act, let me highlight the fact that discipline and modeling pertain to the *comportment* of the teacher—and more generally, to the *comportment* of the school. They do not pertain to the curriculum. It's been my experience, when discussing with teachers these two strategies of discipline and modeling, that almost always some in the audience get angry with me for not becoming concrete and proposing lesson plans, steps, games, dilemmas, and so forth, whereby tendencies can be taught. The objection misses the point. The features of the educational situation in general and the comportment of personnel within that situation influence the tendencies of children to act in certain ways. The situation is not that I fail or refuse to get down to the concrete details of lesson plans, preferring to remain in the philosopher's realm of the abstract; rather, lesson plans are not relevant. If you agree with me that Christian education is for Christian life and not just for Christian thought, and if you are willing to accept the evidence that discipline and modeling influence how people tend to act, then we have to think of the entire educational situation as the educative agent. The formal curriculum is just one component within that totality—overall an exceedingly important component, but when it comes to tendency learning, not the most important.

Further, the curriculum may well be contradicted by other components within the totality; worse, it may be nullified. If in our classrooms we talk about how Christians should treat the earth, and all the while students see the school itself treating the earth differently, we know what's likely to be the outcome: Students will preach as the school preaches and do as the school does. If we want to be effective, we have to get our act together.

These considerations have led me to adopt a different model for thinking of formal education from that with which I operated until just a few years ago. The determining purpose behind a school—the reason for the sake of which the school exists—is that teachers shall instruct students in a curriculum. Until a few years ago, I moved from recognizing this as the determining purpose to assuming that the curriculum was also where the great bulk of the school's educating took place. I acknowledged, of course, that classroom curricular instruction is supplemented by a variety of out-of-the-classroom activities, but supplementation is how I thought of those other activities. The school exists for the sake of classroom curricular instruction, and that, so I assumed, is where the great bulk of the educating that it does occurs.

From there I went on to think of those school personnel who were not involved in the classroom situation as support staff: the administration in all its ramifications, janitors, groundskeepers, librarians, and so forth. I recognized, of course, that significant differentiations could and should be made within this group; nonetheless, I thought of them all together as enablers of education rather than as educators.

The model won't do. Of course, it is true that the school exists mainly for the sake of curricular instruction, and it is true that various other activities of the school function to support such instruction. But what we learn from the studies to which I have alluded is that it's a mistake to identify the education performed by the school with the curriculum of the classroom. The way to think is rather this: The entire situation, and the comportment of the personnel within that situation, play an educational role. The curriculum is just one component within the educative function of the school generally—a decisive component, indeed, for the particular institution that is the school would not exist but for this. Nonetheless, once the school is up and going, the teaching of the curriculum is just one of the ways in which education is accomplished. And when it comes to tendency learning, it's not the main way.

For those of us who are teachers, this alternative model is unsettling. I've already mentioned there aren't lesson plans for tendency learning—though shortly I'll mention an exception to this generalization. But that's not the main source of unease. The main source of unease is the unmistakable implication that the educative role of the teacher cannot be confined to what he or she says in the classroom. For one thing, it cannot be confined to what the teacher *says* but unavoidably includes what he or she *does*. Second, it cannot be confined to what he or she says or does *in the classroom* but unavoidably includes what he or she says or does generally. It's comportment in general that educates, whether for good or ill. The thought is unsettling!

I mentioned that the wisdom of the ages and studies by contemporary psychologists join in telling us that there are three fundamental strategies for influencing how someone tends to act. So far I've mentioned only two, discipline and modeling; it's those two that force us to adopt an alternative model of the educative agent. Let me now mention the third. If we want to influence how someone acts, it helps to give him or her a reason for acting that way.

The offering by a teacher to a student of a reason for acting a certain way can be a component in the curriculum; it's something that can be included in a lesson plan. Notice, though, that such reasons are different from what we mainly think of when we think of curriculum. They don't, strictly speaking, belong to natural science, to social science, to history; instead, they serve to bridge the gap between thought and practice. They are what the philosophical tradition has called *practical reasons*.

Let me close by highlighting some of the implications of what I have been saying. I have the sense that I myself have only begun to discern the implications of the alternative model for school education that I have suggested; these, then, are no more than some of the more obvious implications.

First, having become clear on our goals in Christian education, we must then, keeping in mind that the school as a whole is the educative agent, ask where and how those goals can be advanced—not neglecting the curriculum in arriving at an answer to this question but also not myopically fixing on it as if it were the sole agent of education. In particular, we want to keep in mind that when the practice of the school or its personnel contradicts its message, its message will be rendered ineffective.

Second, the school must become a loving community. Out with authoritarianism and all its relatives. For one thing, if we want to produce love, we must model love. But also, what we learn from the modeling research is that the most effective models in general are those for whom the child feels affection or esteem.

Third, whether we like it or not, we must acknowledge that the comportment and person of the teacher—inside and outside the classroom—are as important as his or her academic competence. The implications for hiring policy are obvious.

Fourth, we have to acknowledge that it's of educational relevance, and not only of relevance to determinations of justice, whether a teacher is male or female, white or black, young or old, and so forth. These all have modeling effects.

Lastly, we have to supplement abstract inquiry by addressing the concrete issues that come a Christian's way in present-day society—war, ecology, family, work, recreation, and so forth. Since society and culture together are our concern, not just culture by itself, we have to develop and offer "bridging reasons."

Perhaps I can summarize what I have been saying like this: Education for Christian praxis requires Christian praxis. If a school is to educate for Christian life, it will in its totality have to exhibit Christian life. The school as a whole is the educative agent.

chapter seven

Teaching for Tomorrow Today

The Christian Parent Controlled Schools of Australia (at that time called the National Union of Christian Parent Controlled Schools), an organization of eighty Christian schools, invited Wolterstorff to be the keynote speaker at their 1984 Education in Focus Conference. The conference was intended to challenge and inspire a practice of distinctive and substantive Christ-centered teaching. The theme for the series of lectures, "Teaching for Tomorrow Today," came out of a strong sense that teachers need to understand the potential they have to influence the development of a faith-view in their students. According to Bob Johnson, the principal who organized the conference, the goal was to inspire, challenge, and motivate teachers by helping them see the investment they make in the future generation of young adults. This chapter contains the four lectures Wolterstorff gave at the conference.

I feel sure that there are some among you who are apprehensive about having a philosopher as your major speaker at this conference. So I have decided that rather than present to you on this occasion a sequentially structured, logically organized, thoroughly integrated philosophy of education, I would do something a bit more personal, something that has a bit of an autobiographical character to it. I propose to take you along with me on some lines of thought that I have been following in recent years and that I find myself forced to bring to mind when I think about Christian education. Some of these lines of thought I have only recently undertaken; some I have been pursuing for a long time now. I'm going to present to you four lines of thought. Then I'm going to bring things together by asking what a Christian school should look like if these lines of thought are correct in their basic contours. If I succeed, you will be thinking along with me about the educational implications of what has been said. I must warn you, though, not to expect all the ropes to be tightly twisted and all the knots firmly tied, for these lines of thought have produced certain perplexities in me that I don't yet know how to resolve.

The Life for Which We Educate

In my own thinking about education, I always begin with the goals or ends of education. I think of all the concrete decisions about education as properly made by backing up from there—curricular decisions, pedagogical decisions, institutional-structural decisions, and so forth. I know, of course, that often they are in fact not made that way. We teachers teach as we were taught, or we follow the fads. The result is that often there is a serious discrepancy between educational practice and professed aim. But I scarcely have to argue to you that that's not the way it should be. And perhaps right here I should remark that I am going to be looking at the education of children and young people, not adults. In my judgment, quite different things have to be said about adult education.

The education of a child is always, I would say, either tacitly or explicitly pointed toward a certain way of being in the world for that child. It's true that in assessing an educational situation we must look not only at what the education is pointed toward but at the quality of the situation itself. I shall have something to say about that later. But always the educator is aiming for certain changes in the child. If that were not so, we would be engaged in mere baby-sitting, not in education. No doubt educators hope that those changes will be relevant to life in the classroom, but they especially hope that many of them will be relevant to life outside the classroom. They hope for carryover. If everything learned in the classroom were forgotten at the door of the classroom, if students displayed that strange sort of scholastic amnesia, then what we think of as education would hardly be taking place. And though the responsible teacher hopes that some of those changes will be relevant to the child's life today, he or she also hopes that many of them will be relevant to the child's life in the future: Teaching for tomorrow today.

I know that often in the past and sometimes yet today adults treat children as not yet persons, as entities waiting to become persons. They stuff them full of things that might someday be useful, without concerning themselves with what would be useful now. Whatever our practice, I trust that no one would any longer defend this. A child has the dignity of a person—which is, at bottom, the dignity of being made in God's image. "Bring the little children to me," said Jesus. So to say it once again, education is unavoidably pointed toward a way of being in the world within the classroom and outside it, today and for the future.

Education: A Way of Being in the World

Which means, of course, that education unavoidably touches religious issues. This is why education is such a battlefield among us. Partly it's a battlefield because of its importance. We all realize that those who control education have a decisive influence on the youth of our society and that those who decisively influence the youth of our society thereby shape our society's future. And partly it's a battlefield because we really don't understand very well how human beings learn, so we have our disputes about that. But these together are not enough to account for the battlefield that education is among us. It becomes for us a battlefield because in pointing toward a certain way of being in the world it touches religious issues, and we in our pluralistic societies disagree on religious issues, disagree profoundly.

Let's follow this thought that education is pointed toward a certain way of being in the world for the child. Something entirely unique about human existence is that new human beings enter the world at a certain point in history and that the world situation into which they enter then becomes their own world situation, in the sense that it shapes them and they shape it. They enter commonalties that are at a certain point in their historical odyssey. They enter nature that is at a certain stage in the process of being shaped by and shaping humankind. They enter culture that is at a certain point in its development. And yes, they enter the history of God's interaction with humankind. In all these ways, they enter the world at a certain point in history, whereupon that world situation becomes theirs and is no longer merely that of their ancestors.

But what is also unique about human existence is that there are, open to each of us, various ways of being in the world. We must not exaggerate the extent to which this is true. We must not adopt the imperial stance of the modern philosophers according to which the self floats freely about the empirical world. We are, all of us, shaped by the world around us. We are embedded in this world. We are creatures of dust and creatures of habit and impulse and disposition and conditioning. Yet we are not only acted upon but we act upon. We and the world *inter*act. We envisage states of affairs different from those that now prevail, and sometimes we have it in our power freely to undertake to bring about those states of affairs. In that way we are confronted with alternative ways of shaping our lives within that world of society and nature and culture and divine/human interaction that confronts us at a certain moment of history. We exist within a structured world within which we, ourselves structured beings, can set a direction for our lives. So education not only points children toward *a* way of being in the world, but it also points them toward one *certain* way from among alternative ways.

It isn't always thought of that way. Frequently, educational debates in our societies are presented as if they were just debates about method: How can children be taught to read more effectively? How can the American child be brought up to the Japanese child in mathematical knowledge and skills? And so forth. Don't get me wrong; some debates among educators are really just debates over method. But the deepest educational debates are debates over how a human being appropriately lives in the world.

Two Major Educational Ideologies

I think a good way to bring this point home is to look at two of the major ideologies of education in the Western world today. We will see that there is vastly more than method at stake here. Religious issues are being debated. For Christian educators, this glance at some major ideologies will perhaps also help us perk up our ears and open our eyes to some of the formative "spirits" of our society.

Some in our society see education as *nurturing* the child so that he or she *matures* into an individual whose desires, interests, and motivations are satisfied. The appropriate criterion for the choices that go into the formation of a person's way of being in the world is, according to this view, what will contribute to the person's satisfaction. The business of education is to serve, in whatever way relevant, the attainment of such satisfaction. Examples of educational theorists who hold maturationists views are A. S. Neill and Carl Rogers, and going further back, Jean-Jacques Rousseau.

Almost invariably the image of biological growth is prominent in the exposition of such theories. The function of the school, says the maturationist, is to provide nourishment for the maturing child. The core idea is that children will turn out happiest if they are allowed to grow without inhibition in a nourishing environment. One hears talk of the need for providing "growth experiences" for students.

Of course, no educator is in favor of immaturity. All are in favor of students becoming mature. But not all educators understand maturation in the same way as the person whom I am calling a maturationist; not everyone holds that the whole business of the school is to contribute to the satisfaction of students' innate impulses and desires.

At the heart of maturational theories are a specific concept of the self and an insistence that it is important for each self to express or realize itself. The fundamental theses are that each self comes with a variety of innate desires, interests, and motivations, that mental health and happiness will be achieved only if these innate desires are allowed to find their satisfaction within the natural and social environment, and that an individual's mental health and happiness constitute his or her ultimate good. Of course, all would agree that these environments are not completely malleable and that the individual has *some* innate desires that cannot possibly be satisfied without ensuing pain. The maturationists tend to hold, however, that no fundamental unhappiness and mental disease will result if such particular innate desires and interests are extinguished. What must be avoided at all costs, though, is imposing the wishes and expectations of others onto the self. Down that road lie unhappiness and disease. The way to the ultimate good that is personal health and happiness is self-expression, not the internalization of others' wishes.

The proper goal of the educator, then, is to provide the child with an environment that is *permissive*—in that it does not impose the wishes of others onto the child—and *nourishing*—in that it provides for the satisfaction of the child's desires and interests. On this all maturationists would agree. Some would say that this is the limit of what they should do: The school should confine itself to providing a permissive nourishing environment in which children can express themselves. Others argue that persons characteristically develop internal blockages of their natural desires and interests and that the school should not only provide a permissive nourishing environment but also work to remove inhibitions on self-expression.

It is easy to see why those holding a maturational view often speak
of the properly run school as "child-centered." Anti-maturationists often
counter this slogan by claiming that one might as well call the properly
run school "subject-centered," since one never teaches some *person* without teaching some *subject* to that person. But that misses the point. The
maturationist holds that the desires and interests of the child ought to
determine the subject matter.

The normative theory underlying the maturationist view is always
either antinomianism or ethical egoism. With the antinomian view, the
categories of right and wrong have no application; nothing is either right
or wrong. With ethical egoism, they do have application, but what is
right for a given person just consists of what satisfies his or her own
desires and interests. The desirous impulsive self is its own norm. Either
way, we hear regularly that we should avoid blaming and praising others for their actions. Blame and praise cause the persons whose actions
are evaluated to internalize the evaluations of the evaluator, and this is
precisely what must at all costs be avoided. That is the prime evil. If the
maturationists had their way, praising and blaming would disappear
from human life.

I have been speaking of those in our society who see education as
consisting of nurturing the child toward the satisfaction of desires. There
are others who see things in almost the opposite way: Education is to
form or mold or shape the child so that eventually he or she becomes
socialized. Children must be imprinted with the rules and roles of the
surrounding society so that they become well-functioning, contributing
members thereof. Whereas the focus in maturational theories is on the
child, the focus here is on *society*. Education is society's way of maintaining and perpetuating itself as a well-functioning organism. Emile
Durkheim and B. F. Skinner are good examples of contemporary socialization theorists; Plato was one as well.

When we look at those groupings of people that are typically regarded
as societies, we discover a massive commonality in beliefs, emotions,
and behavior. The members of society share ideals and rituals and
objects of veneration (whether persons, places, events, or artifacts). They
share understandings of their group's history and significance. They
share practices, institutions, and often religion and theology. What
stamps someone as an American, for example, and not a Frenchman is
less his or her citizenship and more this type of sharing with other Americans. To be fully American is to venerate Lincoln and not Napoleon, to
celebrate Independence Day and not Bastille Day, to prefer potato chips
to croissants. Given the comprehensive goal of inducting children into
such a society and making them well-functioning members thereof, the
socialization theorist believes that education must get children to adopt

as their own the shared cognitive, emotional, and behavioral features of their society. The goal of education is to get children to internalize these shared social phenomena.

But there is more than this to socializing children. Not only are children to become good Australians or Germans or whatever, but they are also to *contribute* to making Australia good or Germany good, etc. They are to play constructive *roles* in their society. In every society we can discern a unique and highly articulate structure of social roles and role expectations. The socialization theorist holds that the educator must acquaint children with these various role expectations and equip them to "play" a particular set of roles. To equip children for their stations and duties is the goal. Thus, the concept of social role and its duties characteristically plays a large part in the thought of socialization theorists.

Naturally, socialization theorists want to find a good fit between a student and the role for which he or she is being prepared. Usually, though, they assume that children are rather malleable. With suitable training each child can be made to fit a variety of social roles. But this will not happen if children are just allowed to "flower." Some of their behaviors must be quenched, others kindled. They must be disciplined. Whereas *freedom* is a central concept for the maturationist, *discipline* occupies central position in the thought of the socialization theorist.

Customarily, the normative theory accompanying this view of education is cultural relativism. The normative laws holding for the members of one society are distinct from those holding for another, for moral norms are simply the creations of a given society. They specify what a society thinks is right to do. Moral norms are social rules. And it makes no sense to ask if the rules are right.

I suggest that these two types of theories, maturation and socialization, are far and away the dominant ideologies of education in the West today. They shape our thought about education from top to bottom. My own sense is that today, at least in the United States, socialization theories are replacing maturation theories in ascendancy—this in spite of the fact that the political liberalism that historically has shaped the United States fits better with the maturation view, while the socialization view fits better with communist and authoritarian societies. In the seesaw battle between these two, one can see a sort of dialectic between the individual and society. Of course, theorists of both sorts recognize that children have to *cope* with their world, but they also realize that such coping occurs within the context of alternative ways of being in the world. At the root of their disagreements on education—nurturing versus forming, maturation versus socialization—are their different views on our proper human way of being in the world: Is it the desires of the individual that are to reign supreme, or is it the interests and rules of the group?

Christians, when confronted with maturation and socialization theories, have many things to say. But one thing draws their eye immediately—the assumption in the one case that the individual, and in the other, that society, can do no wrong; the assumption in the one case that the desires of the individual, and in the other, that the rules and roles of society, are the appropriate critera for determining our way of being in the world. They ask whether certain desires of an individual may be wrong and whether certain roles and rules of society may likewise be wrong. They are not, of course, alone in asking this question; they have allies of various stripes. But they ask it because they have ringing in their ears the words of the prophets and apostles—and of their Lord, Jesus Christ. They ask it because they have heard their words of judgment and their call for repentance. They ask it because they have committed themselves to taking *God* as their authority. Rather than taking individual or society as their norm, they place individual and society under judgment, *God's* judgment. You can see the drift of the argument for yourself: If the maturationist proposes child-centered education and the socialization theorist proposes society-centered education, then the Christian proposes God-centered education.

God-Centered Education: Keeping Faith

But we must understand the phrase "God-centered education" aright, or we will be led astray. Deep in the medieval vision of the Christian's way of being in the world was the conviction that the contemplative life was superior to the active life. All humanity was in search of happiness; on this, the medievals held, there was no variation from person to person. Disagreement came on the issue of wherein lies our happiness. It was the conviction of most medieval thinkers that we are so created that our happiness lies in the life of the intellect, focused on that which is of most worth—God. The true end of a human lies in turning away from this world to engage in knowledgeable and loving contemplation of God. In this and in this alone lies ultimate happiness. Now, an education designed to foster such a way of being in the world—designed to foster turning away from the world toward contemplation of God—might appropriately be called, I suppose, "God-centered education." But this is not the sort of thing I have in mind with this phrase, for my understanding of the authentic Christian way of being in the world is, frankly, a Reformation understanding—though I don't at all want to suggest that it is not to be found outside the churches of the Reformation. It is.

No doubt the alternative can be approached from many different directions. In the past, I have approached it by probing the nature of faith. But here on this occasion I want to get at it from a different angle.

"I am the Alpha and the Omega," says God in the Book of Revelation, the one "who is and who was and who is coming." The picture of God constructed by the medieval theologians was that of God outside of time, dwelling in eternity, ever present, with no past and no future, impassive, immutable. The picture of the biblical writers is profoundly different: God is past and future as well as present, for his *actions* are past and future as well as present. His actions are located within our history as well as constituting the ground of our history. Central to the character of the Christian's way of being in the world is the fact that the God he or she acknowledges is engaged in a history that is both God's and ours, but a history of which God is Lord and we are not.

Recall then the farewell speech of Moses to the tribes of Israel as we find it in the Book of Deuteronomy. Like mighty gongs being struck over and over and over, three themes interweave through the speech: *remember, expect,* and *take heed.* Israel is forever to remember that the God who created the heavens and the earth has liberated her from the bondage of toiling in the brickyards of Egypt. She is forever to live in the confident expectation that God will be faithful to his promise to bless his people and give them land in which to dwell. And in the open space between never failing remembrance and never ceasing expectation, she is to take heed of God's commandments, commandments that do not impose some alien duty but are for the good of Israel's members (10:13), to the end that they may have life (4:1). In society, they shall not pervert justice; justice and only justice shall they follow (16:19–20). And they shall worship before the Lord God, rejoicing in all the good he has given them (26:10–11).

What was to be unique in the life of Israel was that its work and worship would be its way of keeping faith with the God whose actions of liberation and blessing it was forever to remember and expect. I suggest that the Christian way of being in the world, though different in content, is the same in structure. The core of the difference is, of course, that the Messiah foretold and expected by Israel is located by the Christian in Jesus of Nazareth. A fully Christian theology will be a theology of hope and of remembering, as well as a theology of keeping faith with the God whom one remembers and hopes for.

I dare say that you are already beginning to see some of the implications for the vision of education. The ultimate goal of education, as the Christian sees it, is not the maturation of the student, though maturation will find its place. It is not the socialization of the student, though socialization will also find its place. Neither is it the contemplation of

God, though that too will find its place. It is to lead the child into a life of keeping faith with the God whom we remember and expect.

Let me say a bit more about this matter of keeping faith. The picture of the Christian way of being in the world that I have just presented to you is an inescapably sacramental picture. Our world is a sacrament of God. In the stuff of nature and history, we meet God. Reality is drenched with sacrality. Both in its totality as cosmos and in its becoming as history it "is an epiphany of God, a means of His revelation, presence, and power. [It] truly 'speaks' of Him and is in itself an essential means both of knowledge of God and communion with Him, and to be so is its true nature and its ultimate destiny."[1]

And what is the appropriate response to our realization that as we tread our way through our world we have to deal with God? I like what John Calvin says on the matter. Gratitude, he suggests, is our appropriate response: an obedient, worshipful, and appreciative gratitude. Let me emphasize each of these qualifiers: Gratitude will find its manifestation in obedience to the will of God, to the laws of God. Also it will find its manifestation in the worship of God. Of course, worship is itself an act of obedience, but the deepest reason for Christians to worship God is not that they are commanded to worship but that they break forth into worship out of gratitude. And yet a third thing: Gratitude will find its manifestation in the appreciative use of the things around us, in joyful delight and delighted joy. Says Calvin: "If we ponder to what end God created food, we shall find that he meant not only to provide for necessity but also for delight and good cheer. . . . In grasses, trees, and fruits, apart from their various uses, there is beauty of appearance and pleasantness of odor."[2]

When Christians who stand in the tradition of the Reformation try to get at the core of keeping faith with God, so often it is *obedience* that they emphasize. God is perceived primarily as lawgiver and we as called to obedience. We have a task in the world. At bottom, to be human is to be responsible. In the past I have sometimes talked that way myself. But today I want to present a different picture. Obedience is of course present. I would be the last to deny, or even ignore, the place of laws, norms, tasks, responsibilities. But I suggest that there is something deeper in the Christian way of being in the world than obedience to God perceived primarily as lawgiver. That something deeper is gratitude, to a God perceived as loving his children. A *chastened* gratitude, I should perhaps add, for the Christian perceives also the anger of God with those who scorn his gifts and him the giver. Obedience is then one of the manifestations of gratitude, but only one, for there is also worship, along with the delighted and joyful appreciation of our ambient world. Again, I trust that you are getting some glimpse of the vistas that this opens up for education. A few years back I wrote a book called *Educating for Responsible Action*. I argued that a Christian theory of education is one version of responsibility theory. I still think that's true. But it doesn't catch the full picture. The Christian way of being in the world is a life of responsible, worshipful, and appreciative gratitude. Education is for that.

Educating for Shalom

And now I'd like to approach our topic from yet one more angle, this time not from the angle of what it is for us to keep faith but from the angle of the actions of the God with *whom* we keep faith. That God who is and who was and who is coming, that God whose actions we remember and expect and discern—what is the *pattern* of his actions? What is the goal toward which he is working? One answer prominent in the New Testament is that God is working to establish his reign, his kingdom. And what, I want to ask on this occasion, is the *content* of that reign of God?

I suggest that the answer of the biblical writers is that the content of God's reign is peace—or let us use the much better Hebrew word *shalom*. That community in which Christ is Lord is the shalom community. Yes, but what is shalom? Shalom is present when a person dwells at peace in all his or her relationships: with God, with self, with fellows, with nature. When shalom breaks in, then

> The wolf shall dwell with the lamb,
>   and the leopard shall lie down with the kid,
> and the calf and the lion and the fatling together,
>   and a little child shall lead them.
> The cow and the bear shall feed;
>   their young shall lie down together;
>   and the lion shall eat straw like the ox.
> The sucking child shall play over the hole of the asp,
>   and the weaned child shall put his hand on the adder's den.
>
> Isaiah 11:6–8

To dwell at peace in one's relationships, it is not enough, however, that hostility be absent. Letting live is not yet shalom. Shalom is enjoyment in one's relationships. A nation may be at peace with all its neighbors and yet be miserable in its poverty. To dwell in shalom is to *enjoy* living before God, to *enjoy* living in one's physical surroundings, to *enjoy* living with one's fellows, to *enjoy* life with oneself.

Shalom in the first place incorporates right, harmonious relationship with *God* and delight in God's worship and service. When the prophets speak of shalom, they speak of a day when human beings will no longer flee God down the corridors of time, a day when they will no longer turn in those corridors to defy their divine pursuer. Shalom is perfected when humanity acknowledges that in its service of God is true delight. "The mountain of the house of the Lord," says the prophet:

> shall be established as the highest of the mountains,
>   and shall be raised above the hills;
> and peoples shall flow to it.

>   Micah 4:1

Second, shalom incorporates right harmonious relationships with other *human beings* and delight in human community. Shalom is absent when society is a collection of individuals each out to make his or her own way in the world. And, of course, there can be delight in community only when justice reigns, only when human beings no longer oppress one another. When "justice shall make its home in the wilderness, and righteousness dwell in the grassland"—only then will it be true that "righteousness shall yield shalom, and its fruit be quietness and confidence for ever" (Isa. 32:16–17). In shalom:

> Love and Fidelity now meet,
>   Justice and Peace now embrace;
> Fidelity reaches up from earth;
>   and Justice leans down from heaven.

>   Psalm 85:10–11, paraphrased

Third, shalom incorporates right, harmonious relationships with *nature* and delight in our physical surroundings. Shalom comes when we, bodily creatures and not disembodied souls, shape the world with our labor and find fulfillment in so doing and delight in its results. In speaking of shalom, the prophet spoke of a day when the Lord would prepare

> a banquet of rich fare for all the people,
> a banquet of wines well matured and richest fare,
> well matured wines strained clear.

>   Isaiah 25:6, paraphrased

I said that justice, the enjoyment of one's rights, is indispensable to shalom. That is because a community of shalom is an *ethical* community. If individuals are not granted what is due them, if their claim on others is not acknowledged by those others, if others do not carry out their obligations to them, then shalom is wounded. That is so even if there are no *feelings* of hostility between them, because the shalom community is an ethical community that is wounded when justice is absent. But the right relationships that lie at the basis of shalom involve more than right relationships with other human beings, hence more than ethical relationships. They involve right relationships with God, with nature, and with oneself as well. Therefore, a community of shalom is more than an ethical community. It is a *responsible* community in which God's laws for the multifaceted existence of his creatures are obeyed.

And shalom goes beyond even a responsible community. We may all have acted responsibly and yet shalom may be missing, for delight may be absent. It is in this context that we must ultimately see the significance of technology. Technology makes possible advance toward shalom; progress in mastery of the world can bring shalom nearer. But the limits of technology must also be acknowledged; technology is entirely incapable of bringing about shalom between ourselves and God, and it is only marginally capable of bringing about the love of self and neighbor.

I have already cited that best known of all shalom passages in which Isaiah describes the anticipated shalom with a flourish of images of harmony—harmony among the animals, harmony between humans and animals: "The wolf shall dwell with the lamb . . ." That passage, though, is introduced with these words:

> There shall come forth a shoot from the stump of Jesse,
>   and a branch shall grow out of his roots.
> And the Spirit of the LORD shall rest upon him,
>   the spirit of wisdom and understanding,
>   the spirit of counsel and might,
>   the spirit of knowledge and the fear of the LORD.
>
> Isaiah 11:1–2

That shoot of which Isaiah spoke is he of whom the angels sang in celebration of his birth: "Glory to God in the highest, and on earth *peace* among men with whom he is pleased" (Luke 2:14). He is the one of whom the priest Zechariah said, he will "guide our feet into the way of *peace*" (Luke 1:79). He is the one of whom Simeon said, "Lord, now lettest thou thy servant depart in *peace*, according to thy word" (Luke 2:29). He is the one of whom Peter said that it was by him that God preached "good news of *peace*" to Israel (Acts 10:36). He is the one of whom Paul, speaking as a Jew to the Gentiles, said that "he came and preached *peace* to you who were far off and *peace* to those who were near" (Eph. 2:17). He is in fact Jesus Christ, whom Isaiah called the "Prince of *Peace*" (Isa. 9:6).

It was this same Jesus who said to the apostles in his farewell discourse, "The words that I say to you I do not speak on my own authority; but the Father who dwells in me does his works. Believe me that I am in the Father and the Father in me; or else believe me for the sake of the works themselves." And then he added, "I say to you, he who believes in me will also do the works that I do; and greater works than these will he do" (John 14:10–12).

Can we avoid the conclusion that not only is shalom God's cause in the world but that all who believe in Jesus will, along with him, engage in the works of shalom? Shalom is both God's cause in the world and our human calling. Even though the full incursion of shalom into our history will be a divine gift and not merely human achievement, even though its episodic incursion into our lives now also has a dimension of divine gift, nonetheless it is shalom that we are to work and struggle for. We are not to stand around, hands folded, waiting for shalom to arrive. We are workers in God's cause, his peace workers. The *missio Dei* is our mission.

Sometimes the basic category shaping Christian thought has been that of redemption; then what is emphasized is the struggle against sin, personal and social. Sometimes the basic category has been that of creation; what is then emphasized is our calling to develop our world. What I like about the category of shalom is that in pointing ahead it brings these two emphases together; we are to struggle both to open up creation and to liberate those in bondage. It is into such a life that Christian education leads the student. Christian education is education for shalom, and Christian education is education for a life of obedient, worshipful, appreciative gratitude—two ways of approaching the same rich reality.

But, of course, not everyone sees things this way, and so, of course, not everyone will wish to have their children educated for such a life. There are in our society convinced secularists—along with Jews, Muslims, Buddhists, and so forth. They reject the Christian way of being in the world that I have outlined, for themselves and for their children. In my judgment, we must respect their wishes and ask that they extend the same respect to us. Education will have to reflect and respect the pluralism of our society. It too will have to be pluralistic. That is not to say that different communities within the pluralism cannot agree, in a rough and ready way, on some common elements concerning the education of their children. They can. But those common elements will be caught up into different visions. Accordingly, when I set a Christian understanding of the goals of education alongside a maturationist and socializationist understanding of the goals, I do not contend that the education of *all* children in our society should be shaped by this Christian understanding. Christian education is an education for those who accept these goals—or more generally, perhaps, for those who accept or are sympathetic to them. Christian education must not aspire to more than the status of an *option* in our society. But it must indeed aspire to the status of a free and open option. Other visions of education must likewise aspire to no more than that. One is constantly amazed at the number of those who profess to be in favor of freedom and pluralism but who yet betray that profession when it comes to education. I don't doubt that Christians can also participate in programs of education that, in one way or another, do something else than point a child toward the Christian way of being in the world. But here I am not addressing the challenges and dilemmas facing such a person but rather the characteristics of a program of Christian education.

Let me bring my line of thought thus far to a conclusion: Maturationists see themselves as nurturing the child. Socializationists see themselves as forming the child. I suggest that the heart of education as the Christian sees it is *leading* the child. That will include nurturing and forming, but it will include those only as elements. Christian education is leading and guiding the child toward the Christian way of being in the world.

And now for a last point: Such leading or guiding is itself to be an ethically qualified act. It is to be shaped and motivated by care and concern and love for the child. It is of the same order as the care of a mother for her child, of a nurse for a patient, of a spouse for a spouse. The teacher is to be there for the child, to come through for the child, without smothering the child in paternalism or maternalism, longing instead to see the child stand tall and upright as a person of God in the world. The motive behind the teacher's education of the student is not to be one of exerting power over the student, one of baby-sitting the student, or one of perpetuating a familiar social structure. The energizing force should be that of love. Education should be an interaction of love. And need I tell you that it fails as often in this essential qualifier as it does in its appropriate ends. Leading the child toward a multifaceted life of gratitude, a life committed to shalom, and doing so out of love and care is how I see Christian education. Its contents—curriculum, pedagogy, and institutional structure—need to be developed by backing up from here, by asking what will serve that end and fulfill that motive.

The Knowledge We Use to Educate

As I stated earlier, education is always and inescapably pointed toward a certain way of being in the world. Of course, a given teacher may take for granted a certain way of being in the world or a certain style of education to the extent that she doesn't realize this. But we all realize it when we look at education in distant societies or when we confront ideologies for education in our own society that we find profoundly alien.

I also suggested that what is definitive of Christian education is that the teacher leads or guides the student into the Christian way of being in the world. From there I went on to consider what way of being that is. I suggested that it is the way of obedient, worshipful, and appreciative gratitude. Or alternatively, that it is the way toward shalom. I added that these two descriptions by no means exhaust the ways in which we may express the rich reality of the Christian way of being in the world.

A good way to introduce the next line of thought I want to follow is to draw out one of the implications of what I have been saying by contrasting it with an alternative view of the matter.

Teaching Students to Think and Live in Obedience to God

After attending public schools for eight years in the United States, I attended Christian high school for four years and then went on to a Christian college, Calvin College. I remember well that when the apologists for that system of Christian education tried to express the vision that undergirded those schools, they regularly said that the aim of the school was to impart to the student a Christian world-and-life view. What they wished to emphasize, in putting things that way, is that in the Christian gospel we find more than a set of guidelines for ecclesiastical and devotional practice. We find an entire way of looking at things, a complete perspective on reality. Thus, those who said that the aim of the Christian school was to impart a Christian world-and-life view wished to resist any sort of sacred/secular dichotomy. It was this holistic vision that led them to insist on Christian schools, contending that the supposedly neutral education provided by the American public schools was not adequate. Christ, they said, is Lord over all of life; there is not an inch of it that does not fall within his realm. And we, in our education as in our life, must recognize this cosmic lordship.

Now, I did and do find the holistic emphasis of this vision immensely admirable. Yet earlier I presented to you a somewhat different perspective. I did not say that the goal of Christian education is to impart to the student a Christian world-and-life view. I said instead that the goal is to lead the student into a Christian way of being in the world.

Why the difference? Why was I not content to use that old formula so familiar to me? Notice the word *view* at the end. For all its desire to be holistic, a desire captured in the words "world and life," this perspective fails, it seems to me, in its goal. It fails to be fully holistic. It emphasizes thought, intellection, cognition. It stresses the intellect. It sees the school as dealing with a *view*. It says, be it noted once more, that the learning presented to the student must be shaped and reshaped so that it is *Christian* learning. But nonetheless, the goal is to impart to the student a certain *view*.

In my judgment, that reflects the liberal arts tradition of education. Think, for a moment, of the works of high culture that humankind has produced through the ages: works of natural science, philosophy, theology, music, painting, poetry, architecture. The image that immediately comes to my mind is that of a mighty stream, ever widening as it approaches us, flowing down from the distant past. I suggest that the best way to think of liberal arts education is to think of it as education designed to enable the student to interact fruitfully with that stream of high culture. A liberal arts education enables the student to appropriate some of that poetry and some of that music for his or her own; it enables the student to understand some of that philosophy, to attain some of the comprehension offered by that science. And in my view, we shouldn't argue that the worth of this education lies in making us better persons; so often it doesn't. Neither should we argue that it is indispensable for becoming critical thinkers; there are other ways. Nor need we argue that it is indispensable for certain professions, though it is. All that need be said is that science and art enrich our lives; they impart to us some of God's shalom. When science opens our eyes to the astonishing pattern of creation, and when music moves us to the depths of our being, then we experience some of the shalom that God intends for us his human creatures. No more need be said than that. That's enough. Art and theory are gifts of God in fulfillment of our humanity. A life devoid of the knowledge that theorizing brings us and of the images that art sets before us is a poor and paltry thing, short of what God meant our lives to be. In such a life, shalom is wounded. I have gone on at some length about this lest you think that I am against culture—against art and theory—when most emphatically I am not.

Those who taught me saw the genius of the Christian school in presenting this vast stream of culture to the student within a Christian perspective. Other schools also inducted their students into this stream of culture. What was unique about the Christian school is that it did this in Christian perspective. Of course, that presupposed the presence of scholars in the community who were developing a Christian perspective in the various fields of learning.

But I submit that this vision, magnificent though it is in many ways, is incomplete; it is too intellectual in its orientation. The Reformers protested the adulation of the contemplative life that they found among the medieval Catholics; they praised the active life of obedience. But here we have a new adulation of the intellectual life—more comprehensive indeed, since now it embraces not just theology but all the disciplines, yet contemplative.

I do indeed believe that Christians are called to *think* in obedience to their Lord. But they are called to do more than that. They are called to *live* and not just to think obediently—as well as, let us not forget, worshipfully and appreciatively. And what the body of Christians needs are teachers to lead and guide their children into that way of being. All this I, at least, find inescapable. I simply don't think that one can say that the essence of Christian education lies in the imparting of a view.

Nonetheless, having said all this, I now want to pursue this notion of a Christian perspective on learning. But why, you say, would I do that, after warning that we are concerned with more than thought. Because if one is going to lead a child into the Christian way of being in the world, one is going to have to teach him something about that world. If one is going to act for shalom in the world, one will have to have substantial knowledge of the world. All that is pretty obvious. But here is the point I now wish to emphasize and that my own tradition taught me: Knowledge must itself reflect the Christian way of being in the world. It must be knowledge of the world in Christian perspective.

It is so easy and customary to think along different lines. It is so easy to think that we go to the theoretician to get an objective opinion on what society is like, on what nature is like, on what culture is like, and then, once we have gotten this picture of the world, to raise what is seen as the independent question of how to live in this world. It is so easy to divide up the situation into facts and values and then to assign the facts to the scientist, and having learned from him what the facts are, to ask what values we wish to adopt in the face of those facts and what mode of life to live in the light of those facts and those values. But this seems to me all wrong. Theorizing is itself a committed enterprise. It is far from being impervious to values; on the contrary, it is permeated by values.

The Cartesian View

We in the modern Western world are gripped with a certain vision of science and the proper business of the scientist. According to that vision, the notion of conducting one's theorizing within a Christian perspective makes no sense. Worse, it is seen as a travesty of what science properly is. I suggest that we take a bit of time to explore briefly this vision of genuine science that so grips us. Perhaps the best way to do so is to go back to the French philosopher René Descartes, for it was Descartes above all who formed our modern understanding of knowledge, rationality, and science—though the full picture would require adding the contribution of Francis Bacon.

Descartes was profoundly struck by the diversity of human opinion. Reflecting on his own education in one of the best schools of France, he highlighted the fact that his teachers disagreed with each other. A twentieth-century student would have reveled in this diversity. Descartes, quite to the contrary, was persuaded that it was a sign of disease. It was a symptom of the fact that the sciences had not yet been set on their proper foundations.

Do you see what a fateful assumption this was? Descartes was assuming that genuine science will gain the consensus of all rational persons—and that not in some ultimate eschatological future but right here and now and every step of the way. True science is consensus science. Descartes' vision was that in the midst of this enormous diversity of human opinion, it is possible to erect a great tower of science, a tower built by rational consensus, a tower to which each of us can add our small brick, a tower that from generation to generation will show progress, a tower from which all personal idiosyncrasy has been eliminated in favor of the objective, the impartial, the consensual. There is to be no pluralism in the academy. Pluralism is a sign of disease. In science we are to find our unity.

Descartes made a second fateful move. In looking around at the sorry state of the sciences in his day, he thought he saw light at one point. In mathematics he saw a science that measured up; mathematics was not rife with dissension. And why was that? Well, it must be that in mathematics the right method was being used. Accordingly, Descartes proposed treating mathematics as the paradigm science. He proposed extracting from it its method and then using that method in all the sciences. Need I tell you that ever since, mathematics along with mathematical physics have been for us the model sciences?

Descartes then set about analyzing the method followed by the mathematician. The method, he suggested, was this: The mathematician started from what he was certain of and then by steps of inference of whose validity he was also certain, he arrived at conclusions almost equally certain—almost, I say, since Descartes recognized that following proofs requires memory, and he was never willing to ascribe full certitude to memory. In short, Descartes saw mathematics as grounded in certitude. And here we touch on one of the most ancient lures in Western philosophy. The medievals had also construed authentic science as beginning from what we "see" to be true—from what, in that way, is certain for us. And before Descartes and the medievals was, of course, Plato. In Plato's struggle to sort out opinion from knowledge, he concluded that a key component in the difference is that knowledge is certain.

So far, then, we have three fundamental and influential assumptions in Descartes: First, in the construction of a science, we must confine ourselves to that on which we can gain rational consensus. Second, mathematics and mathematical physics are paradigms of science, for in them consensus is being gained. Third, they are gaining consensus because they are following the right method, namely, the method of grounding their conclusions in certitude. Perhaps we may add a fourth assumption that really underlies all of these: Descartes assumed that there are within all of us common shared capacities for the acquisition of knowledge, such that if we use these in the right way, we will achieve the consensus needed for science. In other words, there are in us certain capacities untinged by fallenness, and the road ahead is simply to take those and find out the proper method for their use. He believed the mathematician had done that.

Let's consider one last fateful assumption made by Descartes. Science properly conducted, thought Descartes, will never conflict with the Christian faith. The corollary is that to insert one's faith into the process of building up a science is to pollute that process with the very diversity and lack of consensus that we are struggling to eliminate. We must practice methodological atheism.

I suggest that this cluster of Cartesian assumptions has been profoundly formative in our way of thinking about theorizing. Why has psychology been so much in the grip of the model of the physical sciences? Because we have adopted Descartes' conviction that in those sciences we are in the presence of the finest flowering of human rationality; after all, is there not consensus in those sciences? Here the right method has been found. And why have we thought that in the practice of the sciences we have to keep faith out? Because we have adopted Descartes' conviction that the project of a science is a consensus project, a here-and-now consensus, not an eschatological consensus. In the sciences, one confines oneself to what any rational person would consent to. And the Christian faith most emphatically does not satisfy that condition.

Francis Bacon was, of course, somewhat different, and a full description of our picture of the sciences would have to show how the Cartesian strand interacts with the Baconian. Science, for Descartes, begins from self-evident necessary truths and incorrigible reports of consciousness; only these have the requite certitude. It then proceeds deductively. By contrast, science for Bacon consists of individual facts about the world presented to us by our senses and proceeds inductively from there. But Bacon, no more than Descartes, envisaged a pluralism of the academy. He, as much as Descartes, saw science as a consensus enterprise.

Abraham Kuyper and Worldview

Abraham Kuyper and his associates in nineteenth-century Holland questioned this Cartesian picture at a most profound level. Kuyper argued in effect that we never just absorb the world; we always bring to the world ourselves, with our religious commitments, our loves and hates, our social perspectives, and so on. And these color our way of seeing the world. What we actually come to believe cannot be explained merely in terms of some dispositions that we share with all humanity that then get triggered by the world. What we come to believe is a complicated amalgam of what we bring to the world and the world's action on us. I could quote many passages from Kuyper. Here is a particularly striking one:

> He who has had his bringing-up in the midst of want and neglect will entertain entirely different views of jural relationships and social regulations from him who from his youth has been bathed in prosperity.[3]

And here is another:

> A lover of animals understands the life of the animal. In order to study nature in its material operations, you must love her. Without this inclination and this desire toward the object of your study, you do not advance an inch.[4]

Of course, what Kuyper above all emphasizes is that Christian *believers* see reality differently from their unbelieving colleagues, and this is not distortion but clear vision; their faith puts them in touch with reality. Accordingly, they practice science differently as well. The academy is unavoidably pluralistic.

Now, Descartes might reply to this point—that human conviction is the outcome of an interaction between the world, on the one hand, and a self carrying interests, convictions, attitudes, on the other hand—by saying that yes, that's true. Nonetheless, there are within us certain capacities and certain methods for using those capacities such that those capacities used in those ways yield certitude. Accordingly, it is on that certitude that we should erect science. Kuyper would reply in turn that though this may be true for a few things, it is by no means true of enough for us to construct the sciences with these alone. In the sciences as a whole, we always and unavoidably make certain assumptions, take for granted certain ways of seeing things, which are not and cannot be grounded in certitude. Kuyper went on to say that in the Christian's case, what forms his way of seeing things is, in part, religious convictions.

Furthermore, and this was of first-rate importance, Kuyper insisted that believers were perfectly within their rights to practice science within the perspective of their faith. There was nothing wrong in proceeding thus. Others, after all, look at the world in *their* own way, also without being able to ground in certitude their way of seeing the world. We all see the world in certain ways, unavoidably so, and we all conduct our science within these ways of seeing the world, unavoidably so. But those ways of seeing the world cannot be grounded in certitude. The Cartesian-Baconian picture of science is an illusion.

So Kuyper's advice to the Christian scholar and theorist was this: To your own faith be true. Practice science in Christian perspective—listening, of course, when someone claims to have something to say against one or another conclusion of yours to see whether this objection has a cogency that you ought to acknowledge, listening also so as to learn from others, but proceeding from faith in confidence.

Now, I think this was a profound critique. It has also proven to be a prescient critique, for this whole Cartesian-Baconian picture of genuine science has come crashing down in the last twenty-five years or so, for reasons some of which are related to those that Kuyper gave one hundred years ago. Let me sketch out quickly some of the shattering developments that have occurred.

Shattering Walls of Certitude

We can begin with Karl Popper, who along with his followers has argued that science proceeds neither in the inductive fashion of Bacon nor the deductive fashion of Descartes. It matters not at all, says Popper, how you get your theories, and seldom in the sciences do people try to confirm their theories. What matters is only whether your theories have been falsified. What matters is not how often nature says yes to your theory but whether she ever says no. If your theory has not been falsified, you are entitled to hold on to it whether or not other scientists happen to agree with you. Conjecture and refutation is the procedure of science. Consensus, as Popper sees it, is at best an eschatological hope rather than an initiating insistence.

Various followers of Popper, such as Imre Lakatos, have gone beyond their master and pointed out in turn how slithery is the notion of falsification. Strictly speaking, theories are rarely falsified; what rather happens is that unexpected anomalies turn up, and to cope with these anomalies one has to add more and more ad hoc assumptions. Theories are not put to death by falsification. They die the death of a thousand qualifications. So the full picture that emerges from the Popper school is that the rationality at work in science is very different from what the Cartesian or Baconian traditions thought it was. Science is not grounded in certitude. Lakatos has gone so far in repudiating the consensus view of science as to say that science advances by way of a plurality of tenaciously held-to theories.

An even more radical line of thought comes from Thomas Kuhn and Paul K. Feyerabend, who argue that often the supposedly paradigm sciences of mathematics and mathematical physics show something other than rationality at work. Popper and his followers never really doubted that science represented embodied rationality; they simply disagreed with Descartes and Bacon as to the character of that rationality. These new philosophers of science argue that only periodically does science represent embodied rationality. At critical junctures it shows very different features of humanity at work. Nonrational shifts of paradigm for a given science take place, from Newtonian to Einstenian physics, say, and just plain old-fashioned stubbornness and jealously and political pull and rhetorical giftedness play their role. When we look at science, we do not simply see humanity in the glory of its rationality; we see its glory and its fallenness all intertwined. Whatever yields consensus at a certain point in a given science, we must not automatically suppose that it was rationality working at its highest pitch. I should add here that even before these startling new theories of science emerged, those model sciences of mathematics and physics themselves moved into dark and bewildering terrain. New and profoundly perplexing developments have taken place within them.

The point has also been made that never do we confront the world like clean absorbent blotters. Always we carry along ourselves, chockfull of all sorts of distorting mechanisms. One of the great contributions of the twentieth century has been the discovery of the many lawlike patterns of distortion. The Marxists have had their say, arguing that our faculties for the acquisition of belief and knowledge are not the common property of humanity, neutral and impartial, but are corrupted and polluted by our social situations. And psychologists of all sorts have argued that even perception is polluted by beliefs and expectations, not to mention the indigenously human distortions of our sensory mechanisms.

One last point: Continental thinkers have insisted that the physical sciences must not be taken as the paradigm for all sciences. The goal of physical science is the discovery of explanatory laws. The goal of the human sciences, by contrast, is interpretation resulting in understanding *(Verstehen)*. The human sciences are hermeneutic rather than nomological sciences.

I trust you get the point by now: For all these and yet more reasons, the Cartesian-Baconian picture of science has collapsed in the last quarter century. We live and work in the midst of the wreckage. No comprehensive picture has yet emerged to take its place. But I think one thing is clear at least: As we struggle to form a new image of science, we shall have to give up the vision of science as a consensus enterprise grounded in certitude. We shall have to give up the notion that one must limit oneself to saying what every rational person would agree on. We must instead begin to see science as the articulation of a person's view of life, in interaction, of course, with the world and with one's fellows. Did B. F. Skinner win consensus on his deterministic model of the person before he set about doing his research within that framework? Of course not. Did Carl Rogers win consensus on his self-realization model before he began his work? Of course not. We have to begin taking seriously the actual pluralism of the academy and stop overlooking it or excusing it. The traditional assumption was that pluralism in the academy is proof that things weren't being done in a fully rational fashion. We shall have to scrap this picture. The responsible pursuit of science does not yield consensus but pluralism, for we human beings see things differently, and that divergence in seeing is not always the sign of irrationality on someone's part. The central beliefs with which we each unavoidably operate do not enjoy consensus.

In this pluralized academy, Christian scholars must courageously play their role. They enter their practice of science cloaked with Christian conviction. Their calling is not to try to shed that cloak but with care and discipline to say how things look to them. The contents of their Christian convictions are to function for them as what I have sometimes called "control beliefs." Those beliefs lead Christians to reject certain theories as incompatible with those convictions and to search for theories compatible. And this is not as such the mark of irrationality on their part. It's true that by older theories of rationality it was. But so much the worse for those theories. We today need new and better theories of rationality. The old ones have collapsed on us. Christians will listen to those who say they have objections, and they will learn wherever they can. But what they practice is scholarship in Christian perspective, a form of learning that itself reflects the Christian way of being in the world while at the same time being of service to the Christian way of being in the world.

Obviously, Christian scholarship of the sort I have tried briefly to explain is a prerequisite for authentically Christian education. If Christian education is to succeed, it needs within the body of Christians a group of faithful, dedicated, and gifted scholars practicing Christian learning. It cannot be successful without that, for as I already remarked, and as is obvious to all, to lead a child into the Christian way of being in the world, one must help him or her understand the world. But it turns out that there are different understandings of the world, shaped in part by different religious convictions. So what one needs for leading a child into the Christian way of being in the world is a faithfully Christian understanding of the world, an understanding shaped by those who in their scholarship are themselves faithfully living the Christian way of being in the world. One sees here how important it is to see the Christian school within the context of the Christian community. That is a theme on which I shall have a bit more to say later.

Let me foreclose one likely misunderstanding. I have repeatedly said that the curriculum for the Christian school must be devised by asking what would best serve the end of leading the child into a Christian way of being in the world. I fear that if nothing more is said, this is likely to produce an unduly practical and utilitarian spirit. Remember then that worship and delight are also components of the Christian life: worship of God and delight in his creation and humanity's culture. Shalom, remember, includes delight in our relationships. Where life is grim, there shalom is wounded. Not all the knowledge imparted to the student has to serve some "practical" end. We are also made, I am convinced, to find delight simply in understanding this world in which we are placed; that too belongs to shalom. Christian education must educate not only for that which serves some practical end but also for worship and delight. And since, for those engaged in this education, their engagement is itself a component of their Christian way of being in the world, Christian education must itself exhibit worship and delight.

The Means by Which We Educate

Now I want to talk somewhat autobiographically. Some twenty years ago, I served as the chairman of the Curriculum Revision Committee at my college—a Christian college, specifically, Calvin College. By that time I had already come to the conclusion that the comprehensive goal of Christian education was not just a certain way of thinking but a certain way of being in the world, that its goal was not just to induct the student into a Christian understanding of the world but to lead the student into a Christian way of being in the world.

The committee agreed with me on this. So from there we backed up and asked what sort of curriculum we should set up to achieve this end. This too still seems to me to have been the right move; as I have already suggested, curriculum can be devised only by backing up from your goals and asking, with courage and imagination, what would have the best chance of achieving those goals. The conclusion we came to at the time was that the best curriculum was one that introduced the student to the academic disciplines. We thought we should require a fairly extensive study of a number of disciplines and then an in-depth study of one. We rejected the humanist option, according to which one should simply study the best that has been thought and said, as being too backward looking, and we rejected the pragmatist option, according to which one should focus on contemporary problems, as running the danger of being rendered largely irrelevant by the substantial change of problems. A disciplinary approach, we argued, would give the students the knowledge they would need to find their way in the world.

I now think that our supposition that that sort of curriculum would in fact secure our desired end was a piece of extreme naivete on our part. Of course, it's true that the knowledge one needs for the Christian way of being in the world is, in part, provided by the learned disciplines. The naivete was in supposing that setting abstract sociology and physics and economics and mathematics and so forth before the students would make them inclined to live a Christian life in the world. The naivete was in supposing that this would influence their tendency to live in such a way. It won't. Something will shape their lives, but it won't, to any significant degree, be this abstract theory. We all know the phenomenon of people talking a better line than they live. We as Christian educators have to address that issue head on and not try to walk past it. There is no reason to suppose that putting political theory in front of students, even political theory in Christian perspective, is going to make them act in Christian fashion with respect to war.

The rethinking I have gone through in the intervening years has led me to the conclusion that we must think of the entire school situation as the educative agent, with the curriculum only a component within it, though indeed an important component. I used to think of the formal curriculum as the educative agent, and I called those school personnel who were not classroom teachers "support staff." Of course, I knew that on the college level visiting lecturers and so forth also served to educate, but the picture I had was that the classroom was the focus of education and that the non-faculty staff of the school served to support it. I now think that picture gets things almost entirely upside down. Of course, it's true that if it weren't for what goes on in classrooms, we wouldn't have the schools we have; that is what calls them into existence. And, of course, it's true that administrators and janitors and librarians support that. But the point that has to be made is that once a school is set up, then the entire situation begins to function educatively. And then we have to consider what that situation is teaching, for it may well be that what it is teaching is at odds with what is taught in the classroom. It may well be that the hidden curriculum is in conflict with the open curriculum.

I would like to trace for you the line of thought that led me to change my views on this matter. It began in a quite natural way. Suppose you say that the goal of Christian education—I'm getting repetitious on this point—is to lead or guide the student into a certain way of being in the world, the Christian way. It's clear that knowledge of a variety of sorts will be necessary for living such a life—to some extent different knowledge for different persons, to some extent common knowledge. Hence, the educational program will unavoidably have a cognitive component. Furthermore, it's obvious that to live such a life one will have to have the ability to do various things. Again, some of the abilities that we teach will be common to all students; some will be quite unique to particular students. Put it like this: The school will have to concern itself not only with various *knowings that* on the part of the student but also with *knowings how*.

But on reflection it seemed clear to me that this is not yet enough. The student may well have all sorts of knowledge and all sorts of abilities and yet not be disposed to use that knowledge and those abilities to the end of living the Christian life. He or she may have no tendency to do so. I began to wonder whether our education, if it is serious about its goal, doesn't need something more than a cognitive component and something more than an ability component. Does it not also have to cultivate tendencies and dispositions? I knew, of course, that education can't *guarantee* certain actions on the part of a student, but surely it has an influence on them. So I asked myself this question: What are effective and responsible ways for shaping how a child tends to act?

Earlier I said that though I thought the dominant idea for education is that of *guiding*, nevertheless there is a formative, molding dimension to it. I suppose that it is especially here that the formative dimension comes to the fore. Let me add this, though: Surely one of the ways in which we wish to form children is to the end that they will be able to stand on their own two feet and be self-directing.

Shaping Tendencies

So there was my question: What are effective and responsible ways for shaping how a child tends to act? You see how the question arises naturally once the goal is set for which I have been arguing. Still, posing the question makes people nervous, so before I present what I believe the answer is, let me reflect on this nervousness. I find that when one talks about shaping how a student tends to act, many people become extremely squeamish. Such shaping seems to them to infringe on the freedom of the child and perhaps on the freedom of the parent. The teacher should just impart knowledge and ability to the student and let the child do with it what he or she will.

I think there are deep dilemmas posed on this score by our monopolistic public school system, because I think that this response operates with a deep illusion. It operates with the illusion that one can avoid shaping how the student acts. My own view of the person in the world is very much an interactive view; we interact with the world. We act on it and it acts on us. The behaviorists seriously neglect the dimension of us freely acting on the world, but the various proponents of radical freedom seriously neglect the ways in which the world acts on us. We are unavoidably shaped in our tendencies by the ambient world, including then the school. The only question in this region that doesn't suffer from illusions is this: In what direction should we shape how the child tends to act? The question of *whether* to shape never arises. Unavoidably, in one's interaction with the child one shapes the child. Of course, there are bad ways of shaping, wrong ways, ways that violate the dignity of the child. That is why I always put in that word *responsible*. What are effective and *responsible* ways of shaping how the child tends to act? When the teacher determines which knowledge to impart to students, he or she is making decisions that profoundly shape what students will think. When the teacher determines which abilities to inculcate in students, he or she is profoundly shaping their entire ability structure. It is difficult to see why it is wrong to contribute to the shaping of their dispositional structure. But in any case, it is unavoidable. So the question is academic.

I decided, in order to answer my question, to look into the psychological research on the matter. It is, after all, a matter of educational psychology or, even broader than that, social psychology. And though I am a philosopher, I didn't think that philosophers had any business sitting in their armchairs just thinking about the matter and hoping or expecting in that way to come up with some defensible answers. So I turned to experimental psychology. I discovered that a great deal of the psychology relevant to the issue was focused on moral education. Now, I had other fish I wanted to catch; I was concerned not only with moral education but ecological education, and aesthetic, and political, etc. But the fact that the literature focused on moral education seemed to me no

insuperable defect. I would look to see what was said on moral education and then generalize.

There was a serious difficulty that confronted me, however. I found
that none of the research operated with what I could regard as an acceptable understanding of the moral agent. All operated with distorted or
partial views. Thus, I had to formulate an acceptable picture of the moral
agent and then in terms of this to pick and choose within the literature.
But the great danger is that one simply winds up with incoherence, for
one is picking and choosing from lines of research inspired by different
and contradictory views of the moral agent. That difficulty was connected to another, deeper one. I found that I had no Christian psychological model of the person to guide me through the research. There are
indeed Christian *theological* models. But we exist in the situation in
which there are no Christian psychological models—that is, no models
intentionally faithful to the Christian gospel that interact with alternative psychological models and that inspire psychological research programs. But, of course, one cannot leap out of one's historical situation.
I had to proceed.

Without on this occasion actually spelling out for you my understanding of the structure of the moral agent, let me summarize what I
learned. Perhaps I should mention at the beginning, though, that in
some ways I didn't learn anything. I was simply reminded of what I
already knew and of what has been the wisdom of the ages for centuries.

Attaching Consequences

In the first place, the wisdom of the ages tells us, and contemporary
psychology elaborately confirms it, that if we want to shape how people tend to act, it helps to attach consequences to their actions that they
find pleasant or unpleasant. That's to put it as a radical behaviorist would
put it who wants to eliminate all reference to the life of the mind. (He
wouldn't even, when speaking with care, speak of the pleasant and the
unpleasant.) The right way to put it is this: It helps to *lead them to expect*
consequences of their actions that they find pleasant or unpleasant. For
certain behavior, the behavior will become less frequent to the point of
being extinguished if you get the person to expect certain consequences,
and if you evoke the expectation of certain other consequences, it will
become more frequent. Of course, there are all sorts of subtleties of tim-
ing and sequence that could be introduced here if we had more time:
Frequency of behavior is only a rough stab in the direction. Perhaps we
can call the whole process of shaping behavior in this fashion, discipline. Discipline, thus understood, includes pleasant as well as non-

pleasant consequences, and social and internal consequences as well as physical consequences. In short, discipline is one way of shaping how children tend to act. The mechanism at work here is uniformly called conditioning by the psychologists. There are, however, different theories as to how conditioning works. I have already indicated that, in my judgment, conditioning in the human being involves inducing expectations. Conditioning is not autonomic; it is not mindless.

Once we notice that discipline is one way of shaping action, a flood of questions bursts forth, begging for answers. What, for example, are the most effective ways of conditioning? Are some effective means immoral? And what about the side effects of various types of discipline? It has been discovered, for example, that if you reward persons for doing what they like to do anyway, their liking to do it without reward is diminished. If you find that your students like to do math, a way to diminish that inherent delight is to reward them with lollipops for doing it. Here I cannot get into all the fascinating questions that arise. Suffice it to say, one way of shaping how a student tends to act is discipline.

Providing a Model

A second thing the wisdom of the ages tells us, and that contemporary psychology has by now quite well confirmed, is that if we want to shape how a child tends to act, it helps to act that way ourselves. The phenomenon here is what psychologists call modeling, whereby a person is induced to act in a certain way by presenting him or her with a model who acts that way. Modeling of a vast variety has by now been confirmed by laboratory observation. Yielding to temptation of various sorts can be increased by putting a child in the presence of a model who yields to temptation. The incidence of aggressive behavior can be increased by putting a child in the presence of a model who engages in aggressive behavior. Likewise, the incidence of altruistic behavior can be increased by putting a child in the presence of a model who engages in altruistic behavior. The setting of higher or lower standards of performance on some task can be increased by putting a child in the presence of a model who sets high or low standards of performance for himself or herself on that task. And so on.

In reflecting on this idea, various questions come to mind. Who, for instance, does a given person tend to take as a model, since no one can take as a model everyone who turns up in the environment? The answer is clear: People tend to take as models those persons for whom they feel affection or esteem. Thus, given the esteem that many people in our society feel for sports figures, advertisers know well what they are doing when they show famous sports figures using the products that they want to sell.

A second question that comes to mind is, What happens when a person is confronted with contradictory models? The answer is that the effect is unpredictable. In my judgment, this result has profound implications for the project of conducting a program of Christian education in a non-isolationist setting.

Yet a third question: What happens if a model is presented on film or TV instead of live in the room? The answer is that it makes virtually no difference; the modeling effect is virtually as strong. Obviously, this too is of tremendous importance. A point often made in presenting fiction to children is that we must allow them to be confronted with the evil of the world and not present to them a false, idealized world. I basically agree with that position; yet these modeling experiments bring forcibly home that a film of aggressive or nationalist or racist or sexist or licentious behavior is not something that just remains out there to be observed in cool fashion by the child. It enters into the child, or at least threatens to.

Again, what happens if a model acts one way and preaches another way? What the wisdom of the ages tells us is correct: Actions speak louder than words. The child's actions are shaped by the actions and not by the words of the model. Or rather, the full description of the situation is the most striking: The child tends to act as the model acts and to preach as the model preaches. Hypocrisy perpetuates itself.

Lastly, what happens if a person is presented with consistent models and then suddenly with a mass of those who contradict that consensus, as compared with a person who has had a few counter-models in front of him or her all along plus reasons for not following those counter-models? The answer is that the latter is much more likely to resist the attractiveness of the new models. Inoculation helps.

Giving Reasons

Thus far I have spoken of discipline and modeling. Let us move on to a third major strategy for shaping how children tend to act. The wisdom of the ages tells us, and some contemporary experiments tend to confirm it, that if we want a child to act in a certain way, it helps to give him or her reasons for acting that way. On this strategy the evidence is definitely less ample than on the other two. There's a reason for that, I think: Two of the great twentieth-century ideologies in psychology, Freudianism and behaviorism, join in holding that reasons do not play a causal role in human life. But the hammerlock hold of those perspectives is now diminishing, and it looks as if the offering of reasons performs at least two significant functions. For one thing, reasons help a person internalize a course of action. To some extent we can get people to act in accord with moral law by threatening pleasant or unpleasant consequences. But what about the situation when the person judges that these consequences will not ensue? Surely one doesn't have a moral agent until the person acts in accord with moral law regardless of the pleasant or unpleasant results that will accrue to him or her. The pattern of action must be internalized. It turns out that offering reasons for acting that way helps. And interestingly, "other-regarding" reasons, in which the feelings of other people are cited, seem especially effective.

I am inclined to think that reasons play a second role as well. Sometimes we can increase the likelihood that people will act a certain way by offering them reasons for acting that way that start from principles that they themselves accept. The medievals called this casuistry. It got a bad name for itself, but perhaps we ought to resurrect the name. Casuistry is another strategy for shaping how a person tends to act. Of course, when you show people the consequences of some principles and beliefs that they hold, they may find the prospect of acting thus too frightening, too appalling, and may refuse to act on their convictions. It turns out that in such situations, people try in some way to reduce the dissonance: They give up certain of their convictions, try to show that such convictions do not really call for such action, etc. So casuistry, like the other strategies we have surveyed, is not a surefire strategy for shaping action.

We have examined three major strategies—discipline, modeling, and giving reasons—and it turns out that these strategies support each other. The most effective way of shaping how a child tends to act is for you or someone else that the child takes as a model to act that way, for the child to be given reasons for acting that way, and for appropriate discipline to be attached to acting that way.

One last point must be made: On this occasion I don't have the time to say much about it, but clearly the development of a moral agent requires the development within that agent of a cognitive structure for morality. We don't have a fully moral agent if the person just acts in accord with moral law, however that pattern of action be induced. What is also necessary is that the person acquire the concepts of right and wrong and that the person learn to apply these concepts, thereby coming to grasp moral principles. Morality requires, in that way, the acquisition of a cognitive structure. And, of course, this structure must not just idle in the mind of the person. What is required is that the person *act on* the principles belonging to that structure whenever such action is relevant. There is no moral agent in the absence of this. As some of you realize, it is on this matter of acquisition of a cognitive structure for morality that the Piaget-Kohlberg theory of moral education speaks most directly; indeed, I think it speaks directly *only* to this phase of the matter. In my judgment, we do not yet know to what extent it gives us a correct theory of the matter.

It's really not difficult to see how these conclusions, framed specifically for the moral agent, can be generalized, say, to ecological responsibilities. An ecologically responsible agent must acquire the relevant concepts and the relevant principles. And the agent must learn to act in accord with, and even *on,* those principles. For that, discipline, modeling, and giving reasons are the three great strategies.

Now, I think that all this has both exciting and unsettling consequences for the schools. I will explore some of them with you later. Here let me just circle back to the two main points I made. Do you now see why I concluded that just setting abstract theory in front of people will have little effect on how they tend to act? If we want our students to act a certain way in the economic domain of life, it helps for us and other models to act that way, and it helps for discipline of one sort and another to be attached to acting that way. But just setting economic theory in front of them will do nothing. In short, what we have to think about is building the bridges between theory and practice, for there is indeed a gap to be bridged. Action does not just flow out from theory. Something will be shaping how people tend to act, but it won't be theory. Theory will do nothing more than give them something to use in their actions.

Second, do you see now why I said that the entire school situation becomes the educative agent? The conduct of the entire body of school personnel has a modeling effect upon the student. Classroom teachers can talk as much as they want about love, but if the administration acts spitefully, we know what the outcome is likely to be. Of course, the same is true for the teachers. How they comport themselves becomes of prime importance. Their actions speak as loudly as their words. We teachers would much prefer it if our educative impact were confined to what we say, and more than that, to what we say in the classroom, when speaking in our "official" capacity. But it doesn't work that way. Our conduct in and out of class teaches, whether we like it our not.

My experience has been that some educators are inclined to dismiss or turn away from the things I have discussed in this talk because no lesson plans emerge from it, no classroom strategies. They continue to want to avoid some of its major conclusions. I find this to be true even of some of those who have all along professed themselves to be most pragmatic in their outlook, least purely cognitive. We saw that giving reasons has a place. And when it comes to this, there are things to be done in class. We can discuss the issues that will or do actually confront the child and offer reasons for acting in a certain way. And let me add that to some extent this can and should be done in an exploratory fashion; it needn't always be done by the teacher *telling* them. Let the students themselves reflect on the issues and consider in what way they think they ought to act. Be sure, though, that the question is how they *ought* to act. I have nothing but scorn for values-clarification strategies in which the question is never that but rather what they would feel comfortable doing. Such amoralism has no place in Christian education—to which I may add that there is not a shred of evidence that such amoral discussions contribute to making the positive, enthusiastic, purposeful, proud individuals for which they are supposedly the means. But back to the main point: What we learn from these studies is that much of the education and forming and guiding that takes place in schools has nothing to do with lesson plans, has nothing to do with formal or official curriculum.

It can be quite appalling for teachers to realize that their actions educate as effectively as their words. Let me then speak one word of reminder. Among the things that the Christian adult will model for the child is admission of error and sin. Authentically Christian teachers will not present themselves as if they were perfect. And the Christian adult will model by pointing away from self to Christ, who is our true model and pattern, worthy of being imitated.

Let's consider an objection that has fairly often been put to me when I have discussed these matters. Maybe it expresses an unease that some of you have. This is all so mechanical, it is said. You have left no room for the Holy Spirit.

A number of things should be said in response. The first is that I know what I have said sounds mechanical. What I have done, in the fashion of a theorist, is isolate from the ebb and flow of experience certain facets or dimensions of our interaction with each other that tend to shape how the other person acts. I think we should be aware of them. And all I have really done is bring them to awareness. But we must beware of taking these abstracted factors for the reality. In our interactions with each other, we influence each other. I have isolated three of the ways in which we do so. But we should not assume that these are the whole of the matter. Be aware of these; use them responsibly. But remember that above all our charge is to treat the child with love. And keep in mind what I have said over and over: In all of this there are no guarantees. The person remains a free and responsible agent.

Furthermore, I too believe that the Holy Spirit works in our lives; I believe that we must pray that the Holy Spirit does so. But I don't see that the recognition of that implies that we must just wait around or that we really are not creatures of conditioning and modeling and reasoning. And, though it gives me sorrow to say it, I have noticed in a few cases that those who most repetitively appeal to the Holy Spirit act most repressively toward their children. I put it to you: How do you think those children will turn out? In my judgment, Christians do not think that a choice must be made between acknowledging the Holy Spirit and acknowledging the truth of what we have uncovered. They acknowledge both.

The World for Which We Educate

My language up to this point could readily be interpreted in individualistic fashion. The school is to lead the child into a Christian way of being in the world. If nothing more is said, someone might well draw the conclusion that the school and the child—*individual* child—is the extent of our concern. But in fact that is not at all how I think of the situation. Now, then, I propose to follow a line of thought that will bring out the unavoidably social dimension of the school.

The Christian is not a solitary individual in the world, alone in solitude before God, with everything else as mere context. To be a Christian is to be part of the company of God's people—the church. There is in the world a people, the Pentecost community, called out from all the natural peoples of the world to be a witness to God's work, to be God's agent in the world, and to give evidence of the new life available to us in God. There is in the world "a chosen race," "a royal priesthood," "a holy nation," "God's own people," to use the phrases of Peter—a people called out of darkness into God's marvelous light to declare the wonderful deeds of him who called her. Once this people, spread around the world and taken from many natural peoples, was no people; now it is God's people. To be a Christian is to cast one's lot with that people. It is to sign up with it, to commit oneself to its project in the world, to its calling in history. The Christian school is a project of and by and for that community. This people has by now endured almost two thousand years and encircled the globe. A fundamental task of the Christian school is to make the child aware of this great transnational people.

But this new people is painfully aware that it is only part of humanity. It is painfully aware that not all humanity acknowledges that the Creator of the universe is active within the universe for the redemption of human creatures; and certainly not all humanity acknowledges that the center of life is to be located in the life and death of Jesus of Nazereth. This realization immediately raises the question of how this new people is to be related to general society. Where is it to live this new life to which it is called and to which it is pledged? Is it to seek some place on earth where it can live alone by itself, there in isolation building the new community and making only occasional forays into the outside? Or is it to live mingled amidst all its human brothers and sisters? Is it to establish a separate and separated republic, or is it to share the republics of the earth in common with its brothers and sisters who do not accept its faith?

The Community of Christ in the World: Three Aspects

These are, of course, profound and controversial questions, deserving extensive treatment. Here I can do no more than state my own conviction. It is my conviction—and I take it to be yours as well—that the community of Christ is to live in the midst of general society. The New Testament formula is that this new community is to be in but not of the world. It is to be a *leaven*. Yeast in bread makes a decisive difference; it's not just more of the same, more of what was there before it was introduced. It is something distinctly new. Yet the yeast is to be *in* the bread, not off by itself. By itself it doesn't do its work of leavening. Our model here is, of course, the one who is our Master: Jesus performed his works of shalom there among the people of first-century Palestinian society. It was starkly clear that he was not *of* that society. But also it was starkly clear that he was *in* that society. We are to follow him in this. The great challenge facing the church is to resist accommodating itself to general society while yet not isolating itself from general society. That is also the great challenge facing the school that aims to lead children into participation in the life of the church: neither accommodation nor isolation. Alternative education for life within that alternative community that is the church—a community intermingled with all humanity.

Now, in the Middle Ages people tended to think of their society as natural—part of the givenness of things. Reality as a whole was characteristically thought of as a hierarchy stretching from God all the way down to the most disorganized pieces of inanimate matter. Human society was part of this cosmic scale, itself, in fact, exhibiting a natural hierarchy. People were born into roles within this society. With minor exceptions they didn't choose those roles; those roles were ascribed to them by virtue of the situation of their birth.

By the time of the Reformation, people had begun to think very differently. They began to think of social organization not as part of the nature of things into which a given person was simply born but as one of the creations of human beings. Of course, it wasn't as a whole a deliberate intentional creation; on the contrary, much of it was the unintended consequences of human action.

Just as important, they began to see this human creation that is our structured society as fallen. They did not see issues of right and wrong as confined to how the individual conducted himself within his assigned roles. They surveyed the structure of society and judged that structure itself as fallen, in violation of God's will. Of course, when I say that they perceived social structures as fallen, I do not mean that they perceived them as through and through evil; no, they perceived them as a mixture of blessing and curse.

And one more thing: Especially in the Calvinist Reformation, they began to say that it is the responsibility of all God's people to struggle to revise that structure so that it is closer to the will of God. A profound reformist impulse was here given birth—and has remained with us in the West ever since. One can see why Micheal Walzer says that the Puritans and Huguenots were the first of the modern revolutionaries. They were the first to survey the structure of society, condemn it as fallen, and pledge themselves to structural reform. Of course, the plausibility of this vision presupposed a considerable freeing up of social bonds. People in general will scarcely begin to see themselves as called to work for the reformation of society when they are so repressed as to risk torture and death whenever they stray out of line.

What came to birth there in the Calvinist reform—among the Puritans, among the Huguenots, among the Genevans—was what I have elsewhere called *world-formative Christianity*. It was the vision that in response to the perception of the fallenness of our social world we are not just to turn away from it so as to establish closer union with God; rather, we are called in obedient gratitude to struggle to change that world so as to bring it closer to God's will, closer to shalom. The saints are responsible for the structure of the social world in which they find themselves. That structure is not simply part of the order of nature; on the contrary, it is the result of human decision, and by concerted effort it can be altered. And it should be altered, for it is a fallen structure in need of reform. The responsibility of the saints to struggle for the reform of the social order in which they find themselves is one facet of that discipleship to which their Lord Jesus Christ has called them. It is not an addition to their religion; it is there among the very motions of Christian spirituality.

I think it is helpful at this point to introduce the concept of calling, vocation, *Beruf*, which was so prominent in the thought of the Reformers. I follow Ernest Troeltsch in thinking that the Lutherans' understanding of this was somewhat different from that of the Calvinists. Apparently, Luther's thought was that God's calling to one is to work devotedly in the occupation in which one is placed. The Calvinistic idea was different. God's call to us is not first of all to work devotedly in some occupation, however that be determined. His calling to us is to serve him obediently in the world, devoting ourselves to the good of our fellows. Either way, the Protestant innovation was that *everyone* has a calling; calling is not confined, as it had been in medieval Christianity, to special religious tasks and ways of life. But in the Calvinist view, one first attempts to determine what it is that God is calling one to do, and then one searches around for an occupation in which to carry out that call. Furthermore, one will expect that whatever occupational role is selected, that role will prove in various ways to be fallen, so that one must struggle to reshape it. You see the restlessly reformative impulse that must emerge from such a vision. But there was more yet. The Calvinists did not in general think that it was only through one's occupation that one filled one's calling. One also had a calling as parent and as church member and as citizen.

It seems to me that this notion of calling has almost disappeared from Christian consciousness. When it is still present, it is usually reduced to a question of occupation. When students discuss with me what might be their calling, usually they have in mind what their occupation should be. And it seems to me that too often once they have found that occupation to which they feel God has called them, they sink into it, pretty much accept it as presented to them, and do not inquire whether the fulfillment of their calling may not require the reshaping of that occupation. They act as the doctors around them act, as the attorneys around them act, as the businessmen around them act—only more honestly and more piously. Now, I think it is vastly better to choose an occupation in terms of calling than in terms of prospective financial success. Yet how far has the mighty idea of calling fallen when this is all it comes to.

God asks of us that we commit ourselves to shalom. He calls us to this. This is our vocation, the vocation of all of us. But this does not remain some abstract and general thing. It becomes a differentiated call. God asks of each of us that we take up *specific* roles in society. What God asks of me is different from what he asks of you. What he asks is in the light of our talents and training, the needs of the church, the state of society. The call to commit oneself to shalom is always a differentiated, articulated, particularized call. And the Christian school, as I see it, must help each student to recognize his or her own call and to prepare for answering it. This means, as I see it, that there will be a place for individualized, particularized education. Not everybody is to be led into exactly the same way of being in the world. We have to think through the educational implications of the particularization of our callings.

Furthermore, what God calls a given person to do is itself multifaceted. He calls us to play many different roles. Our callings are more comprehensive than what can be fulfilled within our occupations. In fact, I think that we must face the fact that sometimes the only occupation a person can find is one in which he cannot, to any significant degree, fulfill his calling. This point was most vividly brought home to me a few years ago when a former student of mine wrote me saying that he had just taken a job as a bank clerk. He added that he did not think that God was calling him to be a bank clerk but that he was unable to find any other paying job. He would, of course, act as responsibly as he could within the job he had found. But that which God was calling him to do would have to be exercised, by and large, outside of his occupation. He would wait to see whether he was wrong in these conclusions and whether, after all, being a bank clerk could be a means of carrying out his calling—other than that of supporting his family. But right now he didn't see how it could be. I myself think he may have been right about that—and that in general we must not simply blend occupation with calling.

Let me pull together what I have said so far. I suggested that each of us is called by God to commit himself or herself to shalom. But how we are to work for shalom is always differentiated, particularized by our particular abilities, what the other members of the church are doing, by the state of society, and so on. When things go well, people will be able to find occupations in which they can carry out some important phase of their calling. But occupation will never exhaust one's calling; and sometimes the occupation that one is forced to take is a very poor instrument for carrying out one's calling. As I see it, Christian education must lead each child into the performance of his or her particularized calling, in all its many facets.

To do this, it seems to me that the school is going to have to include three fundamental things in its curriculum. It will have to give students an articulated sense of the character of God's shalom. Second, it will have to give students some sense of the structure of the society in which they will have to identify and live out their callings. It will have to engage in social analysis, in what Kuyper used to call architectonic analysis. Of course, if one's roles were pretty much determined at birth, as once upon a time they were, this would scarcely be necessary. But that is not true for us. And third, the school will have to match up our society against the demands of God's shalom, so as to discern what is to be altered. As you can see, that's a tall order. But if we are to train our students to answer their particular multifaceted callings in a fallen society, I see no way around this. Do you?

I suppose I could break off our discussion at this point of high generality. To do so, however, would be to forestall some of the most fundamental curricular issues that we must face. Hence, I propose to follow our line of thought further and ask what is the fundamental structure of our modern society. Of course, I will have to be extremely brief and even dogmatic. All I can really do is set the issues before you.

The Fundamental Structure of Modern Society

As I see it, there are two main schools of interpretation of the structure of our modern social world, one older and vastly more prominent in the First World, having its roots especially in Max Weber, and the other newer, finding its popularity principally in the Third World.

We may call the former of these interpretations the modernization interpretation. Modernization theorists see our world as containing a large number of distinct societies, each at a certain point in the process of modernization. If one attends to the examples of societies that modernizationists offer, one sees that their maps of the distinct societies of the world come close to coinciding with the political map of the world. The United States constitutes a society, so does Australia, and the like. Naturally, modernization theorists realize that these distinct societies interact, but they see this interaction as the interaction of distinct societies, rather like the interaction of distinct persons.

By comparing societies that they consider to be at different stages in the process of modernization, modernization theorists try to isolate the essential features of modernization and its crucial dynamics. I'm sure you are acquainted with some of the standard suggestions. It is regularly suggested, for example, that one of the hallmarks of modernization is the increase in what Max Weber called rationalized action: Increasingly, people depart from tradition, no longer being guided in what they do by how it has always been done, instead asking what is a better way to do it. Another standardly cited hallmark of modernization is a decrease in ascriptivism: Fewer and fewer of the social roles that people play are ones that they are simply born into; more and more they are ones that they themselves choose or to which they are assigned by some administrator. As to the driving force behind modernization, probably most Western theorists would say that it is the impulse toward expanding the scope of technology, which is, at bottom, a type of rationalized action. In technology, we take the results of science so as to alter our environment or ourselves into something more desirable.

Apart from claims concerning the defining features of the process of modernization, two theses lie at the very core of the modernization theorist's way of thinking: It is in principle possible for all societies simultaneously to reach a high point of modernization without any fundamental structural alteration in the already established, highly modernized societies; and second, the causes of a given society's low level of modernization are to be found in that society itself and not, to any significant degree, in the impact of the highly modernized societies upon that one. Something is amiss within the societies that fail to become highly modernized: a lack of money for investment, the wrong kind of character formation, the wrong kind of religion, or whatever. Depending on what is thought to be amiss, perhaps the highly modernized societies can help with the cure; perhaps they can supply the money needed for investment or the missionaries for a better religion. But in any case, they are not the *cause* of what is amiss.

Many intellectuals in the twentieth century have suggested that the process of modernization is an essentially destructive phenomenon that replaces concrete social formations with abstract formations in which individuals feel alienated from a social order not expressive of themselves. But at least until recently the general public has implicitly regarded modernization as a good thing, typically giving it the honorific title of development. The modernization interpretation of the world is very much the one that shapes the policies of the United States government. Basically, all that the present administration would wish to add to the interpretation as I have presented it is that the Soviet Union distorts and hinders the process of modernization. Of course, everyone would agree that modernization as we know it has carried ills in its wake; the committed modernizationist would say, though, that the cure for these is more of the same—more modernization, more technology.

I think there can be little doubt that the modernization interpretation does not enjoy the popularity it once did. The reasons seem clear: Things have not gone the way the interpretation predicted, and it isn't very plausible to suggest that all failures are due to the malevolent influence of the Soviet Union.

The interpretation that has begun here and there to replace it is the world-system interpretation. Where modernization theorists see the world as containing a number of distinct societies at various stages in the process of modernization, world-system theorists see the world today as containing just one society, or social system, as they prefer to call it. This one social system displays the historically unique features of having a single integrated economy combined with a multiplicity of distinct states and a multiplicity of distinct peoples (nations). It seems obvious that in the world today there is a division of labor that straddles states and peoples; TV sets sold in the United States are manufactured in Hong Kong, not to mention the fact, so painful for Americans, that cars sold in the United States are manufactured in Japan. But this combination of social entities is historically extraordinary. Usually, economies, states, and peoples coincide, or in the case of empires, which comprise many peoples, economies and states coincide. Our world today is different.

Furthermore, our unique structure of one economy straddling diverse states and diverse peoples is by now pretty much worldwide; almost every area of the world has been integrated into one economy, though of course to widely differing degrees.

One thing that the world-system theorist emphasizes is that this world economy is capitalist in its structure. Of course, there are socialist and communist states that participate in the structure. But socialist and communist states, when they enter the world market, prove just as capitalist in their behavior as the most capitalist of individual entrepreneurs.

What the world-system theorist also wishes to emphasize is that the capitalist economy of our world-system has a horizontal structure of *core* and *periphery*. Even a cursory glance at our world-system reveals that wealth is not evenly distributed throughout the geographical areas of the system—and more importantly, that *capital* wealth is not evenly distributed. Today its heaviest concentrations are to be found in North America, in northwest Europe, and in Japan. Those areas of heaviest capital accumulation constitute the core of our system; those of least capital accumulation, the periphery. Today the core of the system is heavily engaged in capital-intensive, high-technology, high-wage production, whereas the periphery is dominantly engaged in labor-intensive, low-technology, low-wage production.

However, the idea behind calling certain areas *core* is not so much that they are the richest in capital but that they have the preponderance of economic voice and power in the system—this being both result and cause of their concentration of capital wealth. The core dominates the periphery, or to put it from the other side, the periphery is subordinate to the core. And a consequence of this domination is that the core exploits the periphery; in the interaction between the two, the core constantly gets the better end of the deal. It gets the better end of the deal because it has certain modes of power at its disposal that the periphery lacks.

It is characteristic of world-system theorists to argue that this domination of a periphery by a core is a necessary dynamic of the system; it is not an accident. The vision of modernization theorists that we can all advance simultaneously into the glorious future of high modernization is a cruel illusion. There are deep and profound reasons why TV manufacturers have moved their production from the United States to Hong Kong: What they find there are low wages and no strikes. If that were not true, they would find some other place to produce TVs.

What is also characteristic of world-system theorists is the argument that this system has been in operation for about four centuries. Accordingly, there has been, in their view, a development of underdevelopment. Two centuries ago Bangladesh was a relatively prosperous part of the world. Today it is impoverished. What made the difference is the inter-action of Britain with the Bengalis.

Obviously, there are issues of tremendous importance here that, on this occasion, we cannot possibly discuss in detail. My own view is that the world-system interpretation is definitely correct in its general guide-lines. On the other hand, though the modernization theory does not seem to me acceptable as an embracing theory, it does seem to me that modernization theorists, in their attempt to pick out the hallmarks of modernization, have pointed to a number of characteristics that, as I see it, are inevitable accompaniments of our world-system in its expan-sion from its European origins to around the globe. The spread of this system does carry with it a destruction of tradition and an increase of rationalized action, it does carry with it a diminishing of ascriptivism, and so on. A world in which a core dominates and exploits a periph-ery—that, it seems to me, is the world in which we find ourselves. I dis-cover that a good many Christians are inclined to shy away from any theorist who discerns domination and exploitation in our society. They immediately interpret that as Marxist and reject it out of hand. My own feeling, however, is that Christians should be the last to be surprised by the presence of domination and exploitation in society. Christians above all should expect exactly that. Their response should be the opposite of rejecting such claims out of hand. "This is exactly what I would have expected," they should say. "Tell me the details of how it goes."

And why has this world-system emerged and expanded during the last four centuries? There is no substitute for careful and detailed analy-sis in trying to answer the question. Let me suggest one category for understanding what has happened. It is the category of *idol*—a category present in the Bible, used often by Augustine, and recently used in a very imaginative way by one of the members of the Amsterdam school, Bob Goudzwaard. Goudzwaard suggests that one of the forces shaping our social system is the idol of *economic growth*. We are in the presence of an idol when some feature of our existence is elevated above normative assessment and when we make all other social goals subservient to this one. The result of an idol is always that the idol one serves begins to enslave those who serve it, so that often those enslaved are at a loss to know how they can be liberated. Economic growth, says Goudzwaard, is an idol among us; it has shaped our entire social existence. And it pro-foundly distorts the proper scope and nature of economic activity. To this I would only add that this is not our only idol. If one is at all to understand our modern world, one has to add nationalism and national security to the list. The Afrikaaner is at a loss to know how he can deliver himself from the idol of nation—or is it just that he dare not do it? And my nation along with very many others is enslaved to the idol of national security. We either do not know how to, or dare not, free ourselves.

A world-system in which core dominates and exploits periphery, shaped by idols that compete with the Lord and by the ordinary lust for wealth and power—that is the social system for which we prepare our children, that is the system within which they will have to identify and carry out their callings. Of course, it is a system that yields benefits for which we must all be thankful. Yet it is also a system that is profoundly fallen. It is a system that squelches shalom. Between it and the shalom community there is profound dissonance.

I know, of course, that others give other analyses of our social predicament. Many Christians in the United States have, in recent years, tended to ascribe most of the evils that they discern—such as abortion—to the inroads of secular humanism. I myself do not doubt that they are correct in claiming such inroads and in seeing many evils as its consequence. Yet for all the alarming trends that secular humanism has set afoot, I do not think that it accounts for the fundamental structure of modern society. It does not account for world poverty, it does not account for the insidious nationalism that one finds in so many places, etc.

I suspect that the matters I have just considered seem like pretty heady stuff to most of you. Leave all that to someone else, you are inclined to say. But I don't see how you and I as Christian school teachers *can* leave it to someone else. If this is the society in which the children we teach will have to carry out their callings, we had better introduce them to an understanding of it. And if the society to which we introduce them is rife with exploitation and idolatry and secularism, we are going to have to take account of the fact that the authentically Christian way of being in the world will have to be an alternative way. But how can we educate for an alternative way of being in the world when we do not propose insulating and isolating the children from that world, with the consequence that that world is bound to have a modeling effect on them? You see how this discussion interacts with our earlier discussion.

Implications and Applications for Christian Schools

Thus far, I have developed four different, though indeed connected, lines of thought. What I propose doing now is to pull these lines of thought together by highlighting some implications and offering some applications.

In thinking about the nature, content, and methods of Christian education, it is of prime importance that we not focus myopically on just one component of the school situation—typically the curriculum—but keep within our range of vision the totality of the school and its personnel. I have two reasons for saying this. In the first place, a school, any school, is not only an institution but is perforce a community. It seems to me too obvious to be worth arguing that a Christian school must be a *Christian* community. By that I mean this: A Christian school is not an institution that offers a distinctive sort of education while, as a community, is an example of an ordinary sort of educational community; rather, as a community it must be Christian. A Christian *educational* community, of course. Christian communities are of many specific sorts: There are Christian churches, Christian businesses, Christian families, and the like. A Christian school must be an example of that particular sort of Christian community that is a school.

An educational community is a community of a quite unusual sort. There are older people who are teachers and administrators, and young people who are students. Among the older people in the community are those who know a great deal about certain subject matters that the young people in the community know very little about. And in spite of all the democratizing impulses that have invaded the schools over the past century, authority and power within a school are unavoidably distributed in a very unequal way, with the consequence that it's easy for that authority and power to be abused—as indeed it's easy for that authority and power to be resented, whether reasonably or not.

I don't think we've done at all well at thinking through this dimension of Christian education, namely, what the school as a Christian educational community should look like. We have not creatively thought through how authority relationships are appropriately to be distributed within that community that is a Christian school, nor how a community with authority relationships thus distributed can excel in its own unique way as a community of love and devotion. I talked with one person who had just this year entered the teaching profession. She told me she had had an open mind as to whether she should teach in one of the Australian state schools, in one of the church parochial schools, or in one of the Christian schools. To help her make her decision, she visited some state schools, then some church schools, and finally some Christian schools. And now I quote almost exactly: "When I visited the Christian schools, I found myself in an atmosphere of love and devotion, and I decided on the spot that that's where I wanted to teach." That's a profound tribute to the Christian schools she visited. Would that her experience were typical!

My other reason for saying that in thinking about Christian education we should not narrow our focus to one aspect or dimension of the school but keep the entire enterprise in our vision has to do with a point I made earlier, namely, that a school as a whole functions educatively;

the totality of how it conducts itself has an educational impact on a student. Disciplinary and modeling effects are dispersed throughout the institution. Accordingly, when, with our goals in mind, we ask ourselves how those goals are to be accomplished, we must not assume that the available means are confined to what teachers say in classrooms; we must think of them as dispersed throughout the institution.

Having emphasized that there's more that educates than the curriculum, I nonetheless now want to point to some curricular implications of what I have been saying. I have organized them under nine headings. I won't have time on this occasion to develop any of these thoughts in detail; what I have to say will have to remain suggestive in nature.

First, it's important to recognize that the knowledge we seek to impart to students may be quite different in its content, organization, emphases, etc., both from that which is to be found in standard textbooks and from that which constitutes the best recent results of theoretical learning.

Depending on what you see as the appropriate goals of school education—socialization goals, maturational goals, culture-transmission goals, Christian goals as I have described them, whatever—you're going to find yourself offering quite different packets of learning to students. What the socialization theorist thinks important is very different from what the maturationist thinks important. Add to this the point that what is described as a "standard" textbook will always have a particular ideology behind it; it won't be neutral. The implication is that the Christian school may or may not find among so-called standard textbooks a book that's satisfactory for its teaching. It may have to strike out on its own.

A related point is this: The goals of the scholar and the goals of the school educator are very different goals, with the consequence that much of what is available in scholarship is not of concern to the school educator, Christian or otherwise, and that some of what is of concern to the educator, Christian or otherwise, may not be available in scholarship. You as a Christian teacher cannot assume that your goals can be accomplished by summarizing the received body of psychological or sociological or physical theory. The Christian school may have to stimulate Christian scholars to pursue new lines of inquiry.

Some of you have been talking with me about what you call an "integrated" or "integral" curriculum in which, instead of dividing up the curriculum along the lines of the standard divisions among the theoretical disciplines, you integrate the curricular content with the goal of enabling the child to live his or her life in the world. I find the idea very attractive. If you divide up the terrain of knowledge in the piecemeal fashion of the academic disciplines, you're likely to produce in the student a piecemeal view of things; conversely, if you want the child to emerge with an integrated vision of God's world and the Christian way of being in that world, then almost certainly you will yourself have to achieve and exhibit that integration, rather than expecting the child to achieve it from the fragments of learning that you offer.

Second, we must be a good deal more concerned than we have been with bridging theory and practice. It's not true that if you impart to students the knowledge relevant to their acting a certain way that then they'll be inclined to act that way—not even if they have the ability to act thus. What they need in addition is the disposition, the tendency. We saw that discipline and modeling shape the formation of tendencies, as does the offering of reasons for acting a certain way—the offering of what philosophers call *practical reasons*. What this implies, as I see it, is that if we are serious about our goal of leading children into a Christian way of being in the world, we shall have to talk with them about the substantial issues that they will face in living that sort of life. We cannot just give them the knowledge and then leave it up to them to decide what they'll do with it. We will have to bring theory and life together. We will have to create bridging courses and bridging components of courses. In my own college, we as professors have rarely talked deliberately and explicitly about the issues of poverty, ecology, and war; I have come to think that that is irresponsible.

Third, though a good deal of what we teach our different students will be common, I have come to think that there must also be a good deal of individualized education. I have two reasons for thinking this, one of which I emphasized earlier. Each of our students will find himself or herself in a distinct calling; callings will not be carbon copies of each other. So if you accept that we must teach for those callings, it follows that there will have to be a significant individualized component to our instruction. The other, related reason is that we're dealing with different persons: different capacities, different aptitudes, different concerns, different modes of delight, and so forth. God does not make human beings like identical marbles. For this reason, too, Christian education has to be substantially individualized.

So often Christian schools, instead of celebrating the freedom that we have in Christ to be our own selves, press students into a mold of conformity. Various excuses are offered for this; one that I hear fairly often is that the need for testing and evaluation unavoidably yields a pressure to conformity. I don't see it, or at least, I don't see that it yields the pressure toward conformity that all too often has been typical of Christian schools. Why can't examinations, to a considerable extent, be individualized? Rather early in my teaching career, I became aware of the fact that students respond differently to different kinds of pressure and to different sorts of examinations. So I do my best, both within a given course and across different courses, to devise a rather wide array of examinations. Take-home examinations, classroom examinations, oral examinations, written examinations, examinations in which students can use their books, examinations in which they cannot use their books, essay examinations, various forms of non-essay examinations. And in addition to these various sorts of examinations, I assign written papers, oral reports, and the like. I don't see that the need for testing and evaluation is a reason for refusing to adapt the education one offers to the unique students one has.

Fourth, we must beware of explicitly or implicitly exalting some callings and some modes of knowing over others. It's always been a temptation in evangelical circles to exalt the calling of evangelist and preacher over all others—a temptation that can be seen as a variant on the medieval practice of exalting the calling of priest and monk over all others and of monk over priest. If you accept what I argued for, that God gives to each of us our own distinct calling, then we are left without any ground for saying that one is superior and the other is inferior. An important implication of this for the schools is that we must not exalt the calling of those who go on to college or university over those who do not. Christian education is not to be primarily aimed at producing learned people—though lest you misunderstand me, let me add that it must aim at *also* producing learned people. Christian schooling requires Christian learning.

Fifth, education in our schools must be internationalized. When I say that, I don't just mean that we should introduce interesting little tidbits about China, Russia, Zimbabwe, or ancient Greece—though I certainly have no objection to that. What I have in mind rather is this: If you and I do really live in a social world in which the various parts around the globe not only interact economically, politically, and culturally with each other but in which certain parts dominate and exploit other parts, then it has to be part of Christian responsibility to make that clear to students. We have to move beyond the old paradigm in which it was assumed that one could understand Australian society all by itself, American society all by itself, and so forth. Furthermore, in the course of introducing students to the reality of a global society, we must somehow evoke in them the realization that the dynamics of evil—and yes, the dynamics of blessing as well—are not just individual, nor even just national, but global.

Sixth, curriculum must prepare students for living within political structures that are pluralistic. For one thing, every polity in which the students of Christian schools find themselves is religiously pluralistic, thereby challenging us to face up seriously to the question, How does the Christian live and speak with Christian integrity within the shared structures of a society in which Christianity is just one of many different religions and world-and-life views? Likewise, every polity in which the students of Christian schools find themselves is ethnically and culturally pluralistic. There are scarcely any issues more important today than these issues of pluralism for the Christian way of being in the world.

Seventh, I have come to think that it's important for us to explore ways of bringing life into the classroom and of bringing the classroom to life. The walls between school and life outside the school must become much more porous than traditionally they have been. Let me explain. I myself had no significant empathy for the plight of the Palestinians until, as the result of some unexpected circumstances, that plight acquired for me a human face and a human voice. I had read about the Palestinians in the newspapers, I had listened to reports on TV, but their plight did not sink into my bones and consciousness until, one unforgettable day, I found myself in the same room with a number of Palestinians, almost all of them Christian, and listened to them pour out their pain. I was transformed.

Since then, I have not only spoken up for the Palestinians, visited Palestine, and read yards and yards of books and journals, but I have also reflected on what happened to me on that occasion. My interpretation of what happened is that actually seeing the faces and hearing the voices evoked empathy in a way in which nothing else did. This is not always the case. Indeed, sometimes fear and loathing block empathy. But often it is. In fact, I have come to think that we are touching here on an important fourth way in which tendencies to act in certain ways are formed in people—in addition to discipline, modeling, and practical reasoning—even though it is, so far as I know, completely ignored in the psychological literature. Black print on white pages does not, for most people, evoke empathy.

The question, then, is how this principle can be applied in the Christian schools. Part of the answer, as I see it, is that if you here in Australia are, for example, teaching about your Aborigines, you must try to get beyond reading about the Aborigines to put your students in touch with them, not, of course, so that the Aborigine becomes an object of curiosity, but so that the aboriginal person can speak and communicate to your students, in face-to-face fashion, what it's like to be an Aborigine. It probably doesn't much matter whether the aboriginal persons come to the school or whether the school goes to them; what matters is genuine speaking and listening. I trust I've said enough to make it possible for you to go on from here to think of other examples of how the principle can be implemented.

Eighth, I have become increasingly convinced that our curriculum must acquaint students with the rich diversity and the deep unity of the church. The church did not begin yesterday, nor did it begin with the emergence of Pentecostalism in Southern California in the early twentieth century, nor did it begin with the Wesleyan revival, nor did it begin with the Reformation, nor did it begin when the Western church split off from the East. It began with the apostles. The church extends all the way from the apostles to you and me, and it is by now indigenous around the globe. To be a Christian is not to be alone with one's inwardness but to be a member of a people spread out around the globe with two thousand years of history. Among the various peoples of the world, it's a very peculiar people; it's the Pentecost people. In calling it that, I mean to allude to Paul's insistence that for membership in this people it makes no difference whether one is Jew or Gentile, slave or free, male or female—or indeed, member of any other natural division. The great mystery of the ages, says Paul, is that God's people are no longer an ethnic people but transcend all natural divisions. The Christian school must communicate this astounding reality and thereby combat the ever present tendency to Christian parochialism. I don't see this as meaning that we must rub out the particular tradition that we ourselves represent within this vast people. What it does mean, though, is that we must learn to understand and appreciate each other's traditions, to talk together across them, and to treat them as distinctly secondary to the unity of the church, Christ's body, across all these distinct traditions.

That leads directly to my last point concerning curriculum. Though I will put it briefly, I regard it as of fundamental importance. A careful, loving, devotional study of Scripture is an indispensable component of the curriculum of the Christian school—for the reason that Scripture is the basis and nourishment of that Christian way of being in the world, which, as I have argued, is the ultimate goal of our enterprise. I'm told by those who teach Bible in the Christian schools in my own country that they find themselves confronted with a serious problem of boredom: Their students are already presented with the Bible in their families and church; to be presented with it again in school seems to them to be overdoing it. I acknowledge the problem. But surely it has to be seen as a challenge to creativity rather than a reason for eliminating the Bible from the curriculum.

Those were suggestions concerning curriculum, nine of them. Each of them is worth a talk of its own; here I've had to content myself with saying just enough to stimulate your own imagination. Let me now close with three more general comments.

First, a comment about controversy. If the Christian school really does what I have been suggesting it should do, it will find that the education it offers every now and then evokes controversy with at least some of its constituents. Dealing appropriately with controversy is important to the maintenance of a Christian school.

My impression is that when parent-controlled Christian schools first begin, it's the strong inclination of the parents to deny, in practice, that the teachers have a distinct calling and office. It's their strong inclination to treat the teacher as nothing more than an instrument for the achievement of their own desires and convictions. But if what I said earlier about callings is correct, then it has to be said that the teacher also has a distinct calling and office in God's scheme of things; teachers are not mere implements in the hands of parents. Consider the minister of a congregation. The minister has a distinct calling and office that calls for respect by the congregation, and that calling and office will sometimes require that the minister say things that the congregation doesn't like to hear. To fail to say those things would amount to infidelity to his or her calling; it would amount to disobedience to our Lord. So too for the teacher, though let it be said that in a situation of controversy, it may be the teacher or school that's wrong and the parents who are right.

Now is not the occasion to offer a full-fledged discussion on the handling of controversies. And even if I had the time, I'm not at all sure that I would have any special wisdom to offer. Let me confine myself to just two comments. Sometimes it will be a matter of Christian integrity on the part of the teacher or the school to teach things that they know are contrary to positions held by some of the constituents. But sometimes, depending on the nature of the controversy, there's another and better way to go, namely, to articulate for students in a fair way the various positions taken on the issue within the Christian community, and then leave it there, without taking the next step of trying to persuade the students of the correctness of one of the competing positions. Let me take what is perhaps the most obvious example: For some eighteen hundred years now, there has been disagreement within the church between those who embrace a pacifist position concerning war and those who embrace a just war position. Given this history, the best service the Christian school can offer its community is a careful presentation of the two positions.

My other comment is that it's been my experience that too often teachers and schools stake out their position on some matter of controversy without ever bothering to explain with care to parents their rationale for the position they have taken. The teacher insists that reading a certain book is necessary for the course, certain parents find the book odious, and horns get locked. When you the teacher find the book essential, whereas some parents find it odious, see it as your responsibility to explain why you find it essential, backing up as far as you have to, perhaps even into the very rationale of the Christian school. That won't always settle the controversy, but I know of cases in which it did. And more generally, a successful Christian school will not only be educating students but will, at the same time, be educating parents. The Christian school, as I have described it, is a countercultural enterprise, and every countercultural enterprise requires constant education of its constituents. It must assume that its supporters have also been influenced in unacceptable ways by the ambient culture, perhaps even without noticing it, or that they have reacted in unacceptable ways. Consequently, it must again and again explain its own particular form of critical engagement with the surrounding culture and offer its rationale for that. In short, the Christian school must take a position of educational leadership in its constituency—always watchful for the arrogance that is the leader's ever present temptation.

My second concluding comment is that in planning your buildings and their surroundings, remember that Christian responsibility includes aesthetic responsibility. So often in the United States, Christian schools are grim and ugly. Usually no notice is taken of this whatsoever; people act as if they're completely oblivious to it. When it is noticed, and it's felt that some excuse has to be offered, the excuse is usually that there wasn't enough money to achieve beauty. Let me say emphatically that beauty does not require wealth; you yourselves can all think of examples of the point. Let me offer a personal anecdote. Some years back I went to Nairobi, Kenya, to visit a former student who had married a native Kenyan, a Kikuyu. On a Saturday they drove me up the Great Rift Valley to his native village. On the way we stopped at a mission compound about fifty miles from Nairobi. The compound was set in a stupendously beautiful valley. But it was one of the ugliest things I had ever seen. It was obvious that it had been shabbily built in the first place; now paint was peeling, doors were off their hinges, and red dust was everywhere. I was overwhelmed with the near-physical sensation that these gorgeous hills were trying to vomit out this nauseous thing that had been forced down their throat. Those who built this compound did so, no doubt, out of a profound sense of calling; I honor them for that. But I submit that ugliness is ingratitude. Ugliness is irresponsible. Can anyone really believe that God approves of ugliness? Scripture presents God as delighting in his creation. Do you suppose that it is in the ugliness of things that God delights? Be aware that the aesthetic quality of your school says something about you, and then ask yourself, Is what it says about me acceptable? And once again, beauty does not require big expense. Indeed, I would offer as a general principle that when people lavish money on their buildings, they almost always wind up with monstrosities.

Lastly this: I have come to believe that the vocation of Christian teacher, if it is to be properly carried out, must have a certain quality of witness-bearing. Do not, in the presence of students, act as if you were a teaching machine. Instead, reveal that you too are on the journey of Christian existence—sometimes successful, sometimes not, sometimes confident, sometimes doubting, sometimes joyful, sometimes discouraged. Do not try to transubstantiate yourself into something other than what you are nor conceal the fact that you have not been transubstantiated. Authentic Christian teaching is autobiographical teaching.

Part 2

Challenges and Objections to Christian Education

chapter eight

Christ Is Lord

During the mid-1970s, Wolterstorff addressed an audience concerning three crises that Christian Schools International (formerly NUCS) schools were facing. He explained that Christian school leaders needed to be concerned with these crises if the schools were to flourish. They also needed to be concerned with concrete embodiments of what it means that Christ is Lord, which centrally involves developing culture in loving service to our neighbor.

Is it worth it? Is the maintenance of Christian schools worth the time, energy, and money that we put into them? We confess that Christ is Lord. But couldn't we better devote the resources that we put into Christian schools to other Christian causes? Couldn't students who are more dedicated and more aware of their surroundings be produced in some other way, less consuming of time, energy, and money?

I often wonder what would happen if there were no Calvinistic day-school movement today on the North American continent. Would the movement get started? Would you be willing to work for it? Would I? Or are we just going along with an establishment that has now become respectable?

We've all heard stories of people who crossed this continent fifty to seventy-five years ago on trains or in primitive versions of the automobile, at considerable discomfort, to speak to tiny groups of people to promote the cause of Christian education. They succeeded in stirring up enthusiasm in some. But in many they evoked hostility, and in others, the feeling that this was strange, "kooky," un-American. Put yourself in those situations, traveling across the continent at great discomfort, with only glimmers of enthusiasm here and there. Would your dedication have risen above that? I have also heard stories of people in the early days of the Christian school movement who found themselves in the painful situation of having to choose between paying tuition and buying shoes for their children. They chose the tuition against the shoes. Would you and I have done the same?

But these are speculative questions. The real issue confronting us is not whether we have the dedication to begin a Christian school movement. We've inherited a movement, for which we should be immensely grateful. The question facing us is whether the movement we've inherited will be passed on in better, stronger, more vigorous shape than it was received.

External signs of success are evident. The National Union of Christian Schools is growing. Monthly there are more schools, more students, new textbooks. Yet if we probe beneath the surface, I think we must come to the conclusion that we are entering a crisis period in the history of the Calvinistic day-school movement. It's the crisis period of comfortable middle-age respectability.

Three Crises

Three points of crisis can be identified. First, at the beginning of the movement, about seventy-five years ago, most of the movement's supporters had a clear fundamental rationale for Christian schools in the Calvinist tradition. There was consensus in the community as to what these schools were all about. That consensus seems to me in good measure to have evaporated. Many supporters no longer recognize the hallmarks of education in the Reformed, Calvinist tradition. They no longer know the case for it. They offer reasons for it that reflect quite different understandings of our position as human beings in the universe and our standing before God than those of the people who founded the movement. That, then, is the first point of crisis. Supporters of these schools no longer clearly understand their fundamental rationale. They no longer agree on wherein lies their worth.

The second point of crisis is one that educators, with their intellectual orientation toward books and speeches, are inclined to overlook. When Christian schools began, they were, as are all schools, an expression of a way of life. They were an expression *of* a lifestyle while at the same time serving as preparation *for* that lifestyle. It was a lifestyle markedly distinct from that of the surrounding culture. Looking back, it's easy to see in it nothing but its "Dutchness," and there was a lot of that. But there was more. In Northern Europe, a distinctly Reformed style of life had arisen. Part of that distinctness was located in what the English poet and critic Donald Davie calls "simplicity, sobriety, and measure." One saw it in Calvinist music, in Calvinist churches, in the Calvinist way of dress. Another part of that distinctness was located in the central role the family enjoyed in the lives of those people. Another part was located in the central role given to the Bible in the lives of the people. Yet another part of it was located in the deep conviction that one's life occupation is not just a way of gaining money and prestige and respectability but a calling from God, a *vocation*. That distinct lifestyle was transplanted in this continent. And the first Calvinist schools here were an expression of and a preparation for it. Few people in those days complained that the products of the Christian school could not be distinguished from others. If anything, they were *too* distinct!

Today that lifestyle has collapsed. In itself, of course, that's not a bad thing, for certainly not everything in that lifestyle was good. What is bad is that nothing has come to take its place except a sort of general "Americanism," to which a bit of piety, spirituality, and morality have been added. We've dropped that "old" lifestyle, but we've not replaced it with an alternative Christian way of life more appropriate to our own age and place. By and large we've only replaced it with the style of the surrounding culture. We've all become respectable. No longer would someone use the words "simplicity, sobriety, and measure," to describe our lives. We participate avidly in the sensate luxury of contemporary society, so that the "over againstness" of our fathers and mothers has disappeared. As a result, people no longer see many differences between our graduates and those of the public schools. And so, of course, they begin to wonder whether Christian education is worth it.

And now a third point of crisis. Most of you know that many of my students are products of the Calvinist Christian school system. When I talk to those students, I am impressed by the deep resentment their

Christian education has stirred up in many of them. An alarmingly high number of graduates say that their Christian day-school was oppressive and arbitrary. They say the love of God was not exhibited to them in their teachers, nor in their institutions. What they saw was only the heavy hand of conformity. They did not see opened up before them an exciting future in God's service but only the dreary prospect of having to conform to the system. So they've become sullen, passive, resentful, and often cynical. That's the third crisis in the Christian day-school movement today. I don't suppose that we do worse on this matter than our forebears did. But all too often the school fails to sell itself to its own products because often its students perceive the school as acting in contradiction to the very gospel that it preaches. So, of course, they wonder whether these schools are worth it.

Christ Is Lord

A good way to come to grips with all three points of crisis is to turn to the main theme of this convention, "Christ is Lord," for each of the three crisis points raises the issue of Christ's lordship—in our lives, in our schools, in our understanding of what these schools are for. But the lordship of Christ is not only the theme of your convention. The hallmark of authentic Calvinist day-school education has always been the insistence that education *like everything else* must be under the lordship of Jesus Christ. That, therefore, is another reason for looking at this theme, as it is expressed in Philippians 2:11. Let's set the verse in context by beginning with verse two. This is what Paul says:

> Complete my joy by being of the same mind, having the same love, being in full accord and of one mind. Do nothing from selfishness or conceit, but in humility count others better than yourselves. Let each of you look not only to his own interests, but also to the interests of others. Have this mind among yourselves, which is yours in Christ Jesus, who, though he was in the form of God, did not count equality with God a thing to be grasped [or, grasped at], but emptied himself, taking the form of a servant, being born in the likeness of men. And being found in human form he humbled himself and became obedient unto death, even death on a cross. Therefore God has highly exalted him and bestowed on him the name which is above every name, that at the name of Jesus every knee should bow, in heaven and on earth and under the earth, and every tongue confess that Jesus Christ is Lord, to the glory of God the Father.

verses 2–11

The context for that closing verse about Christ's lordship is Paul's instruction to the Christians at Philippi on how to live. They are to love one another. And the love is not some vaporous sentiment. It is a love that takes the concrete form of looking to the interests of the other person, making his or her interests my interests. To have this mind among us—and notice that to have this mind among us is to live a certain way, not just to think a certain way—is to have among us a mind that is ours in Christ Jesus. It is ours in Christ Jesus in the quite specific sense that when we look to him, we behold that mind at work. When we look to him, we see love taking the concrete form of a servant.

Paul goes on to say that he who was the servant is now victorious. On account of his sacrificial servanthood, God has exalted him. The servant has become the Master. The slave has become the Lord. To what purpose? To the end that the glory of God may be manifested and that every knee may acknowledge and every tongue confess that Jesus Christ is Lord.

Of what does that lordship consist? What is it that every knee acknowledges and every tongue confesses, when Jesus Christ is acknowledged and confessed as Lord? There is a strong temptation for us in the Protestant churches to turn this matter of confessing Christ as Lord into a subjective matter. We assume that to acknowledge and confess Christ as Lord is to *make* him Lord in our lives. But Paul is quite clearly saying something different. He is not saying that we are to make Christ Lord by doing this or that. He is saying that Christ *is* Lord; our calling is just to acknowledge and confess it. But what is it, then, for Christ to *be* Lord? What are you and I acknowledging and confessing when we acknowledge and confess that he *is* Lord?

Perhaps the most explicit indication of Paul's thought on this matter is to be found in another letter of his, that to the Ephesians. In Ephesians 1 he says:

> [God] raised [Christ] from the dead and made him sit at his right hand in the heavenly places, far above all rule and authority and power and dominion, and above every name that is named, not only in this age but also in that which is to come; and he has put all things under his feet and has made him the head over all things for the church, which is his body.
>
> verses 20–23

From this passage, it is clear that Christ's lordship consists in the fact that, on account of his suffering servanthood, God has given him dominion over all the powers, structures, and authorities that threaten and debilitate our human existence. Christ has been exalted above them all. Thus, none of the life-depressing structures that we find around us need any longer be regarded as inevitable. None is such that we need buckle under them. Christ has dominion over them all; he is Lord over them; he rules them. And that's what it is that one confesses in confessing that Jesus Christ is Lord. One confesses that, due to God's action in Jesus Christ, the thrust of history is now in God's hand toward the goal of human renewal, toward the coming of God's kingdom. What must be added is what Paul adds: Christ's lordship over the powers that oppress human existence and thwart God's purposes is for the sake of the church. It's for the sake of that community that is Christ's body, the community that lives in and out of the love by which Christ lived.

Let me pull together what I have said. For us to acknowledge and confess that Jesus Christ is Lord is to live the life of self-giving love in the conviction that the power of all the enslaving forces of human life have had their ultimate power destroyed. The love and the confession go together.

Two Related Themes

There is yet one more thing to be noted in this marvelous hymnic passage from Philippians 2. In verse 6, Paul says that Jesus was in the form of God. What Paul might just as well have said was that Jesus was in the image of God. The words *form* and *image* are equivalents. And in fact *image* is the word that Paul uses in the first chapter of Colossians, where he speaks of Christ as being in the image of God. So in the language of Colossians, what Paul says in verse 6 of Philippians 2 is that Jesus was in the image of God. It seems to me that in hearing Paul speak of Christ as being in the image of God, we must hear echoes of Genesis 1, where Adam is described as made in the image of God. Indeed, once he has spoken of Christ in verse 6 as being in the form of God, Paul then goes on to speak of him in verses 7 and 8 as being born "in the likeness of *men*" and being found "in *human* form." The allusion to Genesis 1, the echoing of its description of humankind, seems to me unmistakable. We must see in this passage an indication of Paul's standard thought that Christ is the second Adam. That is what is coming to the surface here, without becoming totally explicit.

I hear another echo of Genesis as well. Listen once again to these words of Paul: He "did not count equality with God a thing to be grasped" (Phil. 2:6). By contrast, what we learn from Genesis is that Adam *did* undertake to become like God. He grasped at being like God. Christ, instead of grasping at equality with God and thus imitating the first Adam, emptied himself, taking the form of a servant. So again there's an echo of Genesis, but this time it's the echo of a contrast. Adam grasped at equality with God and was humiliated. Christ did not grasp at equality with God but willingly humbled himself and was exalted.

And now I want to raise a question about these two images. To follow the path of the second Adam, who is and was and will be in the image of God, is to live the life of sacrificial love. But in Genesis, being made in the image of God is associated with having dominion over the earth and all that dwells therein. Do you see the contrast? The image of God that we see in the second Adam is expressed in a life of sacrificial love. The image of God that we see in the first Adam is expressed by having dominion over God's subhuman creatures. The question I invite you to reflect on then is this: Is the second Adam a repudiation of the first? Is the new humanity a repudiation of the old humanity? The mandate of the old humanity, made in the image of God, was to have dominion, to humanize the world, create a culture. Its mandate was a cultural mandate. The mandate of the new humanity, also made in the image of God, is to love one's neighbor as one's self. Its mandate is that of sacrificial love. Is Philippians, then, a repudiation of Genesis? Is the new humanity a repudiation of the old humanity? Is the divine image that is expressed in loving service a replacement of the divine image that is expressed in cultural development?

Most emphatically, no. In the same passage from Colossians to which I have already referred, Christ is explicitly associated with creation. He is spoken of as the firstborn of all creation, for whom all things were created. Thus, any polarity between creation and redemption, between the old humanity and the new humanity, between the first Adam and the second is untenable. In the mandate of the new humanity to form a community whose hallmark is love, there is no discharge of the mandate to the old humanity to form a culture. In the emergence of the second Adam whose lordship consists in servanthood, there is no repudiation of the first Adam whose lordship consists in having dominion. Only his grasping at equality with God is repudiated.

Let me bring things together by suggesting that if there is anything characteristic of the Calvinist tradition, it is the attempt to hold those two themes together: the theme of the first Adam who images God in developing a culture by having dominion and humanizing the world, and the theme of the second Adam who images God in a life of loving service. The acknowledgment of the lordship of Jesus Christ is to be seen in the emergence of a new community whose life is love. But also it is to be seen in the emergence of culture where before there was only unhumanized nature. Love one another and have dominion. The insistence that those two belong together has always characterized the tradition out of which we live. In and out those two themes weave. Where there is no concern for the breadth of creation and its flowering into culture, there you are not in the presence of authentic Christian education as the Calvinist sees it. But equally, where there is no concern for the formation of an alternative community whose style of life has sacrificial love as its foundation, there too you are not in the presence of authentic Christian education as a Calvinist sees it. In Genesis we read, "Let us make man in our image, . . . and let them have dominion" (1:26). In Philippians we read, Jesus, "though he was in the form of God, . . . emptied himself, taking the form of a servant" (2:6–7). The hallmark of Christian education in the Calvinist tradition is to be seen in the attempt to hold together those two passages and the two images of which they speak. To bring Genesis and Philippians together, to image God in developing culture and to image God in loving service to one's neighbor, is the great challenge of the Christian school as understood in our tradition. If the Christian school and its supporting constituencies confess the lordship of Christ by living out the implications of those two dimensions of the image of God, then they will have more than sufficient sustenance to meet whatever crises middle-age respectability may bring upon them.

I suppose that a really good inspirational speech would stop at this point. I would be false to my own convictions if I did stop here, however. It's easy for all of us to feel warm inside in response to what I've said, to say yes, that's how it is, it's nice to be reminded of it, but to do nothing different. It's all too easy for such a speech to make no difference. So I want to close by reminding you that the vision I have put before you comes to nothing unless it is made concrete. To make my point, let me be as specific as I can and use an example: Most of the high schools represented here teach home economics, and I'm sure that you all insist that this subject be taught from a Christian perspective. Some of you are not averse to proof texting, assembling a variety of texts from the Old Testament and the New Testament about God's good gifts of creation. Others will feel that that is a misuse of the Bible. But all will agree that the subject of home economics in a Christian school must be set within a Christian perspective. I submit to you, however, that such setting within perspective really comes to nothing unless the perspective not only shapes our thought about home economics but shapes the style of life to which we challenge our students. Today we know a good deal about the effects of sugar on the body, as we do about the most efficient ways of producing protein. And in general, we know a good deal about how we can best be stewards of God's earth and live a healthy and responsible life. It seems to me that it is the calling of the Christian school, in the light of the most current knowledge available, to confront students with the concrete decisions that they must make if they are to be responsible, loving, dominion creatures. It is the responsibility of the

Christian school to concretize the vision, often entering controversial areas to do so. The unacceptable alternative is that the vision remains all talk and thought.

I intend the above only as an example for my general point. In my judgment, however, it is an important example. After they have left your school, most of your students will not read poetry from the great American tradition. Most will not listen to the music you've tried to teach them. Most will not do much math. But all of them will make decisions about how to eat, how to live, and how to dress. Thus, there is good reason for concluding that home economics, rightly understood, is the central course in the curriculum of the Christian school. Here, above all, things get concrete.

My main point, though, is this: All my words today will mean nothing unless you and I make concrete the vision that I have tried to put before you—unless we make concrete the conviction that we are to image God as we seek to develop culture in loving service of our neighbor. A Christian school is a school in the Calvinist tradition when it seeks to hold together the conviction that the human being is a creature called to culture with the conviction that the human being is a creature called to love. And it is a *successful* school in that tradition when it manages to take that vision and give it concrete embodiment, for remember, this Christ whose lordship we acknowledge and confess did not just hold out an inspiring vision of loving dominion. He emptied himself, taking the form of a servant, even unto death. In his life, we see the visionary concreteness, or if you prefer, the concretized vision, that you and I must strive to imitate. To the vision of imaging God by pursuing culture for love's sake, and to the struggle to give that vision concreteness—to that I urge you all once again to commit yourselves.

Once we do so, we shall see the doubts that it's worth it dispelled!

chapter nine

The Christian School and Its Contemporary Challenges

Is it really true that Christian schools are by and large ineffective in cultivating in their graduates resistance to the dominant American values? In this series of addresses to teachers in the mid-1970s, Wolterstorff addresses three criticisms made of these schools: (1) Christian schools don't let students find out what contemporary society and culture are like; (2) Christian schools squelch individuality and produce conformists; and (3) Christian schools isolate students from society and culture. With each criticism he explains how the idea of a Christian school can be improved to meet valid challenges.

Do you sometimes wonder whether Christian education is worth it any more? Do you sometimes find yourself wondering whether perhaps the

Christian day-schools served a purpose for about a century or so but that now their day of usefulness is coming to an end? Do you sometimes find yourself thinking that the challenges facing the Christian day-school movement today are so great that they can't be met?

There's a sign of hope that we ought to take note of before we do anything else. It comes, as signs of hope so often do, not from the deeds and actions of the powerful but from the helpless cries of the victims. The sign of hope that I have in mind comes from some African American parents who live on the west side of Chicago in a ghetto known as Lawndale. These parents, convinced of the importance of Christian education for their children, applied for admission of their children to the Christian school in the nearby suburb of Cicero. The board of the school adamantly refused to grant them admission, on the ground that racism is so rampant in Cicero that they would not be able to guarantee the safety of the children nor the security of the buildings were they admitted. As proof that they are not themselves racists, they point to the fact that black children are in attendance at another Christian school operated by the same school board in a different suburb.

I'm not sure whether my dominant feeling in response to the pleas of these parents is one of despair or of hope. How about you? But whether or not hope is one's dominant feeling, surely one's response includes hope. If, in spite of all their incredible humiliations, these parents are still in favor of Christian education, then I at least am convinced that there has to be something to it. It can't be entirely outmoded.

Accordingly, let our consideration of the contemporary challenges to the Christian school movement be conducted in a spirit of confidence. Challenges can always be seen either as threats or as opportunities; usually, I suppose, an objective observer would say that there's a component of both. But we would be traitors to our African American brothers and sisters in Lawndale if we did not consider the challenges more as opportunity than threat.

Many people see the dominant contemporary challenge to the Christian day-school movement as economic. As we all well know, the public school receives public tax funds while religiously oriented schools do not. Many in our country are saying that, as a consequence, the nonpublic religiously oriented schools—Catholic, Lutheran, Calvinist, Jewish—cannot long endure unless some redress is granted. It is said that if funds are forthcoming, these schools can continue to play a significant role in American education, whereas if they are not forthcoming, the schools will disappear.

Possibly this argument has some weight in the case of the Catholic schools. There, because of the shift in recent years from religious to lay personnel, the costs are rising with great rapidity; for that reason it may possibly be true—though I myself doubt it—that the Catholic schools will disappear from the scene unless relief is soon forthcoming. I feel confident in saying, however, that this will not prove true for Christian schools in the Reformed tradition. If Christian schools gradually disappear from the scene, it will not be because of the failure to secure financial aid. Conversely, I am not at all convinced that securing financial aid will make it more likely that they will stay in existence. I am very much in favor of state aid to academically qualified nonpublic schools, but I think this should be seen as a matter of justice, not as a matter of survival.

The fact that the state refuses to give tax aid to nonpublic schools, in spite of the fact that it regards the products of these schools as fully satisfactory, is but one manifestation of the century-long hostility between the basic ethos of this country and the nonpublic religiously oriented school. The public school has become an intrinsic part of the American way of life, and in turn, the American way of life is the functional religion of many, possibly most, Americans. The nonpublic religiously oriented school is thus a standing challenge to the fundamental religious orientation of Americans; conversely, that fundamental religious orientation is a standing challenge to the Christian school and to all other nonpublic religiously oriented schools. Therefore, to see the main contemporary challenge to the Christian school as a financial crisis induced by the state's refusal to apportion a fair share of tax funds is to see the main contemporary challenge to the Christian school as originating from outside.

My own conviction, on the contrary, is that the main contemporary challenge to the Christian school movement comes from within the movement, not from without. If this challenge from within can be met, the movement will live on; if it cannot, receiving state funds will not perpetuate the movement but merely prolong its death agonies.

The main challenge, as I see it, lies in the fact that many of the students whom the Christian school graduates are not at all convinced of the worth of the institution that graduated them. The challenge lies in the fact that some of Christian education's most severe critics are products of its system. The challenge lies in the fact that many of its own graduates are its worst salesmen.

As you know, I teach at Calvin College, where a high proportion of the students are products of the Christian day-school system. It's been my experience that a high proportion of these are not at all convinced of the worth of the Christian day-school system. Some of them are in fact filled with deep hostility and resentment toward the system. In my experience, these young college students are not alone in doubting the worth of the system that educated them. I also know a good number of young parents, graduates of the system, facing for the first time the question as to where they should send their children and having the same feelings. Therein lies the challenge to the Christian day-school movement. Any school system is challenged and even threatened when it produces a large number of graduates who are not convinced of the worth of the system.

You might say that this is really only a more subtle version of the challenge from without. These young college students and these young parents have absorbed so many typical American values and attitudes that they no longer sympathize with the basic vision of the Christian school.

I'm sure that's true in some cases—though there is something rather disturbing in the admission that the Christian school is by and large ineffective in cultivating in its graduates resistance to the dominant American values. But I am equally sure that in a good many other cases it is not true. I remember vividly just a week ago talking to a young person who has been attending some spontaneous worship services taking place in Grand Rapids. He told me that he had gone through the Christian school system and attended the Christian Reformed Church all his life without ever catching a glimpse of what Reformed Christianity is all about; finally, he had caught that glimpse in these worship services. He was excited—and angry. Not angry because he thought there was no place for Christian schools. Angry because they had not done their duty by him.

I have done my best to listen to some of these complaints against the Christian school system coming from some of its recent graduates. What I have chosen to do in these three talks is pick out three of what seem to me the most significant of these complaints and to analyze them, to see to what extent they deny the very idea of a Christian school and to what extent they instead challenge the implementation of the idea. That done, when it is the latter that is at stake—the implementation of the idea rather than the idea itself—I hope to make some suggestions as to how our implementation of the idea can be improved. What we emerge with will be, I trust, an image of a new kind of Christian school.

Propaganda or Neutrality

The first of the challenges to the Christian school goes something like this: The Christian school isn't open and honest with its students in its educational program. It tries to keep its students ignorant of many issues in contemporary society and culture. It won't let them really find out what contemporary society and culture are like; everything is carefully screened in advance so that only the clean, the sweet, and the bland find their way into the classroom. Even many of the issues within the contemporary Christian community are banned from the classroom as too hot to handle. Objections to the Vietnam War, the authority of Scripture, evolution—these are just a few of the many that could be mentioned as banned from classroom discussion. And as for the topics that are considered, everything is considered from just one narrow point of view; opposing views, if heard at all, are never given a fair chance. Finally, what the school does decide to teach is forced down the throat of the student. There is no attempt to find out what questions the student has and then to discuss them and provide answers. Rather, the student is told what question he or she *ought* to have and what answers he or she *ought* to accept.

If this is what the Christian school is really like, then it has all the characteristics of a propaganda mill. The core of the first challenge I want to consider is that the Christian school is a propaganda mill.

Some of you probably consider the language I have used excessive; you're thinking that what I have given you is largely a caricature. In particular, you are convinced that when it comes to your own school, though there may be a kernel of truth in the charge, it's a very small kernel. Maybe so. But the sketch I have drawn, caricature or not, is not at all untypical; for that reason we had better give it our serious attention.

I propose that in developing our response we first remind ourselves of that part of the idea of the Christian school that is relevant to this matter. The Christian school aims at equipping a child for living the Christian life in contemporary society. It is this aim that determines the educational program it offers. It selects its subject matter with this aim in mind. Having selected its subject matter, the interpretations it offers, the emphases it adopts, and the evaluations it makes are all in part made—never entirely—with that ultimate goal in mind. More specifically, having selected its subject matter with that ultimate goal in mind, the Christian school then tries to offer its students a *Christian perspective* on that subject matter. By this I do not mean that it *adds* some theology to a neutral consideration of that subject matter; neither do I mean that it just refuses to mention some things. To offer a Christian perspective on the subject matter means that the Christian tells it as he or she sees it. Do not suppose that when the Christian tells it as he or she sees it, and someone else does so as well, the differences will be total. They will not be. Nonetheless, in the total educational program, there will be plenty of differences to make the Christian project worthwhile. In short, the educational program of the Christian school has, or should have, a distinctively Christian slant in its selection of subject matter, its interpretations, its emphases, and so on. That, at bottom, is what makes it a *Christian* educational program.

I said that the selection and treatment of material in the Christian school will in good measure be determined by the aim. This is true of every coherent educational program. One has to select the subject matter; the canon isn't some objective thing just lying there, waiting to be picked up. And since there are always different ways of treating that subject matter, one has to choose a way of treating it. Every educational program, if it is at all coherent, selects and treats its material by reference to the overall aim of the program. It is not possible to avoid that sort of slant.

If the slant fully coincides with the opinions of the surrounding culture, however, it will often not appear as a slant. It will appear that no choices are being made other than the choice to set objective reality before the student. Everything will appear entirely neutral, such as different religions, different comprehensive perspectives, and so forth. But whenever the situation seems that way, it is because the slant adopted is thoroughly in accord with prevailing opinion. It looks as though the school is accepting objective reality rather than making choices.

In short, one should not suppose that as one moves from a Christian school to a public school, one moves from a slanted education to one devoid of any slant. Nor should one suppose—though I will not argue the point here—that one moves from a religiously slanted education to one that, though slanted, is at least religiously neutral.

The differences are rather these, as I see it: The Christian school attempts to offer a consistent Christian slant. Given the religious and ethical pluralism of American society, the slant offered by the American public school is, and has to be, less consistent. The difference even on this point should not be exaggerated, however. The slant in the lower grades is relatively consistent; the slant is basically Americanistic. As one moves into the universities, more and more diversity comes to the surface.

It's my impression that the following difference also exists between the two systems. The Christian school system is forever trying to articulate the vision that shapes its selection and treatment of subject matter. One may think it does a rather poor job of this, but that it is forever struggling with this is indubitable. By contrast, there is considerable pressure in the public school system to avoid the explicit consideration of fundamental issues—to avoid discussing the rock-bottom convictions that lead to one's selection and treatment of subject matter. The hippies and the new left have noted this phenomenon and attributed it to perversity on the part of individual professors. I think it is nothing of the sort but that there is something virtually inevitable about it. When people of fundamentally different convictions have to work together within an organization, they tend to avoid bringing to the surface the deep issues on which they know they disagree. Instead, they remain on a more superficial level where, so they hope, they can work out accommodations.

Perhaps some of those who charge the Christian school with being a propaganda mill are against the very idea of the Christian school. They don't want their children in an educational program that offers a consistently Christian slant in its selection and treatment of subject matter. There are others, however, who are not against the idea as such but are rather against the way the idea has been implemented. Let us then consider some of the ways in which the idea of a school that offers a consistently Christian slant on selection and treatment of subject matter can be implemented so that it does not function as a propaganda mill.

First, and most important, we must stop trying to avoid the delicate and the controversial issues, whether these be posed to us by the surrounding culture and society or by discussions and changes taking place within the Christian community. These are typically the issues that our students will have to face. We must equip our students to deal with exactly such issues, not with issues that they will never have to face. The boys will all have to face the issue of whether they should allow themselves to be drafted to serve in Vietnam; accordingly, there is nothing the Christian schools could better do today than discuss with their students the issues of war and peace. Again, given the prominence of the issue in the Christian community, every one of our students will have to reflect on the issue of creation and evolution; each will have to make up his or her mind. That makes it an issue the Christian school cannot responsibly avoid. Unless the Christian school courageously considers with its students such issues as these, it will unavoidably be a propaganda mill.

Second, we must consider the questions that students have and stimulate in them appropriate questions where none before existed. I mean to say that Christian education must deal with the questions that *students* do and ought to have—not merely questions that the teacher or someone else has, questions that even when posed to students are not taken up by them and need not be. Christian education must address itself to the questions and problems appropriate to students, the ones actually bothering them and the ones that ought to be bothering them. It must not force on them questions that they never have asked, never will ask, and will never have an obligation to ask. Of course, the questions that students actually have on their minds are often exactly those delicate and controversial questions that I mentioned earlier; hence, my first and second points overlap.

As to the answers to those questions that are delicate and controversial, and to those that students are asking, I offer three points. First, honesty at all cost. We have to stop pretending. Second, we teachers should not try to have, and should not give the impression of having, answers to all questions. Often it's appropriate to say, and often honesty will require that we say, we don't know. Third, don't give students the impression that everything has already been decided and that rather than being genuine participants in the discussion, they are merely observers of the conclusions.

Perhaps a few words about pedagogical techniques are also in order. For one thing, I think we must use discussion a good deal more than we traditionally have. Instead of just lecturing at students, we should try to get them to open up, to come to grips with the issues for themselves—guiding them and giving them such assistance as we can but always avoiding forcing things down their throats. I sense that the Christian schools are quite rapidly moving in this direction; it seems to me a very healthy change.

Let students know that Christians have come to different conclusions on significant matters; don't try to conceal this fact. Present to students the various responsible options that Christians have chosen on the issue under consideration. This does not mean that the teacher need conceal his or her own convictions; what it does mean is that the teacher should seek to bring students to the point where they realize existentially that what unites Christians is not just shared answers—though that is definitely part of the picture—but shared questions, some of which have endured for centuries without a consensus as to how they ought to be answered.

When it comes to dealing with issues in the community, why not every now and then invite people to present their views, whether they be alternative views on an issue within the Christian community or in the culture or society generally. Alternatively, instead of bringing the person to the students, why not sometimes bring the students to the person? Those who charge the Christian school with being a propaganda mill are asking not that teachers have no commitments, nor that they conceal them, but that they represent the alternatives fairly. Nothing could better alleviate this charge than interacting with an alternative view. I know, of course, that reading books can accomplish the same outcome, but the great advantage of live presentation is obviously that questions can be asked and answered.

Lastly, I think we have to be more aggressively and perceptively Christian in our treatment of subject matter. Curiously, I think one of the roots of the charge of propaganda is that the Christian school, in far too many areas of thought, has no genuinely and attractively Christian perspective to offer. We have to be much more creative and programmatic than we have been in producing material for students that will enable them to arrive at a genuinely Christian answer to their questions. When there's all shell but no nut, the charge of propaganda arises.

About half a year ago, I received a letter from a man who is principal of a Friends' school in Delaware. He had become convinced that what he especially needed for his program was material presenting a Christian approach to various social issues. So he wrote to both the National Union of Christian Schools and the National Association of Christian Schools asking for material along these lines. From both he got back the answer that they had none. I regard that as scandalous. There is a long tradition of Christian reflection on war and peace. Why has that not been made available? There is a long tradition of Christian reflection on the significance of work. Why has that not been made available? Why are there no new studies on the use of recreation time? And so forth. It's when the Christian school keeps talking about the importance of a Christian perspective but has almost nothing of the sort to offer that the charge of being a propaganda mill will inevitably arise—and rightly so!

Conformity or Diversity

A second complaint is that the Christian school squelches individuality and produces conformists.

The picture that some have of the Christian school—and once again, this includes rather large numbers of its graduates—is the following: The Christian school is a system for perpetuating a particular subculture within American society. This subculture is, in the first place, ethnically oriented; it is Dutch American. Persons without Dutch ancestry are accepted into the group; a few have been thoroughly assimilated. But most continue to feel like outsiders, always wondering whether there is a subtle undertone in certain remarks and practices that escapes them.

Second, the group is theologically conservative. It espouses a brand of Reformed scholastic theology and regards the acceptance of this theology as the essence of being a good Christian. Admittedly, it says that there ought to be faithful action as well, but when push comes to shove, this group's decisive test always proves to be theological. It sees new developments in theology as a threat, and it refuses to join any of the ecumenical movements, on the ground that it might become corrupted. It rejects the argument that ecumenical gatherings would provide a platform for its own voice to be heard; even more emphatically it rejects the argument that it might learn something from ecumenical contacts and be enriched. Its theological and religious stance is essentially one of holding on to the past rather than advancing into the future.

In its morals the group, third, is puritanical, its chief social concern being what it calls "Sabbath observance." Its moral posture in general is legalistic; its dominant goal vis-à-vis the surrounding culture is avoidance rather than engagement. In politics it is located firmly on the right. It's in favor of the Vietnam War, typically saying that the government must be obeyed in all things. It's for law and order. It thinks that the welfare state and the labor unions will ruin us. Its dominant social configuration is bourgeois middle class.

The implicit if not explicit aim of the Christian school, so say the critics I now have in mind, is to induct the child into this subculture of Dutch American ethnic identity, conservative theology, puritanical morals, rightist politics, and middle-class shopkeepers. It is a subtle and complex system designed not to develop the gifts of the individual student but to press him or her into a mold. The aim is to make the student conform—to become a well-functioning non-questioning member of this particular subculture.

So what are we to say to this charge? When I state it as bluntly as I have just now, it probably sounds to many like a caricature. I myself regard it as a caricature of the subculture in question, for the subculture is much more diverse than the picture I have painted of it would indicate. Yet I am sure you have all heard criticisms along these lines, if not quite so bluntly and starkly stated, and I would guess you agree with me that the criticisms cannot be dismissed out of hand. So though the criticism as I have stated it may well be based on a caricature, it's a caricature of something real; it has not been invented out of whole cloth.

Having heard the complaint, let us follow our strategy and remind ourselves next of the relevant part of the idea of a Christian school. The Christian school aims at inducting the child into a community. In offering an inducting education, it is typical rather than unique. Most education aims at inducting the child into the life of some community. Sometimes this is so taken for granted that people scarcely notice that it is being done; at other times it is done with considerable self-consciousness. Either way, education is typically education for induction into the life of a group. The public schools of the United States are for the most part quite conscious of the fact that they are inducting children into the life of the American nation—as indeed over and over throughout history one finds that it is into the life of the nation that schools aim to induct children. In other cases—that of the traditional English schools, for example—education is for induction into the life of some social class within the nation.

The Christian school is thus not at all unique in educating for induction. What differentiates it from other such schools is the particular community into whose life it aims to induct the student. It aims to induct the student into the life of the Christian community. The Christian school is not only a project *of* the Christianity community but a project *for* the Christian community, in that it aims to induct the child into the life of that very community that sponsors the school.

This community is not a geographically determined community; it cuts across all space. Neither is it a temporally determined community; it cuts across all time. It is also not a socially determined community; it cuts across all social classes. Nor is it a racially determined community; it cuts across all races and peoples. Nor is it a vocationally determined community; it cuts across all vocations. And it is not an intellectually determined community; it cuts across all intellectual stratifications. It is the community of all those who are bound together by their allegiance to God in Jesus Christ, seeking to accomplish God's full-orbed work on earth. The aim of the Christian school is to induct the child into that community.

Perhaps some of those who protest against what they see as the conformist program of the Christian schools are protesting against this core idea of the Christian school. Perhaps they are in general opposed to education for induction; perhaps, though not opposed in general to education for induction, they are opposed to an education that inducts the student into the Christian community. No reform would satisfy such a person. Others, however, do not protest against the very idea of education for induction into the Christian community but against how that program of education has been implemented within the Christian day-school movement. It is to these that I wish to reply. How can the Christian school induct the child into the life of the Christian community without stifling his or her individuality and oppressing him or her with conformism?

Before I offer some suggestions, I think we should recognize that the troubles and difficulties of the Christian school are in good measure the mirror image of the troubles and difficulties in its constituency. Let me be specific. The consciousness of a community of Christians, in the sense in which I explained it above, has almost disappeared from our lives. We are conscious of various groups of people, most or all of whom count themselves as Christians; we are scarcely aware of there being a people of God in the world transcending all the demarcations I mentioned above, together doing God's work in the world in fidelity to Jesus Christ. Witness the Christian school tragedy of Lawndale-Cicero. Our white Dutch American relatives in Cicero were not conscious of the fact that the African American people in Lawndale are their brothers and sisters in Christ, together part of the Christian community. They perceived them not as fellow Christians but as black antagonists. In such a situation, how can there be Christian education?

When a living sense of genuine Christian community disappears from one's consciousness, then a curious thing happens—one witnesses the rise of both individualism and conformism. One finds the individual asserting his right to go it alone, to go his own way; at the same time one finds the pitiful phenomenon of each individual being a carbon copy of the other. Where there is a genuine community, both individualism and conformism recede. When genuine community disappears, then people begin stressing all the more the appearance of community. The group begins insisting on conformity while, at the same time, the individual begins insisting on his or her rights, having lost all consciousness of his or her individual contribution to the welfare of the whole.

When the supporting constituency of a school fails to practice the virtues that the school espouses, the school is bound to suffer. In particular, then, when the supporting constituency of a Christian school lacks any strong sense of constituting, along with other Christians, a genuine community, the school will slip, even against its will, into the practice of inducting into a subculture distinct from the Christian community.

So what can be done? For one thing, teachers can introduce material that will enable students to locate themselves within that vast five-century-old tradition and community of Christianity that is the Reformed tradition and community, now spread around the globe. They should be taught what Reformed thinkers are saying and doing, today and in the past, and both the strengths and the weaknesses of the Reformed tradition. But then material should also be introduced that will encourage students in turn to see that tradition and community as just one component within the Christian tradition and community generally. Senior students ought to know, for example, what is going on in the various religious periodicals, and they should be taught not to regard all but one of these as offensive curiosities but rather to see in them the various agonies and gifts of the contemporary Christian community. When this is done, then there can be the beginnings of induction into the Christian community rather than into a highly parochial component thereof.

Second, the Christian school should proactively seek out, for society membership and for instructional personnel, anyone who embraces education in the Reformed tradition of Christianity. Whether these society members and staff personnel happen to be members of Reformed churches, or of Lutheran, Catholic, Methodist, Baptist, Episcopal, or evangelical churches, makes no difference. The Christian school must in this way become as ecumenical as possible without losing its orientation. Ecclesiastical differences among its supporting constituency and personnel should be seen as enriching rather than threatening. Of course, this requires becoming more clear than most of us have been as to what constitutes education in the Reformed tradition of Christianity.

And third, we should welcome students of all sorts to participate in the education we offer. Make clear to parents what sort of education that is; then, open the doors.

Acquiescence or Dissent

Lastly, I want to consider the criticism that is, so far as I can tell, the most influential among young parents who are themselves products of the Christian schools but decide not to send their own children there. The criticism is that the Christian schools isolate the child from society and culture.

It will be conceded by these critics that the best Christian schools do not isolate students in their instructional program. They acquaint students with what is going on in the world, more specifically, in American society and culture. But all of them do so socially. The students go to school with their own kind, play and socialize after school with their own kind, go to church with their own kind, and so forth, with the consequence that throughout their lives they are sheltered, protected, and isolated from anyone with a different background, social status, or religion. Never does the child have the enriching experience of coming into living contact with someone quite different. Never, consequently, does the child enter into the mainstream of American society and culture. Always the child is on the outside looking in. The result is a curious mixture of feelings of arrogant pride and inferiority.

Furthermore, if the intent of all this isolation was to produce in the child a different system of values from that of the society surrounding her, it must be acknowledged that the whole arrangement was a gigantic flop. The graduates of the Christian school are no less materialistic, no less success oriented, no less sex-conscious, no less racist, no less militaristic, no different in their tastes in music, art, film, and clothes than the graduates of public schools.

The Christian school student, deprived of the enrichment that comes from meeting and knowing people of different backgrounds, in this way is stunted, yet he or she emerges with almost exactly the same set of values. The whole system is a vast waste of money.

Having heard the criticism, let us follow our strategy of considering next the relevant part of the idea of the Christian school. Let it be said, first, that it is no part of the aim of a school in the Reformed tradition of Christianity that the education it offers should be protectionist in character. If it has something of that quality, that is at best a by-product, a secondary effect, of its aim. Nor does it aim to produce graduates who will, in their lives, be isolated from contemporary society and culture. On the contrary, the fundamental aim of the Christian school is to equip the child for living the Christian life in the midst of contemporary society and culture. It is characteristic of the Reformed tradition that the Christian life is not to be lived in isolation from society but rather in intimate interaction with that society.

The reason is not that the Reformed Christian finds his ambient society measuring up to God's standards. Quite to the contrary, he finds it to be a fallen society, for we live in a society in which God's good earth is corrupted and polluted as much as it is developed. We live in a society in which the results of science are used to kill almost as often as to cure. We live in a society in which success is measured in monetary terms rather than in terms of service to God. We live in a society in which the walls of partition are scarcely broken down but in which persons are hated and humiliated on account of the color of their skin or the hook of their noses. We live in a society in which few have that exhilarating sense of freedom of which St. Paul spoke but in which many are crushed under the dead weight of rules and institutions and establishments. We live in a society in which ugliness rather than beauty is the dominant feature of our experience. We live in a society in which our novels not only depict our fallen world but revel in its fallenness. We live in a society in which war is thought of as a normal rather than an extreme instrument of national policy. We live in a society in which families are often circles of rising hatred and spite rather than circles of love. We live in a society in which order is far too often praised without perceiving that it is nothing but a curse unless founded on justice. We live in a society in which persons who call themselves Christian are proclaiming that God is dead.

Christians are aware of the discrepancy between the values of Christianity and those of the society and culture in which they find themselves. But the response of the Reformed person to this discrepancy is not, as has historically been the response of a good many Christians, to flee the society. The Reformed Christian's response is rather to work to change that society. With their vivid sense of the corruption in human affairs, they have no illusion of enduring success on this point—though they do indeed hold it out as an ultimate hope.

Thus, they neither acquiesce to their society nor do they try to escape it. Neither do they try to add a bit of Christianity here and there. Their stance is that of those who dissent and seek to reform. "This must not be," they say, and when they see a chance to change what is but must not be, they pursue that chance. The Christian school is called to be a training ground for such a social stance. The society I described is the society in which the Christian school graduate will be living—not off in some protected rural enclave. Can they, in that society, be anything other than dissenters and reformers? The idea of the Christian school in our society is the idea of a school producing dissenters and agents of change in the name of Christ. The Christian school is a training ground for Christian dissent and reform.

Obviously, not all parents in our society will want to send their children to such a school. Thus it is that the isolation, such as it is, occurs. Thus it is that the training ground becomes isolated. But remember, the aim is not that the graduate shall be isolated from society but that he or she will participate in it. The isolation is no more than a temporary provisional thing.

Some of those who criticize the Christian school are probably criticizing this aim itself. They do not want temporary isolation for the sake of dissent and reform. But is it not clear that plenty of others are not criticizing the idea but the implementation of the idea? It is those we have to consider. How can the Christian school lessen its own isolation and the isolation of its graduates and yet remain a training ground for responsible and creative Christian dissent and reform in society?

The most important thing to say, I think, is that we must become far more determined in making the school a training ground for Christian dissent and reform. I sense that the root of much criticism of the isolation of the Christian school, maybe most of it, is that, in terms of the product produced, it seems useless, arbitrary, and irrelevant. The isolation will easily be seen to have a point, and accordingly accepted by a good many critics, if the school really were a source of creative and responsible Christian dissent and change in society.

Of course, it is relevant, once again, to observe that the Christian school needs to be nourished by the practice in its constituency of the virtues the school espouses. The agony that results from discrepancy between school and constituency on this point is vividly illustrated in the Lawndale-Cicero incident, to which I have already referred. African American parents from Lawndale have applied to have their children accepted in the Cicero Christian school. Their application has been rejected since 1965. The rejection is based on two grounds: One is the fear as to what would happen to the school property at the hands of the Cicero community and to the lives of the children if the black children were admitted. The other is the recognition by the board of the presence of rampant racism in the Christian community itself. Recently, half of the teachers in the elementary school wrote a letter to the board protesting the policy, contending that it was un-Christian, contrary to the Word of God. The question starkly posed by the incident is this: Can the Christian school really be a creative and responsible source of dissent against the racism and materialism of American society and an agent of change when that same materialism and racism are exhibited in the constituency of the school? I think the answer to that question is no.

A second thing that can be done is to keep firmly in mind that the educational project of the Christian school must in no way be protectionist except as the maturity of the student requires it. The Christian school must forthrightly introduce its students to contemporary society and culture, not blinking its eyes to the dangers contained therein, instead courageously serving as a guide for the students through the social and cultural expressions of contemporary men and women.

Yet a third suggestion I have to make, perhaps the most "radical," is this. The Christian school should have an open admission policy. I recognize that there are some dangers in this. The temper of the training ground might be destroyed if everyone who wishes is allowed in. Yet there is nothing in principle against it, is there? One has only to apply the policy with discretion. If parents sincerely want the education you offer to be made available to their child, why not allow the child to be admitted? Short of this radical suggestion—if radical it is—what can surely be instituted is a variety of visiting programs and cooperative programs between Christian and public schools, plus, of course, the continuation of interscholastic athletics.

Let me say, by way of conclusion, that I sometimes have the feeling that the entire lifestyle of Christians will have to change, given the radical changes that have taken place in society and culture in our century. The lifestyle of the bulk of those who support the Christian school was formed, for the most part, in the eighteenth and nineteenth century; it's not at all clear that it is particularly relevant to our present day. And that lifestyle is in fact beginning to change.

If there is any truth in such statements, then naturally one goes on to wonder whether Christian schools will be relevant for this new lifestyle, whatever that proves to be. I for one do not think we ought to feel depressed if we eventually conclude that they are not. Just possibly the Christian school was an institution intensely relevant to the life of Reformed Christians in the latter half of the nineteenth and the first three-quarters of the twentieth century but will some day in the future no longer be relevant. My own guess, however, is that the opposite will prove true. They will prove even more relevant to that new emerging lifestyle than they have been heretofore. Of course, it will have to be a new kind of Christian school. If the existing schools in the Reformed tradition of Christianity do not change, I fully expect to see other schools popping up to take their places.

I have talked about the internal pressures, expressed in the form of criticism, that in my judgment are forcing either the demise of the Christian school in the Reformed tradition or its transformation into a new kind of school. I don't in detail know any better than you do what the characteristics of that new kind of Christian school will be. I have, however, thrown out a few general suggestions: It will be less authoritarian, more ecumenical, more open to contacts with the surrounding society and with other Christians, and will prize individuality more highly. In its teaching, it will be more determinedly Christian; it will be a fertile source of creative and responsible dissent and change in society. But these are only hints and guesses. I dare say it will take twenty-five years or more before we really know what the new sort of Christian school is like—if indeed a new sort emerges. In the meantime, you and I can help to bring it about.

chapter ten

Looking to the Eighties

Do Christian Schools Have a Future?

Shortly after the previous article appeared in print, Wolterstorff was invited to speak at the annual meeting of supporters of the Curriculum Development Centre (CDC) in Toronto, Ontario, and his address appeared in their fall 1979 newsletter. The CDC was established to facilitate Canadian Christian school curriculum publications that would help students learn how to have a Christian influence on Canadian society and culture. The materials had a strong social relevance theme, and both content and methodology were chosen on the basis of a Christian view of life.

Wolterstorff describes the difficulty of conducting Christian education that is a true alternative without isolating the children and their families from the surrounding society. The goal of Christian education, he says, is to induct students not only into the life and thought of the Christian community but into the life of discipleship. Christian schools, therefore, must be alternative schools in non-isolationist surroundings.

Does the Christian day-school movement, and in particular the Calvinist day-school movement, have a future?

When I participated in a Christian school convention last spring in Birmingham, Alabama, and got a sense there of the fantastic flowering of Christian day-schools—not racist schools but authentic Christian schools—in the American South during the last five to seven years, I said, "It most certainly does have a future." But when I go to some of the old, well-established, Christian day-schools in the heartland of the United States and there witness the lackadaisical attitudes produced by middle-age respectability, then I say, "I wonder." When I participated recently in a conference of the nonpublic schools in Illinois and there listened to African Americans from central Chicago "chew out" the Calvinists and the Lutherans and the Catholics for having been so quiet about their schools all these years, then I said, "It most certainly does have a future." But on the other hand, when I listen to some of the graduates of the Christian schools pour out their resentment over how they were treated in those schools, then I say, "I'm not so sure." And when I hear, as I do now and then, about the lack of shared vision in some communities and schools, resulting in school systems flying apart into splinters, then I've got to say, "Well, I'm not so sure."

The evidence, in short, is mixed. There are hopeful signs and discouraging signs, promising signs and negative signs. My own guess, for what it's worth, is that the excitement of those new schools springing up will begin to invade some of those old, complacent schools so that by the end of the 1980s the combination will have produced significant new impulses in Christian education. What can also not be ignored is the growing sense in North America of a society adrift. Already this is driving more and more people to see the need for Christian education. In fact, the best statistics indicate that two new Christian schools are being formed every day in the United States. So though the signs are mixed, the future seems to be promising.

The Challenge: Alternative Education in a Non-isolationist Setting

But tonight I really don't want to engage in prophecy and prognostication. Rather than offering predictions as to whether the Christian school movement will flourish, I want to talk about the conditions under which it *can* flourish, for over those conditions you and I have some control. And whether or not the movement flourishes in the future depends on how you and I deal in the present with those conditions.

The great challenge facing the Christian school movement today is the very same challenge that has always faced the movement: Is it possible to conduct alternative Christian education in a non-isolationist setting—that is, in the midst of ordinary North American society? Is it possible, without isolating the children and their families from the surrounding society, to conduct genuinely alternative Christian education? I'm assuming that nobody in this room is seriously persuaded that the course we ought to take is that of isolation. It's clear that alternative education is possible for the old order Amish, under the isolationist conditions that they have chosen for themselves. But the question I want you to think about is this: Is it possible in a non-isolationist setting to conduct a genuinely alternative Christian education?

Let me begin by explaining what I mean by "alternative education" and "non-isolationist setting." I grew up in a Reformed community on the prairies of central United States. My memory of what was said about the goal of the Christian day-schools, which I attended for part of my lower school education, is that it was to communicate to the child a Christian world-and-life view. I'm sure that formula has also been popular here in Canada. What was the impulse behind that formula? What were those who used it driving at? Quite clearly, in adopting that formula they were giving expression to one of the fundamental features of any authentic Reformed vision of Christianity, namely, to its passionate concern with wholeness, with integrity, with the totality of things. What they were saying was this: The Christian gospel does not speak just to our theological thought. It does not speak just to our ethical thought. It speaks to all our thought about the world and life. And Christian education must reflect that "totalism" of the Christian gospel. What they were deliberately avoiding was any formula that says the goal of Christian education is simply to imbue the child with a Christian theological perspective. What they were also deliberately avoiding was any formula that says that the goal of Christian education is simply to imbue the child with a Christian ethical perspective. Instead, the goal of Christian education is to imbue the child with a Christian world-and-life view. Behind that formula lies the conviction that Christ's lordship is to hold sway over all thought, not just over some theological or ethical corner of thought. Let me say that I profoundly agree.

But now I want you to listen once again to the phrase as I emphasize its last word: a Christian world-and-life *view*. Traditionally, Christian schools have seen their goal as that of imbuing the child with a certain view—a view pertaining to all of life, indeed, but a *view*, nonetheless. They have seen their goal as above all a *cognitive* goal. Their concern has been with the thought of the child. They have wanted to shape thinking. Seeing that, the question comes at once to mind: Doesn't that very same impulse toward wholeness, toward integrity, toward allowing everything to come under the lordship of Jesus Christ lead us beyond saying that the goal of Christian education is to impart a *view* toward saying that the goal of Christian education is to shape a way of *living?* A Christian way of life includes, of course, a way of thinking. But there is more to the Christian life than thought. Christian education is a project of the Christian community, and its goal is to induct the child into the life of that community, not just into its thought—into the life of discipleship.

And that—this is my next point—is an alternative mode of life, is it not? Isn't the significance of Pentecost in part that the life of the Christian community will always, until the end of the age, be an alternative mode of life? Once upon a time God's chosen people was a natural grouping of people, a race. It's true that others could enter it and that members of the race could defect. But, nonetheless, God's chosen people was Israel. After Pentecost, no longer. No longer is it to be identified with any nation, any social class, any sex. Now it is a supranational grouping with all the profound implications that has. The gospel tells us to expect that whenever that new people, the church, finds itself present in a nation, it's going to find itself living and called to live an alternative mode of life, for this new people trusts ultimately in God through Jesus Christ. Natural humans always trust in other things.

Every society and every community educates its members for life in that community. American society does so; Canadian society does so. The community of Christians does so as well. Keeping in mind the point made above, I come to the conclusion that Christian education must be alternative education. It's education for a mode of life that is an alternative mode of life. The Christian community requires an alternative mode of education. In so far as the Christian school genuinely educates for Christian life, it conducts an alternative mode of education.

Of course that's the ideal. In fact, it all too often doesn't go like that. When I survey the Christian schools of the Calvinist tradition, I see, over and over, that the supporting community constantly urges its teachers to be, in effect, rebels and reformers, but it fails to hold out the same challenge to others. It constantly urges its teachers to reform sociology, philosophy, psychology, physics, chemistry. It urges that the subjects be rethought and reconstructed so that they can be taught in Christian perspective. In short, the Reformed community constantly asks of its teachers that *they* work out an alternative mode of thought and conduct education in an alternative manner, but it seldom makes the same demand on others. The lawyers of the community act pretty much like other lawyers, and little is said by way of challenging them to act as rebels and reformers in American law. So too for doctors and farmers and businessmen. But of our teachers it is asked that they work out a genuinely Christian alternative.

How is this paradox to be explained? As follows, I think: We expect our doctors and our attorneys and our farmers and our businessmen to *think* like Christians, plus act piously and morally, but outside of that we expect them to go about their business like everyone else. In my judgment, it is the case that the Christian school and its community have concentrated on a *view*. They have concentrated on getting the *thoughts* of the student straight. The Christian businessman acts pretty much the same, but he *thinks* differently. And it is the business of the Christian school and its teachers to provide those alternative *thoughts*.

But that is all confused, isn't it? Christian education, to say it once more, is for Christian life, not just for Christian thought. The Christian life is an alternative mode of life. Consequently, Christian education will have to be an alternative mode of education, not just in the sense of communicating alternative thoughts but in the much more radical sense of equipping students for an alternative way of life.

I trust you see now what I meant when I said that the basic challenge facing the Calvinist day-school today is the same one that has always faced it: Can an alternative Christian educational program succeed in a non-isolationist setting?

Psychology and the Wisdom of the Ages

But why do I see that as a challenge? Wherein lies the difficulty? If you agree with me that the school aims at life and not just thought, then the school cannot be concerned just with *knowledge*. Nor can it be concerned just with knowledge plus *abilities*. It has to be concerned with what the student does with his knowledge and abilities. It has to be concerned with how the child *acts*. Of course, neither the school nor anyone else can guarantee that the child will act a certain way. What it can do, though, is shape what he tends to do, what he is inclined to do, what he is disposed to do. So I come straightforwardly to this conclusion: If what I said concerning the goal of Christian education is correct, then Christian schools must be concerned with shaping how the child tends to act—concerned not just with knowledge, not just with abilities, but with tendencies to *act* in certain ways.

And that leads to this large next question. How can teachers and parents effectively and responsibly shape how children tend to act? I add the word *responsibly* because there may be effective ways of shaping how people tend to act that are irresponsible. So both words are needed, *effective* and *responsible*. If you are concerned with how children are going to live and not just with how they're going to think, how do you exhibit that concern? What do you do?

Over the last twenty years, a great deal of information has been accumulated by psychologists by way of an answer to this question, most of it, in my judgment, confirming the wisdom of the ages but interesting and valuable nonetheless. In this brief overview, I will single out just one of the most important conclusions.

The wisdom of the ages tells us that if you want to shape how a child tends to act, it helps if *you* act that way. If for some reason you're suspicious of the wisdom of the ages, all you have to do is read what is by now a massive amount of psychological literature on the phenomenon that psychologists call "modeling." The idea behind the use of the word is clear. Someone serves as a model for the child. It has been shown, in dozens of different situations, that modeling powerfully shapes in the child a tendency to act as the model acts.

Let me give you a brief indication of some of the situations that have been studied. It's been shown that you can increase a child's tendency to yield to temptation by confronting him or her with models who yield to that temptation. It's been shown that you can increase the tendency of a child to act aggressively by presenting models who act aggressively. It's been shown that you can increase a child's altruistic and generous actions by presenting models who act generously. It's been shown that you can induce a child to raise his or her standards of performance for a task by presenting models who exhibit high standards of performance. It's been shown that you can induce a child to lower standards of performance in a task by presenting models who have low standards of performance. And so on. If you want a child to act a certain way, it helps for respected and loved people in the environment to act that way.

Questions about Modeling

Floods of questions come to mind at this point. Let me pose and answer just three. What happens if a model preaches one way and practices another? The experiments are stunningly unanimous. What shapes the practice of the child is the practice of the model and not the preaching of the model. We all knew that already, didn't we? As the old saying goes, "Actions speak louder than words." However, the full description of the situation is this: If a model preaches one way and practices a different way, the child tends to preach the way the model preaches and act the way the model acts. Hypocrisy perpetuates hypocrisy. Hypocrisy, like everything else, is communicated by models practicing hypocrisy.

A second question is this: What happens if people whom the child regards as models act inconsistently? That is, rather than a given person practicing one way and preaching another, one model acts one way and another acts in a way inconsistent with the first. The answer is this: You can't predict the results. Some children will follow one model, some, the other. And when you average out the behavior, it becomes unpredictable.

Here's a third question. What if the model in question is presented on TV or film instead of live in the environment? It makes virtually no difference. It's been shown in a great many studies that people are just as much influenced by what they see on film and TV as by what they see live. The aggressive behavior of children and adults is increased just as much by presenting them with models on TV or film as by presenting them with live models who act aggressively.

Do you now begin to see why one of the great challenges facing the Christian school is how to educate for an alternative style of life in non-isolationist surroundings? Your children and mine are not reared in isolation. Consequently, they are repeatedly presented with models that contradict what you and I try to model, on film and TV if not in person. They are repeatedly confronted with conflicting styles of life. And what we have learned from the modeling experiments makes us wonder how the goal of training and educating them to live the Christian life can ever succeed without isolation. How can this project that Calvinists have set for themselves, of not isolating themselves from the surrounding society while yet educating their children for an alternative mode of life, possibly succeed? Haven't we just been living with illusions all these years? Don't we have to flip one way or the other, give up as illusionary this project of an alternative education or go the Amish way of isolation?

Before I give you some answers, I want to make one more point. I put the situation as if the child were confronted by teachers and parents who consistently model the Christian way of life and also by people on film and TV who act in contradiction with that. But that's not really the situation, is it? We have to confess that we don't consistently model the Christian way of life. The life of the Christian community is not, in many respects, all that different from that of the surrounding society. So the challenge to be faced is this: How can the Christian school possibly succeed when not even its supporting constituency is consistently presenting the child with a model of the new life in Jesus Christ? The school can preach that alternative mode of life, the parents can preach it, the church can preach it, but we know that if those who preach don't *practice* what they preach, we'll only perpetuate hypocrisy.

Doomed to Isolation?

It's time for me to present some answers, for answers there are. The situation is not really as bleak as I have pictured it.

Let me make two points. The first, is this: We really can succeed, in general, only if the church, the home, and the school are *living* that alternative mode of life. There is no way around this hard truth. So let me say it once again. The school can expect to succeed in its goal of educating for an alternative mode of life only if the church, the home, and the school model that way of life for the child. To suppose otherwise is to live with illusions.

What that means, concretely, is that the church and the home and the school must themselves be communities of love if the school is to succeed in its educational goals, for what we know is that children tend to model themselves after people whom they love and respect. A supporting, loving community has a powerful formative impact on the members of that community. So if someone lives with great responsibility in ecological matters but treats his children without love, all his ecological endeavors will be of little effect. When students come to me and complain bitterly about their Christian education, what they complain about is seldom its inferiority but rather its hypocrisy and the lack of love that they sensed. In so doing, they are pointing at an absolutely decisive defect. If the Christian school is not a community of love, it cannot succeed.

But second, there is now a large body of research that shows that it helps immensely in shaping how a person tends to act if you give him or her *reasons* for acting a particular way. When the child is confronted by violence and aggression on TV, the effects of those models can be diminished by giving reasons for not acting that way. The inarticulate model who says nothing is much less successful than the model who explains. Christian parents who explain why they act as they do are the truly effective models. To counteract the discrepant, the inconsistent, the dissonant models in the surrounding society, the Christian school must do what the Christian parent must do and what the Christian church must do: give the child reasons for acting the right way.

And here, at last, we get into curriculum. I am convinced that if we want to make Christian education succeed, we must first ask what kind of life we want the students to lead when they leave school. Then we must back up from that point and construct a curriculum. Forget what secular educators in Ontario and Michigan are doing. Instead, ask yourself what's necessary to equip the child to live the Christian mode of life, and then frame a curriculum in terms of that.

This means that we will have to get into the hard controversial issues that face Christians in the living of their lives. It's not sufficient to throw abstract sociology and philosophy and psychology and so forth at the child. We have no right to expect that our children are going to act responsibly on ecological matters, matters of war, matters of poverty, matters of how they spend their money, and so forth if we just throw at them abstract academic disciplines. The school that wants to succeed must give the child detailed reasons for acting in definite ways in the surrounding society. I confess, to my embarrassment, that ten years ago I was under the illusion that it was sufficient, at least for college students, to give them these abstract disciplines, and they would put them to use. I now see that that was naive nonsense. It won't work. It never has worked, and it never will work.

In its curriculum, the school must not just give abstract interpretations of history and so forth but must concern itself with the difficult, hard, controversial areas of Christian living, working out answers and offering to students reasons for acting in what the school judges to be the right way.

In conclusion, here is what I see as our program for the 1980s. To acknowledge, as I think we have not done up to this point, that Christian education is for Christian life and not just for Christian thought. Second, to come to realize that Christian life is shaped by the entire conduct of the school, its teachers, by how they act, by how they comport themselves, and not just by what they say, not just by the curriculum. And third, to begin to work out a curriculum in which we give students articulate, soundly based Christian reasons for acting the way in which it seems to us they ought to act. If we manage to do this, then not only will the 1980s be an exciting decade for educators, but at the end of that decade Christian education will also be more exciting and vastly more effective than it has ever been before.

Part 3

Christian Education in a Pluralistic Society

chapter eleven

Religion and the Schools

In the mid-1960s, a series of three articles by Wolterstorff on the topic "Religion and the Public Schools" appeared in *Reformed Journal*. Not too long afterward, these articles were published in the form of a monograph. The monograph, printed here in its entirety, addresses three questions: (1) Should Christians in a pluralistic society, who insist on freedom of religion for themselves, work to protect the religious freedom of people of differing faiths, or is it their duty to work toward creating a Christian society in which the full rights of citizenship are granted only to those who affirm Christian beliefs? (2) What should Christians see as the proper place of religion in public schools? (3) What should Christians see as the proper place of the nonpublic religious school in American society?

The Pluralistic Society

Since the founding of the public school in the mid-nineteenth century, the place of religion in the public school and the place of the non-

185

public "religious" school in society have been issues of serious interest to reflective Americans. Today, the interest has deepened to concern, and as never before, Americans generally are engaged in rethinking the traditional place of religion in the public school and the traditional place of the nonpublic religious school in society. That this general rethinking should have been so long in coming is perhaps surprising, for there have been several large-scale movements in American education that might reasonably have led Americans generally, long ago, to rethink the traditional relationship between religion and the schools.

One such movement is the parochial and Christian school movement. In the nineteenth century, the various states made the decision to set up in each community just one tax-supported school system. In response to this decision, the members of the Catholic community did not merely *protest;* they at once carried their protest beyond words into deeds by setting up their own schools and foregoing all tax support. Furthermore, they made it clear that in so doing they were protesting the *Protestant* orientation of the public schools. Thus, no one could overlook the fact that they were expressing a fundamental criticism of the entire public school system. But the consequence of this criticism was not that Americans began to rethink what they had done. The consequence was rather that hostility and resentment were turned on the Catholics. The Catholic schools were accused of being divisive and un-American. It was openly suggested that "the Papists" should never have been allowed to creep into this fair Protestant land of ours.

The Christian day-schools set up by Dutch Calvinists, from the late nineteenth century onward, also had little effect on American educational thought. These Calvinists also expressed a fundamental criticism of the public school system, but few people discerned that, partly because the movement always remained small. In addition, since the public schools were generally thought to teach a nonsectarian Protestantism, it was easy to regard the action of those Calvinists as nothing more than an attempt by a group of unassimilated Dutchmen to preserve their national identity and to propagate their own sectarian religion. Perhaps some of the things those earlier Calvinists said invited this interpretation of their actions. At any rate, though the Calvinist schools as well as the Catholic schools annoyed people and were accused of being divisive and un-American, their existence did not prompt many Americans, even among those few directly acquainted with them, to rethink the relationship between religion and the schools. The Lutheran schools, too, seem to have been regarded with little more than bemused annoyance.

Another tendency that might have caused Americans to rethink this relationship was the gradual shift, throughout the last hundred years, in the religious orientation of the public schools themselves. Originally, nonsectarian Protestantism constituted the basis of public school education. Those values and beliefs thought to be common and acceptable to all Protestants formed the framework within which education was conducted. But along with the growing religious diversity in American society, this common-denominator *Protestantism* was gradually eroded down to a common-denominator *religion;* the slogan "nonsectarian religion" replaced the slogan "nonsectarian Protestantism." I confess that my understanding of what nonsectarian religion might be is extremely limited. I suspect, however, that most people equated it with theism. The religion of the public schools was to be a religion acceptable to all theists, or perhaps more narrowly, to all theists who regarded themselves as standing in the Judeo-Christian tradition. Now, *mere* theism is certainly a comedown from *mere* Protestantism. Yet it seems that this considerable change in the religious foundation of the public schools did not lead to reconsideration among Americans.

Not only was the original Protestantism of the schools eroded down to a vapid theism, but another and clearly non-Christian ideology frequently moved in to fill the vacuum left by the disappearance of any form of vital Protestantism. Yet not even this caused any widespread reconsideration. The ideology I have in mind is pragmatism. Pragmatism was many things to many people. To almost everyone, however, it was a hymn of praise to democracy. To a degree that should have been alarming, the ideology of the public schools became a religion of the democratic state, a religion whose object of veneration was American democracy. Repeatedly, it was preached that the main business of the schools was the inculcation of democratic values—whatever those might be. Thus, in a profound sense, American education began to resemble Marxist Russian education and Nazi German education and pagan Roman education. In all these cases, a veneration of the state was the moving force in the educational system. Of course, different sorts of states were being venerated.

But none of these far-ranging movements and tendencies in American education is the cause of the present rethinking of the relationship between religion and the schools. All these movements left Americans generally feeling very satisfied with their schools, convinced that their foundations were securely laid. The public school was widely proclaimed as one of the greatest achievements of American democracy and thus of humankind.

So why the present concern? What seems to me to be the true answer to this question is so simple as to be almost incredible. The direct cause of our present willingness to reconsider the matter of religion and the schools is, if I discern at all rightly, two simple and utterly predictable happenings. First, the adamant and highly vocal insistence by a few people during the last couple of decades that the final vestiges of commitment to the Judeo-Christian tradition must be ripped from the public schools. Second, the recent decision by the U.S. Supreme Court that Bible reading in the public schools and prescribed recitation of prayers, no matter how insipid, are in violation of the First Amendment to the Constitution. These two connected developments have finally jolted Americans into the suspicion—I do not say the conviction—that perhaps the public school system as we know it is not our democracy's greatest achievement, that perhaps it is rather an arrangement that is bound to cause endless dissatisfaction in society and endless litigation in the courts by impinging inescapably on some people's freedom.

The schools raise, in an acute form, a problem facing every society that contains conscious religious diversity within one social body: How can people of diverse religions and irreligions live in peace and justice within one society? How can people of diverse life commitments and diverse frameworks of belief concerning reality and human existence live together in harmony and equity within one social organism? The problem obviously becomes more acute the greater the diversity. It is more acute in twentieth-century American society than it was in eighteenth-century American society. Furthermore, it is a problem that, throughout our history, has been prominent in the American consciousness. America was given birth by people fleeing religious persecution and religious antagonism, and on into the nineteenth century, the American wilderness was settled by people fleeing the religious oppressiveness of European societies. Thus, the structure that American society has assumed cannot be understood apart from an understanding of how the American people have responded to the presence of religious diversity within their society.

Since the problem of the proper relationship between religion and the schools is only a specific example of the more comprehensive problem of the proper relationship between religion and social institutions generally, I propose that, before we concern ourselves with the development of a Christian view on the place of religion in the public schools and on the place of the nonpublic religious school in American society, we develop the main outlines of a Christian address to the broader problem.

One key premise in the way Christians have addressed this problem is their conviction that all of life is to be the exercise of their faith in God as revealed in Christ. To be a Christian is not just to accept certain dogmatic beliefs, not just to cultivate certain spiritual feelings, not just to engage in certain acts of worship. It is to be a disciple of Christ in all one's life, for this age and the next. The gospel of Christ speaks to our "secular" and "natural" existence as well as to our "religious" and "spiritual" existence. It speaks to our whole existence—to the whole framework of our beliefs, to the whole complex of our feelings and attitudes, to the whole pattern of our actions. Therefore, to accept this gospel is to do more than engage in Christian worship, more than practice Christian ritual, more than listen to Christian sermons, more than follow Christian morality, more than offer Christian prayers, more than engage in Christian devotions, more than accept Christian dogma. It is to commit oneself to a way of life that is Christian. The Christian is a new person in the entire width and breadth of his or her life. In their entire existence, Christians are pointed toward the true person, Christ. So Christians do not seek to renounce all "secular" activities and to withdraw into some special area of the "religious." Nor do they see in these activities a neutral clearing fenced off to faith. Rather, they see in each of these activities a means of exercising obedient trust in Christ.

A second premise in the Christian's address to the problem of how religion should be related to social structures is the conviction that the community of Christians must be in, yet not of, the world. A person, in becoming a disciple of Christ, becomes an organic member of the community of believers, of the household of faith, of the church. The restoration of harmony between humans and God is inseparable from the restoration of harmony among humans. The church, understood not as the ecclesiastical institution but rather as the fellowship of believers, is always the context and fulfillment of the Christian life.

But not all humans become members of this people of God. Not all are called out. Thus, a cleavage is introduced into society, and the question comes forward with insistence: How is the city of God to be related to the city of the world? This new life of the Christians—where is it to be lived? Are they to flee the society in which they find themselves and set up their own separate society? Are they at all costs to avoid contact with the people of this world and with the culture that they produce?

Certainly not. The body of Christians is not to take flight from the society in which it finds itself; rather, it is to exercise its common faith in the midst of that society. For one thing, flight never does any good. The world is within as well as without. "That which I would not, that I do." But second, to take flight is to fail to live fully the Christian life. Christ has departed from his earthly existence. It now remains to his followers to be a light in a darkened world, a healing balm in a diseased age—in short, to witness to the world of the renewed life available to each person in Christ. To some extent the church, by sending out missionaries and evangelists, has always recognized this. But if the earlier point is correct, that in Christ one finds a new life and not just a new set of dogmatic beliefs and ritual practices, then the church can never identify its witness with its sending out of missionaries and evangelists. On the contrary, Christian life and Christian witness, Christian vocation and Christian mission will have to be seen as opposite sides of the very same coin. And since a Christian's witness must be in the world, so must his or her life. The community of believers lives not for its own sake; it lives for the sake of the world. As Christ was a servant to us, so we are to be a servant-community to those around us. This is our life, and in being our life, it is our witness. When the Christian life is lived in isolation so that it is no longer a witness, then it is no longer the Christian life. It is no longer the life of service to God and other people.

If Christians are indeed to exercise their faith in all the affairs of human life, and if they are to do this as part of the community of believers in the midst of human society, then it follows that Christians will have to seek a society in which they along with other believers are *allowed* to live and act thus. If to have faith in God is to be committed to living a transformed life in the midst of some mingled human society, then that society must be one in which the members of the Christian community are free to live such lives—a free society, a society in which there is freedom of religion. And by freedom of religion it will be obvious that we cannot merely mean freedom of conscience and freedom to associate for the purpose of worshiping as one sees fit, for once a person is convinced that one's faith touches not just one's way of worship but one's way of life, then obviously freedom of religion will have to include freedom to act, freedom to associate for the purpose of acting on one's religious commitments in all spheres of human activity. Freedom of religion will comprise not only the freedom to establish and participate in churches that are expressive of one's religious beliefs and commitments. It will also comprise the right to establish and participate in schools that are expressive of one's religious beliefs and commitments.

Christians, then, must insist on religious freedom for themselves. Should they insist on the same sort of religious freedom for others— freedom to engage in activities expressive of one's religious (or irreligious) commitments? Christians will be intolerant of any infringement on their own religious freedom. Should they be equally intolerant of any infringement on the religious freedom of others? Certainly. Of course, the good order and health of society must be preserved, but within these limits, Christians should strive and plead for a society in which everyone—Catholic as well as Protestant, Buddhist as well as Morman—is allowed the freest possible exercise of his or her religion or irreligion. What is there in the Christian gospel that could possibly give Christians the right to make a person's response to God anything other than free? It will be said that no one has the right to violate God's commands, but what could possibly be the point of forcing someone who does not have faith in God to engage in those activities that Christians use as a means of *exercising* their faith in God? What could possibly be the point of forcing an atheist to say prayers or a Buddhist to swear an oath to God? Can one by Senate and court *really* get people to obey God's commands?

The Christian will strive and plead for what I call a *pluralistic society*, that is, a society in which people, no matter what their religion or irreligion, are allowed to exercise their ultimate loyalty in action as they see fit—limited only by the good order and health of society. They will strive for a society in which the city of God and the city of the world freely coexist in one earthly brick-and-mortar town. They will not strive to make the state Christian, in the sense that it forces everyone to act as the Christian thinks proper, nor even in the sense that it gives special favors to Christians. Rather, they will strive to make the state impartial among all religions and irreligions. In such a society, freedom of religion in its legal dimension will consist of the right of the individual to choose and adhere to whichever religious or irreligious beliefs and commitments he or she wishes; to express and to act on, and to join with others in association for the purpose of expressing and acting on, those beliefs and commitments in whatever way chosen; and to suffer no civil disability on any of these accounts.

Underlying this vision of a society in which all religions and irreligions are freely allowed public expression in word and action is the conviction that people of different world-and-life views, operating out of fundamentally opposed loyalties and fundamentally divergent perspectives on reality and human existence, can yet cooperate in the affairs of state and market. It should be noted that seldom throughout history have people seriously believed that this can be. Over and over they have succumbed to the belief that if society is not to fly apart, there must be some *fundamental*, religious-philosophical agreement among the members of society. Seldom have they risked believing that the Christian and the utilitarian can both be good citizens, though for vastly different reasons. Almost always they have wanted to press people into conformity. Almost always they have wanted to find some fundamental ground on which to stand and then to relegate religious diversity to a sphere in which it makes no difference. Almost always they have dreaded the prospect of a society in which profoundly divergent loyalties are given equal rights in public affairs. But such a society is, I think, what Christians must work for.

I have argued that a proper understanding of the relationship between faith and life and a proper understanding of the role of the Christian community in society lead to the conclusion that Christians should seek a pluralistic society. Let me now point out that different views on these two issues will naturally lead to different views concerning the proper relationship between religion and social structures.

Many Christians have held, and many continue to hold, that in human life and activity we should distinguish between the "secular" or "natural" on the one hand and the "sacred" or "spiritual" on the other. The Christian gospel, they hold, speaks primarily to our spiritual existence. It tells us about the supernatural, about that which lies beyond this bourne of time and space, about that which is inaccessible to experience and reason. It may, *in fact*, also pronounce a judgment on our secular existence and our natural understanding. But it need not. *In principle*, it is only an addition to our secular existence and our natural understanding, not a correction, for it lies in the capacity of all people to order their secular existence by consulting natural law or right reason or self-evident principles. Thus, our secular existence is, in principle, religiously neutral. One's faith in Christ is not the ground of one's whole life but is rather something added to that secular existence and that natural understanding that one shares with all others.

If this is one's understanding of human life and the Christian religion, then one will naturally seek not a pluralistic society but what I call a *neutral society*. One will seek, that is, a society in which the scope of religious diversity is confined to people's private consciences and their ecclesiastical associations, a society in which all institutions and organizations dealing with one's secular existence are neutral toward all religions and irreligions. According to this view, the concern of the state is wholly with our secular existence, and in the exercise of this concern, the state is to ensure that all institutions falling under its jurisdiction are religiously neutral. To this neutral secular existence citizens may then add, for their private delectation, whatever religion they wish. Freedom of religion in its legal dimension will then mean the right of individuals to choose and adhere to whichever religious or irreligious beliefs and commitments they may wish, to expound their beliefs and commitments and engage in acts of worship expressive of their beliefs and commitments and to join with others in association for the purpose of so doing, and to incur no civil disabilities on any of these accounts.

Obviously, the freedom of religion permitted in a neutral society is considerably more constricted than that permitted in a pluralistic society, for though freedom of religion, according to this conception, comprises the freedom to establish and participate in churches that are expressive of one's religious beliefs and commitments, it does not comprise the freedom to establish and participate in schools that are expressive of one's religious beliefs and commitments. The churches are not expected to be religiously neutral, and all that is demanded of the government with respect to the churches is that it treat them all impartially, not that it demand religious neutrality of them all. Of the schools, however, it is required that they be religiously neutral, not just that the government treat them all impartially. By way of comparison, the pluralist holds that religiously committed organizations of various sorts, not just ecclesiastical organizations, should be permitted in society and that the impartiality that the neutralist recommends that the government display toward all the religiously committed churches should be displayed toward all religiously committed organizations.

There are also many Christians who have held, and many who continue to hold, a different view as to the relationship between the Christian community and society than the one just espoused. They believe that it is the duty of the Christian community to set up a Christian society—that is, a society in which the full rights of citizenship are granted only to those who affirm Christian beliefs or participate in Christian worship or belong to Christian churches. They dispute the view that the city of God and the city of the world must live commingled, with equal rights, in one earthly society. They do not agree that the person of unfaith should have the same rights and freedoms as the person of faith. They say that one must pay the price for one's unfaith by enjoying something less than full freedom to speak and act. Henceforth, I shall call such a society a *sacral society*.

Those who hold to the ideal of a sacral society will frequently also speak of freedom of religion. Normally, they will mean by it roughly the same thing as that which the person who holds to the ideal of a pluralistic society means by it: Freedom of religion, in its legal dimension, is to include the right to associate for the purpose of expressing one's religious beliefs and commitments in all manner of institutions, not just in ecclesiastical institutions. Sacralists differ from pluralists, however, in that they wish to confine this freedom of religion to certain religiously qualified members of society—to all orthodox Protestants, or to all Protestants, or to all Christians, or to all theists. It is in this context that the concept of nonsectarianism has found its most frequent use.

American history is in large part the struggle between those who espouse the ideal of a sacral society and those who espouse the ideal of a neutral society. The ideal of a pluralistic society has entered the arena only on rare occasions. In this struggle, the members of the Christian churches have often been on the side of the sacralists. They have usually, indeed, been willing to introduce a measure of nonsectarianism into the sacral society that they desire. Yet there can be no doubt but that many of them have traditionally wanted ours to be a Protestant, or Christian, or religious nation, in the sense that only those who are Protestants, or Christians, or theists are granted full freedom of word and action. They have been willing to impose civil disabilities on others and to give legal advantage to Christianity. In this respect, they stand in the heritage of the medieval church and of John Calvin's Geneva—though of course many of them would be embarrassed to admit this.

On the other hand, the U.S. Supreme Court in recent decades has consistently espoused the ideal of a neutral society. It has consistently interpreted the First Amendment as demanding a neutral society, and it has consistently demanded that the governmentally regulated institutions of the American people fit this interpretation. The abuse that the Court has received on account of its decisions with respect to religious freedom has come, in the main, from those who still hold in some measure to the ideal of a sacral society.

Religion and the Public School

We have explored the concept of a pluralistic society, that is, a society in which all religions and irreligions are given equal right to express their beliefs in word and action, insofar as that is consistent with the public welfare. Such a society was distinguished from a neutral society, that is, a society in which religious diversity is confined to the individual consciences of people, their private lives, and their ecclesiastical associations, and in which all other affairs are conducted with religious neutrality. It was also distinguished from a sacral society, that is, a society in which full freedom of word and action is granted only to those who adopt certain religious beliefs or engage in certain religious practices. Further, I have argued that the conviction of Christians that their whole life is to be an exercise of their faith in Christ and that their life of faith is to be lived as part of the Christian community in the midst of human society should lead them to seek a pluralistic society.

With these matters as background, I now wish to consider the question, What should be the Christian's view as to the proper place of religion in the public school? And let me say in advance that by the public school I mean that one elementary and secondary educational system in each community that is supported by public tax money. If tax money were dispersed to what we now know as private and parochial schools, as well as to what we now know as public schools, then automatically all schools would become public—or alternatively, it would become useless to call any of them public. We could speculate as to what would become, under such an arrangement, of what we now know as the public school. But such speculation is useless for our purposes here. Let us rather consider the proper place of religion in the public school under the present arrangement.

It must be noted, in the first place, that the public school in our present-day American society has no choice but to infringe to a significant degree on the religious freedom of some members of society. It cannot possibly be fully impartial and nondiscriminatory among all the religions and irreligions in our contemporary society, for in our society we find a large group of people who believe, as a matter of conscience, that the education their children receive should *not* be set in the context of a religion or irreligion and should *not* incorporate religious practices. But we also find in our contemporary society large groups of people who believe, as a matter of conscience, that the education their children receive *should* be set in the context of a specific religion and *should* include the religious practices appropriate to that religion. The public school must discriminate, coercively, against the members of one or the other of these groups.

Suppose that the public school, to avoid going contrary to the conscientious convictions of the latter group of people, adopts as its policy and practice to provide an education that is explicitly set in the context of a religion and that includes the practices of that religion. The school will then be doing something contrary to the religion or irreligion of members of the former group, and it will also be doing something contrary to the religion of those members of the latter group who, though they are convinced that their children should receive an education that is set in the context of a religion and that includes the practices of a religion, think it should be a different religion from that which the school happens to have picked. Given the makeup of our society, therefore, the public school, if it followed such a policy and practice, would be discriminating against and infringing on the free exercise of the religions and irreligions of those people whose conscience forbids that they allow their children to have such an education; such people would have to start their own schools and forego the benefit of state funds. If the public school is to respect the religious freedom of all, it cannot provide an education that is set in the context of a religion or irreligion and that includes religious practices.

Suppose the public school, to avoid going contrary to the convictions of those who want their children to receive an education that does *not* include religious practices and that is *not* set in the context of a religion or irreligion, decides to provide this type of education. The school will then be going contrary to the parents who believe that the education their children receive *should* be set in the context of a religion and *should* include the practices of that religion. Given the makeup of our society, the public school, if it followed such a policy and practice, would be discriminating against and infringing on the free exercise of the religions and irreligions of those people whose conscience forbids that they allow their children to have such an education; such people would have to start their own schools and forego the benefit of state funds. If the public school is to respect the religious freedom of all, it cannot provide an education that is *not* set in the context of a religion or irreligion and that does *not* include religious practices.

It is not necessary for the public school to adopt one or the other of the policies and practices mentioned. There is one other course open— it can adopt no policy and practice on the matter, in which case it would presumably be at the pleasure of the individual teacher to determine what to do. But that would be offensive to *all* parties concerned. Thus, given a society that contains the sort of diversity that ours contains, it is impossible for the public school to respect the religious freedom of all. The public school ill fits the pluralistic society. It cannot possibly display, in our society, the impartiality that the state and all its agencies in a pluralistic society ought to display.

The question then becomes, Whose freedom is to be infringed on and whose is to be respected? If the public school begins with prayer and Bible reading, and if Christian doctrines are espoused in the teaching of the various subjects, then the religious freedom of atheists and Buddhists and many others is being infringed on. If prayers and Bible reading and the espousal of Christian doctrine are forbidden, then the religious freedom of various Christians is being infringed on. Who, then, is to be coercively discriminated against?

To discern what seems to me to be the right answer to this question, let us note that one may offend someone, and thus display one's lack of impartiality between that person and some other, either by saying and doing something or by *not* saying and doing something. Bias may be manifested and produced not only by what one says and does but also by what one does not say and do. In the dilemma just explored, we saw that some people are offended when education *is* set in the context of a religion or irreligion, whereas others are offended when it is *not*. Let us, accordingly, distinguish between what I shall call *affirmative* impartiality and *full* impartiality. The state displays affirmative impartiality with respect to the religion and irreligion of two parties if nothing that it says and does manifests a lack of impartiality on its part. It displays full impartiality if, in addition, it manifests impartiality in what it does not say and do. What we have seen above is that full impartiality on the part of the public school is impossible in our society.

It is important to add here that an affirmatively impartial state must not be understood as one that neither says nor does anything that violates the religion or irreligion of any of its citizens. To understand the concept of an affirmatively impartial state in this way would be to make it a worthless, useless concept, for a state that was impartial in this sense could not perform its function of ensuring the common welfare of its citizens. Worse, there could be no such state in our society. This can be made clear with an example. Municipalities should certainly undertake to give police protection to peddlers operating within their confines. But police protection costs money, and on this ground, a municipality may reasonably decide to charge all peddlers a license fee. Jehovah's Witnesses have traditionally refused, on religious grounds, to pay any such license fee. But one cannot therefore claim that a municipality charging such a license fee is hostile to Jehovah's Witnesses and that it is discriminating against them and that it must drop its license fee if it is to be impartial. On religious grounds, some people in our society are opposed to war, some to pacifism, some to integration, some to segregation—in our society there can be no such thing as a state all of whose policies and practices are in accord with the conscientious convictions of all its citizens.

For the state to be affirmatively impartial, therefore, it is not necessary that it not say or do anything contrary to the tenets of any religion or irreligion. Rather, what is demanded is that it not have *as its purpose* to lend support or opposition to any religion or irreligion. In addition, what is demanded is that whenever one of its legitimate purposes can be achieved without violating the tenets of some religion or irreligion, it should be so achieved.[1]

Affirmative impartiality with respect to the religions and irreligions in American society has been the traditional goal and ideal, if not always the practice, of the public school. The public school has traditionally been conceived of as the place where Americans muffle our differences and deal only with that which does not violate the conscience of any one of us. Parents may believe that what their children then wind up with is woefully incomplete for the full education of the child. But the remainder, we have said, is the task of the home and the church. Americans have traditionally talked in terms of the unabridged right of parents not to have alternative religious views forced on their children, rather than in terms of the unabridged right of parents to educate their children in full accord with their own religious convictions.

Underlying this ideology of the public school and accounting for it is the conviction, deeply embedded in American patterns of thought, that religious differences are divisive and that, if our democratic society is to hang together, religious disagreements must for the most part be relegated to the sphere of the private life. They cannot be allowed to enter the public arena. The American solution to the age-old problem of religious strife has not been to give all religions equal sway in public life but rather to make all religions equally isolated from public life. The public school system has always been an integral part of this American ideology, both expressing and perpetuating it. The following passage from Justice Frankfurter's opinion in the *McCollum* case states this nicely: "The sharp confinement of the public schools to secular education was a recognition of the need of a democratic society to educate its children, insofar as the state undertook to do so, in an atmosphere free from pressures in a realm in which pressures are most resisted and where conflicts are most easily and most bitterly engendered. Designed to serve as perhaps the most powerful agency for promoting cohesion among a heterogeneous democratic people, the public school must keep scrupulously free from entanglement in the strife of sects" (*McCollum v. Board of Education,* 333 U.S. 216–17 [1948]). "The public school is at once the symbol of our democracy and the most pervasive means for promoting our common destiny. In no activity of the State is it more vital to keep out divisive forces than in its schools" (231).[2]

What is demanded by the goal of affirmative impartiality has, of course, changed throughout history. In the mid-nineteenth century, when America was *overwhelmingly Protestant,* most communities could afford to let a nonsectarian Protestantism permeate their public school. This was not divisive. Today, obviously, this is no longer the case. It is true that many members of Protestant churches have not reconciled themselves to this change and have continued to insist that the public schools ought to be a training ground for Christianity. But it is interesting that none of the major Protestant denominations has been willing to say, in recent years, that Protestant Christianity, or even Christianity, should be the underlying philosophy of public school education.

There are, of course, many parents in contemporary American society who cannot in good conscience enroll their children in an educational program that is committed to affirmative impartiality among all the religions and irreligions in our diverse society. The rights of such parents demand respect. But those parents who desire that their children should have an education in which religious differences in the community are suppressed as far as possible certainly also have a right to the satisfaction of their desire in our free society. Since the public school is by long tradition the institution designed to satisfy this very desire, and since it has been thus designed not by force of tyranny but by due democratic process, I think it is but right that it remain so. I conclude, then, that it should be part of Christian social policy to recommend that the public school hew more and more strictly to affirmative impartiality among the religions and irreligions in contemporary American society. In this way it remains true to its fundamental tradition.

It is sometimes said that an educational program of the sort I am recommending for the public school—one that is affirmatively impartial among all the religions and irreligions in our society—would perforce itself be based on a sort of religion, "the religion of secularism." It is further said that the public school, if it adopted such a program, would on that account violate the First Amendment to our Constitution, which declares that there shall be "no law respecting an establishment of religion, or prohibiting the free exercise thereof." Consequently, to complete my argument, I must show that there is no likelihood at all that the Supreme Court would accept such an argument. In its decision in the recent *Schempp* case, the Court said, "It is insisted that unless these religious exercises are permitted a 'religion of secularism' is established in the schools. We agree of course that the State may not establish a 'religion of secularism' in the sense of affirmatively opposing or showing hostility to religion, thus 'preferring those who believe in no religion over those who do believe.' . . . We do not agree, however, that this decision in any sense has that effect" (*Schempp v. School Dist. of Abington*, 374 U.S. 225 [1963]). From this passage and its context, one gathers that what the Court demands of the public school, in the name of the Constitution, is that it avoid "affirmatively opposing or showing hostility to religion" or irreligion. It is clear, I think, that a school system practicing affirmative impartiality among the religions and irreligions in our society will fulfill this demand.

It is my own view, however, that the Court has disposed of its problem here much too glibly, and that, as I have already argued, a public school system practicing affirmative impartiality in our society discriminates, coercively, against certain religions. What the Court says, apparently in defense of its view, is that such a school system cannot justly be accused of "preferring those who believe in no religion over those who do." Even if this were true, it would not answer the charge of discrimination, for even if a school system practicing affirmative impartiality among the religions and irreligions in our society does not prefer those who believe in no religion over those who do, such a school system certainly *does* prefer those who conscientiously believe that religion should not pervade the education of their children over those who conscientiously believe that it should. Further, such an educational program will unavoidably, it seems to me, encourage a certain highly prejudicial understanding of the significance and scope of religion in human life. As already observed, beliefs and attitudes are often as effectively inculcated by our not doing or saying something as by our doing and saying something. Suppose, for example, that parents wish to teach their child that belief in God, though not reprehensible, is still a matter of no great importance—that it is, for the consideration of most human issues, irrelevant. One way of instilling this attitude would be to express these convictions openly to the child. An equally effective way would be to avoid all reference to God in conversation with the child. Silence will then speak so loudly that words are superfluous. Similarly, in its exclusive concern with the so-called secular, the public school unavoidably gives aid to the view that religion is at best a matter for one's private and ecclesiastical life. Justice Goldberg saw something of this, I think, when he said in his concurring opinion in the *Schempp* case: "Untutored devotion to the concept of neutrality can lead to invocation or approval of results which partake not simply of that noninterference and noninvolvement with the religious which the Constitution commands, but of a brooding and pervasive devotion to the secular and a passive, or even active, hostility to the religious. Such results are not only not compelled by the Constitution, but, it seems to me, are prohibited by it" (374 U.S. 306).

Given the increasing religious diversity of American society, we must expect that the public school, if it sincerely tries to implement the policy of affirmative impartiality, will increasingly have to constrict its educational program. More and more things will have to be left unsaid and undone. Perhaps this is an alarming consequence, especially when our homes and churches seem no longer to be the effective educational agencies that once they were. But I see no alternative. In a society as religiously diverse as ours, there seems to me no hope of having a public school education that is anywhere near the full scope that such education has traditionally had without departing from the policy of affirmative impartiality. And insofar as more and more is left unsaid and undone, more and more people, I suppose, will be bothered by the lack and distortion in a child's thought and life that an affirmatively impartial educational program is likely to produce.

All this is perhaps most evident in the field of moral training. Traditionally, the public school has been regarded as a source of moral leadership in the community. The public school has been charged with instilling in its students a regard for democratic values, for the values of Western civilization, for the higher values of humankind. Thus, the state has been required, through its public schools, to instill in its citizens moral principles and virtuous inclinations—that it seek to produce good and moral citizens.

It is evident that the fundamental moral principles of human beings are often, if not always, comprised within the tenets of their religions and irreligions. What is even more evident is that the principles thought to be the proper principles of morality are not shared in common among people. A few individual abstract principles may be shared among all the various religions and irreligions in our society, but the moral structures as a whole differ. Some religions preach love, some hate; some tolerance, some intolerance; some activism, some passivity; some violence, some nonviolence; some asceticism, some sensualism. Thus, the public school, if it attempts to inculcate moral principles beyond those of the most elementary, essential, and inevitable housekeeping sort, will almost certainly violate the conscientious convictions of various of its constituents. As we have seen, the fact that the public school teaches something that goes counter to the religious convictions of some of its constituents does not by itself entail that the school has departed from the policy of affirmative impartiality. If the aim of the school in conducting such teaching is an important and legitimate aim on its part, and if the aim cannot be achieved without violating someone's religious convictions, then the school is justified in its practice. But what is not at all clear is that the aim of the public school to produce good and moral citizens, *as it conceives of good and moral citizens,* is an important and legitimate aim on its part. By what right does the state determine the moral codes by which its citizens are to live their lives? Are we not, by virtue of living under a constitutional democracy, to be delivered from just such spiritual tyranny?

There are other aspects of the school's program—its teaching of mathematics, of science, of history, of literature—that it cannot possibly surrender without surrendering its function as a school. Yet in its teaching of these subjects too we must expect that the public school in our diverse society will find it impossible to avoid, in what it says and does, offending the religions and irreligions of various members of its constituency. It will find it impossible to be neutral, either fully or affirmatively, in regard to the religions and irreligions in its constituency. Many of the points I would want to make in this regard have been made by Justice Jackson in the following eloquent passage from his opinion in the *McCollum* case (333 U.S. 235–36):

> I think it remains to be demonstrated whether it is possible . . . to isolate and cast out of secular education all that some people may reasonably regard as religious instruction. . . . Music without sacred music, architecture minus the cathedral, or painting without the scriptural themes would be eccentric and incomplete, even from a secular point of view. Yet the inspirational appeal of religion in these guises is often stronger than in forthright sermon. Even such a "science" as biology raises the issue between evolution and creation as an explanation of our presence on this planet. Certainly a course in English literature that omitted the Bible and other powerful uses of our mother tongue for religious ends would be pretty barren. And I should suppose it is a proper, if not an indispensable, part of preparation for a worldly life to know the roles that religion and religions have played in the tragic story of humankind. The fact is that, for good or for ill, nearly everything in our culture worth transmitting, everything which gives meaning to life, is saturated with religious influences, derived from paganism, Judaism, Christianity—both Catholic and Protestant—and other faiths accepted by a large part of the world's peoples. One can hardly respect a system of education that would leave

the student wholly ignorant of the currents of religious thought that move
the world society, for a part in which he is being prepared.

But how one can teach, with satisfaction or even with justice to all
faiths, such subjects as the story of the Reformation, the Inquisition, or
even the New England effort to found "a Church without a Bishop and a
State without a King" is more than I know. It is too much to expect that
mortals will teach subjects about which their contemporaries have passionate controversies with the detachment they may summon to teaching
about remote subjects such as Confucius or Mohammed. When instruction turns to proselytizing and imparting knowledge becomes evangelism
is, except in the crudest cases, a subtle inquiry.

I fully share Justice Jackson's skepticism as to the possibility of teaching even the so-called secular subject matters without offending one or
another person's religious convictions and without stepping over that
thin line between teaching *about* religious beliefs and *inculcating* religious beliefs. There is some hope, perhaps, of the public school achieving affirmative impartiality; there is no hope, it seems to me, of its achieving neutrality. The public school that was so hopefully designed to
eliminate religious controversy can scarcely avoid contributing to it.[3]

The Place of the Nonpublic Religious School in American Society

I argued that the Christian should recommend that the public schools
in our country commit themselves to a policy of affirmative impartiality with respect to the religions and irreligions in American society. I
also argued that the Christian conviction that all of life is to be an exercise of faith in Christ and that the life of faith is to be lived as part of the
Christian community in the midst of human society should lead Christians to seek a pluralistic society, that is, a society in which all are free
to express their religious or irreligious beliefs in word and action as they
see fit—limited only by the good health and order of society. Now I wish
to consider what the Christian's view should be regarding the proper
place of the nonpublic religious school in American society.

Let me first, however, point out that the principles laid out in the previous parts of this discussion provide the basis for what seems to me a
rather decisive line of thought in favor of the Christian day-school movement. Protestant Christians generally have held that the parent or
guardian of a child has the right and the duty to determine that child's
education. This view, so far as I can discern, is shared by most other
Americans. In the 1920s, the State of Oregon passed a law giving the
state the ultimate right to determine the child's education. The law in

question required all children to attend the public schools of that state. But the law was struck down by the U.S. Supreme Court with the famous words, "The child is not the mere creature of the State; those who nurture him and direct his destiny have the right, coupled with the high duty, to recognize and prepare him for additional obligations" (*Pierce v. Society of Sisters*, 268 U.S. 535 [1925]). Most Americans would now agree, I think, that the Court's decision was right.

What, then, will *Christian* parents set as the main purpose of their child's education? Our previous discussion makes the answer to this question clear. Christian parents, in directing the education of their child, will seek to train that child to live the Christian way of life as a member of the Christian community in the midst of human society. The children of Christian parents are already members of the household of faith, but they are immature members. It is the duty and responsibility of Christian parents to bring their membership to maturity.

It should be noticed that the primary aim of the education that Christian parents give their child is a positive one—preparing the child to do something in society. The primary aim is not a negative one—secluding and isolating the children from society, quarantining them against infection. The Christian view of faith, life, and society justifies no such fearful and apprehensive negativism.

Thus, the question as to whether Christians should maintain separate Christian day-schools will have to be wholly determined by their judgment as to whether, without such schools, they can adequately train their children to live the Christian way of life in contemporary society. It will have to be wholly determined by their judgment as to whether the public schools, plus their homes and churches, are adequate instruments for that end. There can be little doubt that homes and churches together are adequate instruments for teaching children the proper devotional practices and the proper theological beliefs; one scarcely needs separate day-schools for that. But the question is whether homes and churches plus the public school are adequate instruments for training children to live the *whole* Christian way of life.

How *could* the public school supply what Christians must demand of the school to which they send their children? For, to repeat, the public school must be affirmatively impartial in its educational policies and practices. It cannot with propriety undertake to be a training ground for the Christian way of life. It cannot rightfully, in our religiously diverse society, systematically inculcate Christian standards for the assessment of art and literature, Christian economic and political principles, the Christian understanding of work, the Christian view of nature, the Christian understanding of the source of evil in human affairs. Yet exactly these things—and many others of the same sort—are what the Christian wants inculcated in the child, for the inculcation of such things is indispensable to training the child to live the whole Christian way of life. It cannot be overlooked that the gospel speaks to our this-worldly secular existence as well as to our other-worldly existence. I think it is difficult, therefore, to avoid the conclusion that Christians need Christian schools for the education of their children. And once more—they do not need them to teach children the Christian way of worship; they need them to teach children the Christian way of life.

What, then, should be the place of such schools and other religiously committed schools in American society? The right to religious freedom cuts many ways. It cuts down any infringement on the free exercise of Buddhism and humanism and atheism; equally it cuts down any infringement on the free exercise of evangelical Christianity. I have just argued that Christians will exercise their faith by establishing and maintaining Christian schools. If they are also required to assist in the maintenance of other schools and get no assistance in turn, it seems to me absolutely clear that the free exercise of their religion is being seriously infringed on. The government can coercively discriminate against a person's religion in a variety of ways; one of the more effective is to make that person pay extra on account of it. So I think that if the views of faith, life, and society sketched out earlier are correct, then the conclusion is quite inescapable that schools with diverse religious orientations ought to be given equal standing in our society. The state must show no preference whatsoever in the dispersement of funds for education. It must not demand affirmative impartiality of all the schools to which it disperses funds. It must rather be impartial in its dispersement of funds.

The proper aim of the government in the field of education is that all its citizens be educated. The government in our country has acknowledged that nonpublic as well as public schools can properly fulfill this aim. At present, however, the government achieves its end in such a way that a financial burden is placed on those with certain conscientious convictions that is not placed on those lacking these convictions. If the government cannot achieve its end without imposing such unequal burdens, then, this being a legitimate end, it cannot be accused of discrimination and lack of impartiality. But if the government *can* achieve its end without the imposition of this unequal burden, then to fail to do so is to act in a discriminatory, partial manner. It is clear that the government *can* achieve its end in such a way as not to impose such unequal burdens—it can disperse funds to all schools, regardless of their orientation. I conclude, then, that it is obliged to do so. Nothing short of governmental support for *all* schools can secure genuine freedom in education. Only this will yield a truly pluralistic society.

But would it be legal for all schools to receive public tax money regardless of their religious orientation? What I have proposed would involve a profound restructuring of American education. Is there any chance that it would be allowed by the Supreme Court? And, further, is there any chance that the Court would be an ally to those seeking such a restructuring? Or have we been sketching out a utopia?

We must be clear on what is being asked here. I am not trying to predict what the Court would in fact decide on such issues. I am rather asking what the Court, if it follows principles of constitutional interpretation that it has itself laid down, would decide. The distinction is necessary, in part because the Court is a body of nine people raised in America and thus imbued, to some extent, with the prevailing veneration of the American public school system as it now exists. On that account it might resist the ultimate but natural consequence of its own lines of thought. All we can do then is inquire into those lines of thought.

Two questions must be asked: First, is aid to all schools *permissible* under the Constitution? And second, is aid to all schools *required* under the Constitution? Let us consider these questions separately, and let us be reminded of what the First Amendment says. It declares that there shall be "no law respecting an establishment of religion or prohibiting the free exercise thereof."

Two court cases have dealt directly with aid to nonpublic schools, the *Cochrane* case and the *Everson* case. The former concerned the practice in Louisiana of giving certain textbooks free to children in nonpublic as well as public schools. Opponents of this practice argued that it was an illegitimate use of tax money, on the ground that the money was being spent for a private rather than a public purpose. The *Everson* case concerned the practice by a certain community in the State of New Jersey of offering free bus rides to parochial as well as public school children. Opponents of this practice argued that it constituted an establishment of religion. In both cases, the Court sustained the practice, and in so doing it laid down this principle: If the primary aim of a certain law is the general welfare of the people, then the fact that one or another religious institution is benefited in the execution of that law is irrelevant to its constitutionality; such a law does not violate the Establishment Clause. The Establishment Clause does not require the state to discriminate *against* children attending nonpublic schools when distributing funds aimed at the general welfare.

The interest of the state in education is that all children should be educated up to certain minimum standards; beyond a doubt this is conducive to the general welfare. So if, in the attempt to secure this general benefit, some state decides to disperse funds to all schools meeting these minimum standards or to all students attending schools that meet these minimum standards, such a decision, according to the Court's own principle, would not constitute an establishment of religion.

It should be mentioned that there has been considerable disagreement with the Court's interpretation of the Establishment Clause, some of that disagreement coming from dissenting members of the Court itself. Some have claimed that the Constitution does not merely prohibit laws whose purpose or avoidable effect is the benefit of some religious institution but rather that it prohibits laws that *in fact* are to the benefit of some institution in which religious exercises are conducted or the tenets of some religion promulgated. The merest reflection shows that such an interpretation is little short of idiotic. It would mean that a fire department could not save a burning church or a Quaker meeting hall, that policemen could not control traffic around evangelistic meetings or atheist rallies, that the post office could no longer grant below-cost second-class mailing privileges to Catholic schools or to ethical culturalist societies, that an employee of the government could no longer use part of his salary to make a contribution to his church. Such an interpretation of the First Amendment would obviously put so intolerable a burden on the exercise of people's religions that it would be in violation of the Free Exercise Clause. And as the Court stated in the *Everson* case, "New Jersey cannot hamper its citizens in the free exercise of their own religion. Consequently, it cannot exclude individual Catholics, Lutherans, Mohammedans, Baptists, Jews, Methodists, Nonbelievers, Presbyterians, or the members of any other faith, *because of their faith or lack of it,* from receiving the benefits of public welfare legislation. . . . We must be careful, in protecting the citizens of New Jersey against state-established churches, to be sure that we do not inadvertently prohibit New Jersey from extending its general state law benefits to all its citizens without regard to their religious belief" (*Everson v. Board of Education of Ewing Township,* 330 U.S. 16 [1947]).

The fact that a given law aids one or another religious institution must be viewed as constitutionally irrelevant. Rather, the test for a violation of the Establishment Clause "may be stated as follows: What are the purpose and primary effect of the enactment? If either is the advancement or inhibition of religion then the enactment exceeds the scope of legislative power as circumscribed by the Constitution" (*Schempp v. School Dist. of Abington,* 374 U.S. 222 [1963]).[4]

The other issue to be considered is whether all schools meeting certain minimum standards have a *legal right* to public tax monies. Certainly the Court would be reluctant to overthrow an arrangement that has so long been part of American life; it is justly wary of infringing on the legislative function. But the Court has, I think, laid down various principles of constitutional interpretation that, when put together, make questionable the legality of giving tax monies to just one school system.

In order to establish that the Constitution requires that nonpublic religious schools as well as public schools receive public tax funds, one must establish first that an educational program committed to affirmative impartiality among the religions and irreligions in our society violates the religious convictions of some citizens. As we have seen in another context, the Court has already said, in effect, that a public school program committed to affirmative impartiality among the religions and irreligions in our society does not manifest hostility to religion.[5] The Court's line of thought runs something like this: Not starting the school day with prayer does not constitute hostility to prayer; not teaching the Christian doctrine of creation in a biology class does not constitute hostility to the doctrine of creation; and, more generally, not conducting religious exercises nor espousing religious beliefs in the schools does not constitute hostility to religion.

Surely this is correct. The fact that one does not pray on a certain occasion does not constitute hostility to prayer, and the fact that one does not espouse the doctrine of creation on a certain occasion does not constitute hostility to this doctrine. However, total silence on religious matters may *induce* hostility. But even this is not decisively to the point, for the issue is not whether a school system founded on affirmative impartiality would manifest hostility to *religion in general*. The issue is whether it would manifest hostility to *some particular religion or other*. Quite obviously it would. It manifests hostility, for example, to those who conscientiously believe that the education of their children should be set in a Christian perspective, and it aids those who, for whatever reasons, do not believe that the education of their children should be set in a religious perspective. It does not as such manifest hostility to those who think it sometimes appropriate to pray, but it does as such manifest hostility to those who think it obligatory that their children pray a Christian prayer at the beginning of a school day.

Not only does an educational program committed to affirmative impartiality discriminate against some people's religions, but it can also be shown that under our present arrangement it does so in a *coercive* manner. It is often said that the rights of those who cannot in good conscience send their children to the public school are adequately protected by allowing them to establish their own schools. In our country, those who, for whatever reason, dislike the public school do have the long-established right, the *legal* right, to establish their own schools. There is, therefore, as it were, an exemption clause in the requirement of public school attendance. Now, the Court has declared, in its school cases, that if a regulation by the government manifests preference among religions and irreligions, the fact that an exemption clause is attached does not save the regulation from being discriminatory and lacking impartiality. In this case, what is worse is that the exemption operates coercively, for to exercise one's right to provide one's children with a non-public school education, one must be willing and able to give financial support to two different school systems. Common sense, as well as various of the Court's opinions, tells us that a legal arrangement whereby a financial penalty is attached to the exercise of someone's religion can constitute an infringement on the free exercise of that religion—that is, can constitute coercive discrimination against that religion.

Justice Stewart states the issue forcefully in his opinion in the *Schempp* case (374 U.S. 312–13 [1963]):

> There is involved in these cases a substantial free exercise claim on the part of those who affirmatively desire to have their children's school day open with the reading of passages from the Bible.
>
> It has become accepted that the decision in *Pierce v. Society of Sisters*, 268 U.S. 510, upholding the right of parents to send their children to non-public schools, was ultimately based upon the recognition of the validity of the free exercise claim involved in that situation. It might be argued here that parents who wanted their children to be exposed to religious influences in school could, under *Pierce*, send their children to private or parochial schools. But the consideration which renders this contention too facile to be determinative has already been recognized by the Court: "Freedom of speech, freedom of the press, freedom of religion are available to all, not merely to those who can pay their own way" (*Murdock v. Pennsylvania*, 319 U.S. 105, 111 [1943]).

This statement of Justice Stewart occurs in a dissent. If we are to find a legal basis for the claim that attaching a financial penalty to the exercise of a person's religion can constitute coercive discrimination against it, and therefore an infringement on its free exercise, we must look at some of the Court's own opinions. One relevant passage is the one from *Murdock v. Pennsylvania*, cited by Justice Stewart in the passage just quoted. An entire case relevant to the matter, however, is the recent *Sherbert v. Verner* (374 U.S. 398 [1963]). This case was brought by a Seventh-Day Adventist woman who was refused unemployment compensation by the State of North Carolina on the grounds that she had refused to accept a job offered her. The woman refused the job because it entailed her working on Saturdays. The Court declared that North Carolina had infringed on the free exercise of this person's religion, and in the course of its opinion, it said the following: "Government may neither compel affirmation of a repugnant belief—nor penalize or discriminate against individuals or groups because they hold religious views abhorrent to the authorities . . . ; nor employ the taxing power to inhibit the dissemination of particular religious views" (402). "The ruling forces her to choose between following the precepts of her religion and forfeiting benefits, on the one hand, and abandoning one of the precepts of her religion in order to accept work, on the other hand" (404). "It is too late in the day to doubt that the liberties of religion and expression may be infringed by the denial of or placing of conditions upon a benefit or privilege" (404). "To condition the availability of benefits upon this appellant's willingness to violate a cardinal principle of her religious faith effectively penalizes the free exercise of her constitutional *liberties*" (406).

From these passages it is clear that, in the Court's view, a person's religious freedom can be impaired if, by virtue of some legal arrangement, a special financial burden is attached to the exercise of his or her religion. In the *Schempp* case, the Court said that "it is necessary in a free exercise case for one to show the coercive effect of the enactment as it operates against him in the practice of his religion" (374 U.S. 223 [1963]). The Court itself clearly holds that a financial burden resulting from an enactment can have a coercive effect.

Furthermore, if having to pay extra for the exercise of one's particular religion does not constitute an infringement on its *free exercise,* it may well be asked why none of the justices suggested to Mrs. Murray that she set up her own school if she thought that the reading of the Bible impaired the moral health of her children. Granted, the case was officially decided on the Establishment Clause; Justice Brennan at least argued explicitly that it could also have been decided on the Free Exercise Clause. Yet he nowhere suggested that Mrs. Murray already had the free exercise of her religion or irreligion. Why not? Presumably because he as well as everyone else knew that a penalty is attached, a financial penalty.

The last proposition that must be established, if one is to show that nonpublic religious schools have a legal right to tax money, is that the government's concern that all its citizens be educated can be achieved in such a way as not to impose financial burdens that are unequal depending on one's religious convictions and that then it ought to be so achieved. That it *can* be achieved in this alternative manner is obvious; the government can, as it does in many European countries, disperse its funds to all approved schools or to all students attending such schools. That it is, accordingly, obliged to do so by the Constitution, on pain of coercively discriminating against and infringing on the free exercise of some religions, follows from the principle enunciated in the following Court opinion: "If the purpose or effect of a law is to impede the observance of one or all religions or is to discriminate invidiously between religions, that law is constitutionally invalid even though the burden may be characterized as being only indirect. But if the State regulates conduct by enacting a general law within its power, the purpose and effect of which is to advance the State's secular goals, the statute is valid despite its indirect burden on religious observance unless the State may accomplish its purpose by means which do not impose such a burden" (*Braunfeld v. Brown*, 366 U.S. 607 [1961]).

Therefore, on the basis of principles that the Supreme Court itself has enunciated, one can make a strong case to the effect that the government is obliged by the Constitution to disperse funds to all schools meeting certain minimum standards, regardless of any religious orientation that the school may have. But once more, this is not a prediction. The Court's decisions on religious freedom cases are scarcely models of clear and unambiguous formulations of principles of constitutional interpretation. And there is ample evidence that no matter what argument is presented, Justice Douglas will decide that the dispersement of funds to nonpublic schools or to nonpublic school children is unconstitutional.

I close my consideration of the legal aspects of the problem with a curiosity. During the last war, a state university in California required students in attendance at the university to participate in military training instruction. A student protested that this violated his religious convictions. The Court disallowed the protest on the grounds that attendance at the university was not compulsory (*Hamilton v. Regents of the University of California*, 293 U.S. 245 [1934]). Later, it said that this decision was irrelevant to cases dealing with the place of religion in public elementary and secondary schools, since attendance at these schools is compulsory (*West Virginia Board of Education v. Barnette*, 319 U.S. 624 [1943]). But how curious of the Court to have overlooked the fact that attendance at public elementary and secondary schools is *not* compulsory. All that is compulsory is attendance at elementary and secondary schools—public or not.

In conclusion, let me say that one of the first and best things that supporters of nonpublic schools can do is follow the example of Grand Rapids, Michigan, and establish in each city a Coordinating Council on Education, consisting of representatives from all the school systems in the community. In this way, some redress of financial imbalances can be secured. Far more important, in this way it can be shown concretely that the various religious groups within a society can cooperate in securing their common goal of an educated citizenry. Too long the various school systems in our communities have lived in hostile isolation. By cooperative planning of the total educational program of a community, it can be shown concretely that a truly free and pluralistic society is both possible and desirable. Until the day that the ideals of a pluralistic society are achieved in American education, there can be no fully satisfactory or even viable solution to our urgent and perplexing problem of the place of religion in the schools.

chapter twelve

Human Rights in Education

The Rights of Parents

The Illinois Advisory Committee on Non-Public Schools, representing sixteen associations of nonpublic schools, works with the State Board of Education to strengthen educational opportunities for all children in that state. In 1978, they invited Wolterstorff to speak on the topic of the rights of parents.

Do Parents Have the Primary Right to Determine the Character of Their Child's Education?

There are those in the contemporary world who say that parents do not have the primary right to determine the character of their child's education. I think, for example, of A. S. Neill of Summerhill fame, though

211

he is but one representative of a position widely shared in the Western world. Neill was of the view that *nobody* has the right to determine the character of a child's education—nobody other than the child himself. Only the child has the right to decide whether he or she will learn this rather than that, cultivate this ability rather than that one, develop this habit rather than that one. Children as well as adults must be allowed self-determination. Children come with a cluster of innate desires and interests such that mental health and happiness will be achieved if, but only if, these are allowed to find their satisfaction within the natural and social environment of the child. Furthermore, each individual's mental health and happiness constitute what is for him or her the ultimate good. Accordingly, adults have no right to lead children into the way that they, the adults, think they should go. Their responsibility is solely to provide children with an environment that is *permissive,* in that there is no attempt to impose the views and rules of others onto the children, and that is *nourishing,* in that it enables children to satisfy their innate desires and interests.

I cited A. S. Neill as a well-known representative of this position. Actually, I know no better brief statement of it than the following paragraph from the American psychologist G. Stanley Hall:

> The guardians of the young should strive first to keep out of nature's way and to prevent harm and should merit the proud title of the defenders of the happiness and rights of children. They should feel profoundly that childhood, as it comes from the hand of God, is not corrupt but illustrates the survival of the most consummate thing in the world; they should be convinced that there is nothing else so worthy of love, reverence and service as the body and soul of the growing child.[1]

That then is one answer to the question whether parents have the primary right to determine the character of their child's education. Nobody other than the child has a right in this regard.

Others in the contemporary world would also say no to the question but would offer a radically different reason for doing so. If we look beyond the Western world, I dare say that there are more of these others than of the A. S. Neill type. The people I have in mind are those who say that it is not the parents but *the state* that has the primary right to determine the character of a child's education. Parents may have the right to nourish their child in years of immaturity. Parents may have the right to be their child's guardians for a number of years. But when it comes to determining the character of education, parents have only a right that is secondary to and derivative from that of the state, for children cannot just be allowed to flower in a permissive and nourishing environment. They must be shaped and formed for the welfare of the entire citizenry. They must be made to *internalize* those rules and convictions that will benefit society. The officers of the state have the authority to determine *which* rules and convictions those are, for they are in charge of the welfare of the community—that being the ultimate good of the citizenry. Accordingly, the officers of the state have the responsibility and the right to ensure that the rules and convictions conducive to the welfare of the community will be imprinted on the student. Otherwise, the community perishes.

One thinks here of all the ideologically totalitarian regimes with which our contemporary world sadly provides us so many examples. But lest we adopt an attitude of complacent revulsion toward this point of view, let me quote a brief passage from the Education Code of the State of Ohio: "The natural rights of a parent to custody and control of . . . children are subordinate to the power of the state to provide for the education of their children." Every totalitarian regime would be content with that statement exactly as it stands. The view is much closer to home than some of us might have thought.

I am sure you all know that deeply embedded in the Jewish and Christian traditions on which our society was founded is the conviction that parents do in fact have the primary right to determine the character of their child's education. But those traditions are becoming increasingly attenuated among us. Accordingly, today it is no longer persuasive for the defenders of that conviction simply to appeal to the deliverances of the Judaic and Christian traditions. The deep-lying issues must be probed. That I shall try to do as I seek to make the case that parents do have this primary right, for I am profoundly persuaded that the right of parents to determine the character of their child's education is one of the most fundamental of all human rights, more fundamental than the right to free speech. When this right is no longer acknowledged, then much of what is most precious in human existence is endangered.

Before I offer my reasons, I must make some explanatory comments about the concept of *rights* that I was and will be using. One defense of the view that American citizens have the right, let us say, to own firearms would be to point to the law—in this case, primarily to the Bill of Rights attached to our Constitution as its first ten amendments. When we look at the law we see that, yes, it's true, American citizens do have the right, though not indeed the *unqualified* right, to own firearms. Similarly, one might try to defend the view that parents have the primary right to determine the character of their child's education by pointing to the law. In this case, admittedly, one could not point to the Bill of Rights, for that says nothing on the matter. I suspect that it says nothing on the matter for the simple reason that those who formulated the first ten amendments regarded this right as something that goes without saying. You remember that the men who wrote the Constitution even regarded the content of the Bill of Rights as going without saying—which is why it is not part of the Constitution itself. But even though we cannot point to the Bill of Rights, I do take it to be the case that the rights of parents on this matter are fixed in our law—though for all I know they may not be very firmly and unequivocally fixed. We would need a legal scholar to give us the full picture, and that I am not. The only part of the picture with which I am directly acquainted is the famous passage from *Pierce v. Society of Sisters,* a passage that I find curiously cautious and guarded: "The child is not the mere creature of the State; those who nurture him and direct his destiny have the right, coupled with the high duty, to recognize and prepare him for additional obligations" (268 U.S. [1925]).

But when I said that I was going to argue for the view that parents have the primary right to determine the education of their child, I was not referring to the legal right. I was referring rather to the *moral* right, the *human* right—the right that, whether or not honored by our legal code, *should be* honored by it and even, so I shall argue, *ensured* by it, for a good legal code is one that (at the minimum) honors the human, moral rights of the citizens, ensures (guarantees) some of them, and does so in a fair, equitable, and just manner.

It seems to me that moral rights are always the correlatives of moral responsibilities. Some of my rights are the correlatives of responsibilities on my part toward others. They consist fundamentally in my right to exercise those responsibilities. They are what might be called my *freedom rights*—my rights to be allowed to act so as to be able to carry out my responsibilities. Others of my rights are the correlatives of responsibilities on the part of other people toward me. Since they have the responsibility to act toward me in a certain way, I have the right to be so treated. These are what might be called my *rights of treatment*. But either way, moral rights are never free-floating entities. They come as correlatives of our responsibilities. And often the best way to determine whether we have such and such a moral right is to scrutinize our responsibilities.

My thesis then is that the primary right of parents to determine the character of their child's education is a *freedom right* on their part. It is a straightforward correlative of their having the primary responsibility for determining the character of their child's education. If they do indeed have the primary *responsibility* for doing so, then they also have the primary moral *right* to do so. Our legal code should then honor that right. It should not violate it—unless absolutely necessary.

Therefore, is it primarily the moral responsibility of parents to determine the character of their child's education? The child comes into the world as the result of the physical union of his parents—as the product of their physical substance. "Bone of my bones and flesh of my flesh" (Gen. 2:23) is how the ancient biblical writer spoke of the relationship. And we human beings are so created that almost invariably the result of this relationship is natural affection on the part of the parents for the child—normally indeed the deepest of *all* natural affections, wonderful and mysterious, one for which we have nothing even approaching an adequate scientific explanation.

Surely, this natural affection is something good, something to be prized. When it is missing, as every now and then it is, we witness a sad deficiency in the lives of those parents, a lamentable absence of a deep human joy. Being good, being something that gives to parents legitimate joy, it is something that others have the responsibility to respect and that parents accordingly have the right of treatment to exercise. Furthermore, if this right is respected and the child is allowed to live with his or her parents, thereby enabling them to lavish on the child their natural affections, then of course they have the responsibility—and correlatively the freedom right—to nourish the child in his or her early years. Child neglect is a grievous wrong.

As the child grows and matures, the parents' natural affection for the child as offspring normally develops and expands into something rather different, into love for the child as a *young person*. It doesn't always, and when it doesn't, then once again we witness a sad deficiency in human life, for such love is a good thing. Accordingly, others have the responsibility to respect it, and parents have the correlative right of treatment to enjoy and exercise it.

But beyond their natural and normal inclinations, parents have a *responsibility* to love their child. When the right of the parents to the joys of natural affections is honored by allowing the child to live with them, then gradually as the child matures it becomes the responsibility of the parents to go beyond feeling affection for the child as offspring and to begin to love the child as a *person* in his or her own right, albeit a young person. When the child is not treated as a young person in addition to being an object of affection, then too a grievous wrong is inflicted on the child. Correlative with this responsibility on the part of parents is the freedom right on their part to act in accord with those responsibilities. They have the *right* to treat their child as a young person, to whom they feel the ties of natural affection.

Much indeed goes into the responsibility of the parents to treat the child as a young person—one for whom they have affection. But prominent within it, according to my view, and I should think according to the view of anyone who acknowledges that there are responsibilities, is the act of seeking to nurture the child in such a way that his or her promise and dignity as a human being will be actualized. Prominent within it is the act of seeking to rear the child in such a way that he or she will mature into a person who acts responsibly while at the same time finds joy in his or her existence.

And that requires education. One might even say that education properly conceived just *is* seeking to rear the child in such a way that the child will mature into someone who acts responsibly while at the same time finds joy in his or her existence. But in any case, parents who have the responsibility and the correlative right to love their child as a young person thereby also have the responsibility and correlative right to see to it that their child is educated.

What Constitutes Education for Responsible Action?

If our human situation were such that we all agreed on what constitutes responsible action, that we all agreed on what constitutes the legitimate joys of human existence, and that we all agreed on how to educate for these things, then there would be no point in going further to speak of the parents' right to determine the *character* of their child's education. The character would be fixed, agreed on. It would be sufficient to speak of the responsibility and right of the parents to see to it *that* their child was educated. But, of course, one of the most fundamental features of our human situation is that we do not agree on those things. We do not agree on what constitutes responsible action. We do not agree on what constitutes the deep and legitimate joys of human existence. We do not agree on how to educate for these things. Accordingly, the parents' responsibility and right for the education of their child extends to their responsibility and right to determine the *character* of their child's education. It extends *into* the classroom, not merely to the point of having brought the child to the door of the classroom.

To see this clearly, go back to the beginning of our argument. I said that parents' natural affection for their child is a precious and good thing and that parents accordingly have the right to be treated in such a way that their offspring can live with them and their natural affection can be satisfied. I went on to say that as the child grows and matures in intimate interaction with his parents, this affection for the child as offspring develops naturally and normally into love for the child as a young person. That too is a good thing, and parents accordingly have the right to be treated in such a way that they can exercise this love. Indeed, I went further and said that such love is not only a natural and normal development that is good but that it is a *responsibility* on the part of the parents toward their child, with once again the correlative freedom right to exercise this love. From there I went on to say that treating the child as a young person includes helping him or her to mature into someone who acts responsibly while at the same time finds joy in his or her existence. But, of course, this maturation process includes *the parents'* view of a person who acts responsibly and finds true joy in existence. It would not be love but perversity on the part of parents to help their child mature into someone whom they view as an irresponsible agent living a joyless existence. That is why allowing parents to exercise love for their child requires allowing them to determine the fundamental character of their child's education. It requires allowing the parents to decide whether the child shall be reared as an aggressive secularist, or a Christian, or a Buddhist, or with a strong black consciousness, or whatever.

You might reply at this point that my argument does indeed show that parents have a right to determine the character of their child's education, but that it doesn't show that they have the *primary* right. At best it shows that the parents have *a* right, for other people are also responsible for treating the child as a young person. Other people are also responsible for this child's becoming a responsible agent who will find joy in his or her existence. Why then should it be thought that parents have the *primary* responsibility? Is it not instead the case that the responsibility is spread evenly among all the members of the community—I as much responsible for your children as you are for mine?

The answer to this objection is that human responsibilities always come in what might be described, metaphorically, as concentric circles of intensity. My responsibilities to my own children, who have been living intimately with me for years, are more intense than my responsibilities to the children down the block; my responsibilities to my own colleagues in the college where I teach are more intense than my responsibilities to the professors at, say, the University of Nairobi. And in general, my responsibilities to those near me or with whom I intimately interact are more intense than my responsibilities to those at a distance from me and whom I don't even know. I readily admit that the acknowledgment of these concentric circles of responsibility, varying in intensity, may lead to a vicious parochialism. A person's responsibility to his own nation may loom so large in his eyes that it blocks out all sight of his responsibilities to other nations. Yet the fact remains that those with whom I am most intimately entangled in the affairs of life are those to whom I am most deeply responsible. That is why the parents, with whom the child has been living in intimate interaction, have the primary responsibility for determining the character of his education.

All radical social reformers from Plato onward and all ideologically totalitarian regimes would respond in a certain way to the argument I have presented. Whenever there is a conflict, they would say, between the welfare of the individual and that of the commonwealth, the welfare of the commonwealth must rule supreme. They go on to observe that when left to their own devices, parents will often give a character to their child's education that is injurious to the commonwealth. To prevent that from happening, those who are primarily responsible for the welfare of the commonwealth, namely the officers of the state, must also have primary responsibility for determining the character of education in the commonwealth. Whatever may be said in praise of the beauty and goodness of parents' love for their child, that love must be sacrificed on the altar of a higher good.

Some such line of thought almost invariably lies behind the conviction that the state has the primary moral right to determine the education of children. My response is simple and straightforward: The first step taken by all ideologically totalitarian regimes when they come to power is to get control of the education of children. That means, conversely, that the best way to frustrate the rise to power or the consolidation in power of a totalitarian regime is to prevent the state from determining the character of the education of children. Right here lies the ultimate battle line for freedom and human dignity. We have more than enough evidence to show that nothing causes so much human suffering, nothing leads to such grievous assaults on human dignity as ideologically totalitarian regimes. Those rich and precious goods of parental affection and love that these regimes propose to sacrifice are not, it always turns out, sacrificed on the altar of higher good. They are sacrificed on the greedy, bloody altar of despotism and totalitarianism. There is indeed a good of the commonwealth, but that good will slip through our fingers once we no longer see the exercise of parental affection and love as an indispensable ingredient in it, and in consequence, no longer allow parents the primary right to determine the character of their child's education.

But what about the objection of A. S. Neill and others that nobody has the right to determine the character of a child's education—not the state but also not the parents? Part of the answer is that it is sheer illusion to suppose that adults can *avoid* bringing influence to bear on the habits and commitments of children. But a more fundamental response is to observe that what is at stake here is the fundamental issue of the place of responsibility in human existence.

I said that to love children includes caring for them in such a way that they will mature into responsible agents who find joy in their existence. I spoke thus because in my vision of human existence—which, let me make clear, is the Christian vision—the essence of human dignity, the essence of what is unique to us among all God's creatures is that we are responsible agents. Accordingly, it is my view that when parents fail to do what they can to rear children so that they will become responsible agents, the parents fail them at the most fundamental point of all. They treat the children as if they were only complicated animals, creatures devoid of dignity. Likewise, to fail to rear children is to fail in one's responsibilities to others, for though we can argue as to the cause of the phenomenon, the truth of the matter is that children are all too often mean and cruel. Accordingly, simply to allow children to pursue their own inclinations and interests is to allow them to wreak their passion for meanness on others, and to allow that to happen is to act irresponsibly toward those others.

With none of this would Neill, so far as I can tell, agree, for the entire concept of responsibility has fallen out of his thought, as it has fallen out of the thought of many others in the contemporary Western world. Or better yet, it has been pushed out. To push out the concept of responsibility is—let it not be overlooked—also to push out the concept of human rights. The goal of human existence is seen as simply the pursuit of one's own mental health and happiness—though to that too no one has any *right*. There is one exception: Neill—and on this he is like most other contemporary antinomians—reserves for himself the authority to order the children to desist when their actions threaten the very existence of Summerhill. Yet according to Neill's view, there is no *ground* for such an order to desist. He himself has no *right* to issue such an order, neither does the child have a *responsibility* to treat the community in a certain way. Thus does libertarian antinomianism turn into sheer authoritarianism.

Should the Right of Parents to Determine Their Child's Education Be Protected by Law?

One link in my argument remains to be forged. From the fact that you and I have some human, moral right, it doesn't follow that the legal code of our society should ensure that right to us. The law couldn't possibly ensure to us all our moral rights, nor should it try to do so. So the question remains whether the human right of parents to determine the character of their child's education should be ensured to them by the legal code of our society. In this particular case, the reason for thinking that this human right should become a legal right is obvious. It is unavoidable that our legal code assign to someone or other the right to make decisions concerning the character of a child's education. And because assigning it to anyone other than parents would be an active violation of their human rights, because it can be assigned to parents, that is where it should go.

I rest my case. I have contended that the legal code of our society should secure to parents the primary right to determine the character of their child's education. And let me add that, a fortiori, that means our legal code should secure to a *unified community* of parents the right to determine the character of their children's education and thus to pass on to them their way of life. I could have defended this conclusion by appealing to one and another *social benefit* to be expected from a society so ordered. I could, for example, have argued that a society so ordered will encourage competition in education and that in turn will yield an assortment of social benefits. I could have argued that a society so ordered will promote community identity, and that is a good thing. I could have argued that given the psychological depth of the parent/child relationship, a society so ordered will produce better education, since nobody over the long haul will care as much for the education of the child as the parents. I could have argued that only a society so ordered will secure religious freedom in a society that is religiously diverse. All those conclusions I believe to be true. But here I have tried to show that among our fundamental *human* rights is the primary right of parents to determine the character of the education of their child. Because that is a universal human right, I have concluded that every society should secure, with as few encumbrances as possible, the primary right of parents in the education of their child.

The picture sketched would be misleadingly incomplete, however, if I did not go on to say at least a few words about the rights of others with respect to the character of a child's education, for beyond a doubt, others do have moral rights in the field of education: teachers, members of the society at large, the child himself, groups and institutions.[2]

I begin with the state. What are the rights of the state with respect to determining the character of a child's education? None! None at all. In fact, not only does the state have no right to determine the character of a child's education, but it has no rights whatsoever that our legal code should respect with regard to how our children are educated. But then, neither does it have rights in any other field that our legal code should respect—other than just the (non-absolute) right to be obeyed. Perhaps the radical tone of that contention shocks you. But reflect: The business of the state is to honor and ensure *your* rights and *my* rights, along with the rights of our communities, associations, and institutions, and to do so in a just manner. In order to carry out that task, the state has the right, though most emphatically not the *absolute* right, to ask obedience of you and of me and to exact punishment when obedience is not rendered. But that is the end of the matter. The state's whole business in the field of education is to honor and secure the educational rights of persons and groupings of persons.

What then about teachers? What are their rights with respect to determining the character of a child's education? Also none. Teachers do indeed have rights with respect to the education of children—principally as I see it the right to exercise their professional competence in their teaching. But teachers have no right whatsoever to determine the *character* of the child's education. Parents have that right and that responsibility. So to carry out their responsibility, they come to the teachers, asking that the teachers be of service to them. And the teachers offer their services.[3] But if the parents find those services not to be in accord with their fundamental convictions, they have the right, indeed the responsibility, to go elsewhere. The teachers' moral rights with respect to the education of the child are limited to exercising their professional competence within the framework desired by the parents.

Of course, if we were going to discuss the matter in more detail, we would have to sharpen this line between issues pertaining to the character of education and issues to be settled by judgments of professional competence, for often the inclination of the teacher is to regard as an issue of competence what the parents regard as an issue of overall character. Let me say only that, for most of the disputes arising in public schools that I have read about in recent years, my inclination has been to side with the parents. To cite but one bone of contention: A parent has the *right* to ask the child not to read J. D. Salinger. The judgment that it would be good for the child to read *Catcher in the Rye* is not a judgment based purely on professional competence.

Third, what about the rights of other members of society with respect to the character of a child's education? And here, as when I get to the rights of the child, I must limit myself to speaking of those moral rights that it would be good to have secured to us as legal rights in our society. The society in general and the child have, in my judgment, a good many moral rights vis-à-vis the parents that it would not be good to enshrine in our legal code—in part but only in part because there is so much disagreement on those rights.

On the matter of your and my rights with respect to the education of the child of other parents, I think that in the first place we can do little better than adopt the formula that has guided us in free speech cases in this country for fifty years now. If a mode of education that a group of parents is offering to their children is such that it constitutes a clear and present danger to our society, then your and my rights as members of that society are being infringed on. And for the sake of protecting those rights, the state may and should intervene. (It is perhaps debatable whether from this one can get the right of which our courts speak—society's right to an "informed electorate.") Second, when the mode of education that parents give their child is so grossly deficient, given the society in which we live, that the child will almost certainly grow up to be a burden on society, then again your and my rights as members of that society are being infringed on. For the sake of protecting those rights, the state can and should intervene. But those should be the limits of the legally guaranteed rights of others with respect to the education of a child. Always there has been in our society the powerful urge to go further—to insist that the Amish use certified teachers and that they educate their children through high school, to insist that all children be taught reverence for the flag, and so on. All such pressures are violations of the human rights of the parents.

Last, what about the rights of children with respect to the character of their education, rights that should be secured in law? In the first place, children have the right to be educated, and not only that, but to receive an education relevant to life in the community that they will likely enter. It is a violation of their rights to condemn them to being unhappy, nonfunctional misfits. Second, they have the right to be treated non-abusively and not submitted to substantial and avoidable physical danger in their education. When either of these rights is denied them, then the state may and should intervene to protect those rights.

It would be remiss on our part if we closed this discussion on the rights of parents and others in the education of children without inquiring into the state of our union with respect to the fundamental human rights that we have been discussing—the primary right of parents to determine the character of their child's education. Can we in the United States rest content on this matter and turn our attention to the deprivation of this right in other countries, or to the deprivation of other rights in our own as well as in other countries? Does our legal code secure to all of us this right with as few encumbrances as possible? Does the actual structure of our society assure it to all of us with as few encumbrances as possible?

Is the right of Catholic parents to determine the character of their child's education secured to them in our society with as few encumbrances as possible? Is the right of Lutheran parents to determine the character of their child's education secured to them with as few encumbrances as possible? Is the right of Orthodox Jewish parents, of Calvinist parents, of black parents concerned to promote black consciousness in their child, of parents in New York City struggling with the teachers' union to get more autonomy for the local school district—is the right of all these to determine the character of their children's education secured to them with as few encumbrances as possible?

The list could go on and on. Only those blinded by their privileged position in the present arrangement can fail to see that in our society there is a massive deprivation of human rights in the field of education. I am constantly amazed that some of the same people who guard so fiercely and zealously our right to free speech, that some of the same people who when doing social work stress the great importance of the family, stand passively unconcerned when masses of parents in our society, in order to educate their children in accord with their convictions, must pay heavily for it while others are offered it free, or must engage in a titanic struggle with a teachers' union, or must fight off the encroaching bureaucracy of a state board of education.

Of course, I know the stock response, at least to the religious groups I have mentioned. The reply is always that these groups are perfectly free to start their own schools where they can educate their children as they wish—within limits. But this answer exhibits the most elementary confusion, which only its constant repetition could obscure from anyone. Earlier I distinguished between freedom rights and rights of treatment. Among our rights of treatment are certain rights that might be called *benefit rights*—the right to receive a tangible benefit or service from another person or from the community at large. Already in the nineteenth century, the various states in our union decided that parents of children had the benefit right to receive financial aid from the community at large for the education of their children. Accordingly, the public school system was established across our country. Thus, in the field of education, we in America for over a century have recognized two distinct, though related rights: The freedom right to educate one's child in accord with one's convictions, and the benefit right to receive financial aid from the community at large for the education of one's children.

All people in this country are secured the freedom right to educate their child in accord with their convictions. (I don't wish to downplay the existence of threats to this right.) For that we are all grateful; there are countries in which it is not so. But the benefit right to receive financial aid from the community as one educates one's child in accord with one's convictions is distributed with gross inequity in our society. Millions of parents have been saying with full clarity for over 150 years that the public school education offered them free is one that they cannot in good conscience accept—that it is out of accord with what they believe should be the character of their child's education. Accordingly, they are inequitably deprived of a benefit right. To reply to their grievance by saying that they have all the rights everybody else has, because they, like everybody else, have the freedom right to educate their child as they wish is obviously and grossly beside the point. Nobody contends that this freedom right is distributed inequitably. The contention is that the benefit right is distributed inequitably. To that charge there is no answer. Obviously, it *is* distributed inequitably—when we could distribute it much more equitably if we wished.

How did we get into this situation? And what is it that keeps us in it? Several things. One is the deep conviction among many Americans that unless the vast bulk of our students go to a common school, there to be inculcated with what is nowadays called the American civil religion, our nation will fly apart. Another is the equally deep conviction among many Americans that diverse religions are really sectarian versions of one and the same basic religion, so that religious liberty is fully achieved if our publicly supported institutions are based on what is supposedly common to all and the sectarian variations are confined to the private life of family and church. Yet a third is the deep conviction among many Americans that both the religious person and the secular person share a common morality and a common science so that even if all vestiges of religion must be removed from our public institutions so as to achieve consensus, then still it is the case that the fundamental convictions of everybody are being honored. And a fourth, less fundamental than any of those but fully as important nowadays, is the tendency of our governmental institutions in general to remove decisions from the people in the interests of bureaucratic efficiency and effectiveness.

All those, and more yet, are the currents in our society that have led us to neglect this deprivation of human rights in the field of education. It is high time that we Americans, who in my judgment are rightly concerned with the deprivation of human rights around this small globe of ours, should reverse our field at home and devise new patterns for the support and control of education that will lift these burdens of oppression from the backs of so many of our fellow citizens.

But I must end with a word to parents. All that I have said is based on the premise that the right of parents to determine the character of their child's education is grounded on the *responsibility* of parents to determine that education. If parents do not exercise this responsibility, all that I have said will be but hollow talk. Then the control of education will inevitably drift to the state and federal bureaucracies and to the powerful teachers' lobbies and unions. Where else could it go? And parents will be left helpless.

Once upon a time, in the religious traditions on which this country was founded, parents saw a child as a precious gift from God of which they were the guardians until his or her years of maturity. They saw themselves as charged by God with treasuring this gift and nurturing it so that it would reach its potential and dignity as a human being. That vision we must try to recapture. When parents fail in their responsibility to nurture their child so that the child will grow up as a responsible agent finding joy in his or her existence, then the parents have failed the child as badly as anyone can fail a young human being. And when the bulk of parents in our society begin to act thus, then a society in which people can live in freedom and with dignity is lost beyond saving. When responsibility goes unexercised, then the legal *right* to exercise it will eventually be seized from us.

chapter thirteen

The Schools We Deserve

Wolterstorff's following contribution to the book *Schooling Christians* is as apropos today as it was when it was written in 1992. Wolterstorff argues that what is wrong with schools is not simply the consequence of inappropriate teaching on the part of school personnel. Rather, it is the consequence of structures and dynamics that are deep within the American system. We are getting exactly the schools we deserve, and educational reform cannot succeed without social reform. He describes the circumstances under which we might expect to have school systems that express alternative images for our common life.

Though the line of argument in the first part of my paper may prove somewhat complex, the main point is simple: It is as true for American society today as it has been for most societies that fundamental ailments in its educational practice not only cause but are caused by fundamental ailments in the society itself and cannot be cured without a cure of those social ailments. We Americans at almost every turn talk and act on the opposite assumption. We typically assume that, in the interaction between society and school, school is culprit and society victim. The consensus of those in political power over the past decade has been that throwing money at the schools solves no problems; their own solution, insofar as they have had one, has been to deliver hortatory speeches. My own view is that throwing money and delivering hortatory speeches are equally futile. But whether it is money that is thrown or exhortations that are delivered, the assumption is that our society is not getting the schools it deserves.

I shall argue in the first part of my paper that we *are* getting the schools we deserve. Our present educational morass is the consequence of ideological convictions, social structures, and social dynamics deep in the American system. I am not a social determinist; American schools and schooling might be different in many of their details while social structures and dynamics and our formative ideologies remain the same. Nonetheless, the extent and mode of deficiency of our educational practice is not simply the consequence of sloth, turpitude, or wrongheadedness on the part of school personnel.

Once I have argued this case, I will, all too briefly, indicate where we could have taken, and where we still can take, some different turns—though I shall also warn, in the light of the preceding discussion, against naive optimism as to the success of such turns.

Educating for the Wrong Goals

First, let us have before us a clear specimen of treating the school as culprit and of thinking, correspondingly, that by a combination of hortatory talk and pressure of one kind or another we can correct what ails our educational practice. So as not to take cheap shots, let us look at one of the better examples of oblivion to the fact that schools are not only *for* society but also *by* society, namely, the thoughtful symposium on educational reform published a few years ago in *Harper's* under the title "How Not to Fix the Schools."[1] All nine participants agreed that our schools need fixing, and all agreed that the then current rage for fixing the schools by imposing tighter regulations and tougher requirements would prove no cure at all. What ails the schools, they said, is not insufficient money or inadequate regulation but the goal that the schools set for the education they offer. The symposiasts suggested that the dominant goal of American schools today is to induct students into the job market—to teach them the knowledge and skills necessary for entering the economic system as productive workers. The cure for the sickness of the schools is for them to adopt a different and better goal.

Let me halt for a moment to observe that although the *Harper's* symposiasts regarded themselves as painting a dark picture of the American schools, in one important respect it was not dark enough. Quite clearly our society presently operates on the assumption that the productive side of our economy can proceed quite nicely even if a rather large proportion of the members of our society receive at best minimal education for holding down a job. In particular, we assume that urban blacks are pretty much dispensable and disposable. It's simply not true that our society does its best to educate everyone so that he or she can become a productive worker.

But let's proceed. We need a better goal for the schools, say the symposiasts. What might be that better goal? One of the participants, A. Graham Down, stated that education's "abiding, all-encompassing purpose must be to equip people with the taste for lifelong learning." And Ernest Boyer insisted that one of the two fundamental purposes of education is "personal empowerment." But neither of these is the purpose that gained emphasis in the discussion. Instead, what Boyer proposed as the other proper aim of education—namely, "civic engagement"—did. Our schools are to aim at equipping students to perform the role of citizen. Here is how Walter Karp put it:

> One simple concept includes *all* those purposes: Americans do not go to school in order to increase the social efficiency or economic prosperity of the country, but to become informed, critical citizens. A citizen is not a worker. The Soviet Union has workers, the American republic has citizens. A citizen is a political being; he has private powers and a public role. As Jefferson wrote, the education of a citizen must "enable every man to judge for himself what will secure or endanger his freedom."
>
> In practice, that goal is persistently betrayed. It is essential that citizens be able to judge for themselves and have the courage and confidence to think for themselves. Yet America's high schools characteristically breed conformity and mental passivity. . . . Our schools do not attempt to make citizens; they attempt to break citizens.[2]

That is the most eloquent and most insistent statement of the point. But others in the symposium expressed the same view, leading the moderator, Mark D. Donner, to summarize the drift of the conversation this way:

> You educators seem to be in a rather embarrassing minority position here. You think of schools as places where people are taught how to think critically and how to become vigilant citizens, whereas most adults and stu-

dents apparently believe the schools exist to keep kids out of trouble for a few years and help them get jobs.[3]

The fundamental ailment of our schools is that the education they offer is aimed at the wrong goal; adopting a better goal is the cure. The assumption is that schools can pull themselves up by their own bootstraps. The assumption is that while society remains fundamentally unchanged, our schools can adopt this new goal for the education they offer and, that done, can succeed in achieving it. The assumption is that educational reform can succeed without social reform.

Educating for Character and Virtue

But let's dig deeper and look at the particular proposal offered by the *Harper's* symposiasts. The symposiasts suggested that our schools should aim at producing a certain quality of character and the virtues and skills that go with that type of character. They proposed that the schools should aim at inculcating a certain *ethic*. They suggested that the illness of the schools lies in the fact that they see their task as teaching only how-to-do-it matters when they ought to be inculcating in their students a way of living. Let me say that with this assumption I heartily agree.

But immediately a difficulty faces us. When a society is committed to common schools and its members agree on the sort of character and attendant virtues they wish their children to exhibit, it is then immediately relevant for the society to reflect on how its schools must be organized and their education conducted so as to encourage the formation of that character and those virtues. Correspondingly, when a society is not committed to common schools nor do its members agree on the sort of character and attendant virtues they wish their children to exhibit, it is then relevant for the subcommunities of that society within which there is agreement on the ethic desired for their children to band together and organize schools and education with that ethic in mind. But when a society whose members do not agree on the sort of character and attendant virtues they desire in their children nonetheless commits itself to a common school, then prior to all how-to-do-it questions, that society faces the difficult question, *Whose* view as to good character and *whose* view as to right virtues are the schools to adopt? American society is this last kind of society.

The proposal of the *Harper's* symposiasts for the reform of the schools coincides with one of the classic American answers to this question. The public educational institutions of our land are to cultivate in students such qualities of character and such dispositions as are required for playing the role of citizen in our liberal-democratic, republican polity. They are to cultivate the ethic of citizenship. The *Harper's* symposiasts do little to defend this view. But a defense regularly offered for this position goes as follows: Our society has the right to impress its formative Idea on its citizens; the formative Idea of American society is that of a liberal-democratic, republican polity; and this Idea incorporates the ideal of every adult playing the role of citizen.

Let me make some brief preliminary comments about this line of thought before I probe the issue that will lead into our main topic.

For one thing, I myself think that to describe the formative Idea of American society as that of a liberal-democratic, republican polity is to give an idealized formulation of that Idea. We Americans not only tolerate but also actively embrace various forms of duress; that too, then, belongs to our formative Idea. Of course, American society is not peculiar in this regard; the formative idea of any society will be, to use scriptural language, a "fallen" idea. But anyone who suggests that our schooling be guided by the formative Idea of American society is in effect recommending that we perpetuate bias and oppression of certain sorts.

Let it also be noted that the content of the ethic of citizenship is by no means clear and uncontested. The ethic of the physician is the subject of vigorous debate in our society; so too is the ethic of the lawyer. It is no different for the ethic of the citizen. In their fascinating and controversial book, *Habits of the Heart*,[4] Robert N. Bellah and associates argued that an essential component of the character of the republican citizen is concern for the common good over private interests; the *Harper's* symposiasts say nothing about that but insist instead that the citizen needs a critical habit of mind. Both of these may be right, yet there is, if nothing more, a stark difference of emphasis here. And whose voice is to be decisive in determining the content of the common good?

Third, for the schools to shape their education by the ethic of the citizen is by no means for them to be as neutral as might at first appear. For one thing, there are people in our society who consciously and reflectively reject the ethic of the citizen in a liberal-democratic, republican polity. I suppose it might be said, in response, that such people are here only by a kind of sufferance. So let me go on to note that the policy of letting the ethic of the citizen in a liberal-democratic, republican polity shape the education of our common schools is not even neutral among all those who have no particular objection to this ethic. This can be seen by noting that although an ethic of the citizen is perhaps more comprehensive than would at first appear, nonetheless, for the schools of our land to confine themselves to the inculcation of this ethic is to leave a great many facets of character, disposition, and action untouched.

One of the burning moral issues in our society is abortion on demand. But the Supreme Court of the United States has declared that one can be a fully entitled member of our society and not only advocate abortion on demand but secure one on demand. Hence, if the education conducted by the schools is to have the ethic of citizenship as its sole content, the schools will have to avoid taking a stand on this moral issue. Instead of cultivating sensitivities on one side or the other, they will have to confine themselves to cultivating such qualities of character as are necessary for participating in debates on the matter. The same will be true for a vast number of other moral issues. For those who not only agree that the school should inculcate the ethic of citizenship but are also content to have the rest of the ethical education of their children occur in one place or another outside the common day-school, there is no problem. But there are some in our society who are persuaded that education for citizenship in our earthly commonwealth will always be distorted if treated outside the context of life before God. Such people will regard a day-school education shaped purely by the ethic of the citizen as not so much falling short of their educational goals for their children but, in its falling short, as inimical to those goals. We begin here to spy a dilemma about which I will say more later.

But rather than dwelling on any of these points, important though I think they are, I wish instead to argue that our kind of society is inimical toward any ethic whatsoever shaping the education of our common schools, be it the ethic of the citizen or some other. We get the schools we deserve. I shall begin with some fairly standard sociological observations.

A drama is a set of interlocking roles that persons can repeatedly perform. It proves illuminating to think of a society as structured like a drama. Every society creates an interlocking set of roles—that is, coherent and typical ways of acting—that members of the society then learn to perform. In most of the world's societies, a high proportion of the social roles that people played or were expected to play were simply ascribed to them, rather than allotted on the basis of their choice. The eldest son of the king was born to be king; it was his nature to be king. The son of a serf was born to be a serf; it was his nature to be a serf. Such ascriptivism has increasingly disappeared in modern Western society. It is true that a person's choice of social role in our society is often made under considerable duress and that the availability to a given person of certain social roles is conditioned on that person's possession of various indigenous abilities. Nonetheless, role assignment in modern society is grounded on *will* to an extent never before known in history. And this, of course, invites us to think of our personal identity as something *behind* all our social roles rather than as in part determined *by* our roles. Our roles are mainly things that we can and do put on or take off as we decide to do so, with our perceived self-identity being that which abides amidst all our actual and contemplated changes of garment.

Not only is the proportion of social roles allotted by ascription much lower in our society than it was in previous ones, but the roles themselves are also typically both different and understood differently among us. Traditionally, to play a certain social role was not just to act in a certain typical and coherent way but to see oneself and be seen as subject to a specific cluster of *requirements*, the fulfillment of these being enforced and reinforced by social expectations. One who had the role of serf was required to spend a high proportion of one's time laboring for the lord of the manor; one who had the role of lord was required to provide protection and security to one's serfs. These requirements were for the most part not legal requirements. Neither were they merely instrumental requirements—that is, causal conditions for achieving one's goals. They were *moral* requirements, matters of duty and right, and in good measure they were not just *general* moral requirements pertaining to all persons in all roles. Rather, a particular role comprised a specific ethic. To occupy a certain station in life was to be subject to a specific set of duties and to enjoy a specific set of rights. In Christian Europe of the Middle Ages, one can see the beginnings of our modern idea of *human* rights and duties—that is, of rights and duties attached to all human beings whatsoever. But these were almost obscured by the array of rights and duties pertaining to particular roles: There was an ethic of the knight, an ethic of the goldsmith, an ethic of the physician, and so on. Furthermore, the recognition of all these moral requirements, specific and general, was customarily caught up in a picture of the universe according to which all of us not only have duties with respect to human beings and social institutions but also with respect to the sacred, the divine. Indeed, the duties and rights comprised in one's social roles were understood as grounded, in one way or another, in one's duties to the divine.

It was in the context of societies thus structured and the understanding that accompanied them that the role of citizen of a republic emerged—first in some of the city-states of ancient Greece, then later in some of the cities of Renaissance Italy, in the provinces of seventeenth- and eighteenth-century Netherlands, in the villages of nineteenth-century America, etc. To play the role of citizen was to act in a certain coherent and typical way. But more than that, it was to see oneself and be seen as subject to a specific complex of rights and duties. It was to see oneself and be seen as subject to the ethic of the citizen. Typically, of course, only certain of the adults within the community were allowed and required to play this role, the allotment depending not on one's will but on one's gender, age, race, freedom, inherited religion,

property, and so on. Speaking of nineteenth-century America, Bellah
and his associates remark that

> the basic unit of association, and the practical foundation of both indi-
> vidual dignity and participation, was the local community. There a civic
> culture of individual initiative was nurtured through custom and personal
> ties inculcated by a widely shared Protestant Christianity. . . . These
> autonomous small-scale communities in the mid-nineteenth century were
> dominated by the classic citizens of a free republic, men of middling con-
> dition who shared similar economic and social positions and whose ranks
> less affluent members of the population aspired to enter, often success-
> fully. . . . Tocqueville's America can be viewed as an interlocking network
> of specific roles: those of husband, wife, child, farmer, craftsman, clergy-
> man, lawyer, merchant, township officer, and so on. But the distinctive
> quality of that society, its particular identity as a "world" different from
> other societies, was summed up in the spirit, the mores, that animated its
> members, and that spirit was symbolized in the representative character
> of what we can call the independent citizen.[5]

Only traces of such ascribed and ethically infused social roles are left
in the lives and consciousness of contemporary Americans. Perhaps the
clearest trace is to be seen in the role of son and daughter. Not only do
we not choose to occupy the role of child of parents, but probably most
of us still understand this role as incorporating a specific complex of
rights and responsibilities. One has duties to one's parents that one has
to no one else, just by virtue of being their child; they, correspondingly,
have duties to their child.

One of the principal causes of the near disappearance in reality and
consciousness of such ethically infused social roles has been the rise
and spread of industrial and post-industrial capitalism—and let me make
clear that when I speak of "capitalism," I have in mind not only the capitalism of non-command economies but also the state capitalism known
as communism. A prominent feature of the spread of capitalism into
new sectors of society is that more and more things are put on the market, with the result that the presence of contractual relations among
human beings is increased enormously and the loyalty—and expectations of loyalty—to persons and institutions characteristic of traditional
societies is destroyed. Under capitalism a worker puts his or her labor
on the market and makes a contract with some owner of capital whereby
for such-and-such quality and quantity of labor the worker will receive
such-and-such pay; in most societies there was no such thing as a labor
market. Under capitalism land is put on the market and contracts are
signed whereby title is transferred for such-and-such payment; in most
societies it was impossible to transfer title to land by contract. Under

capitalism the ethic of contract becomes more and more the pervasive ethic of society. The range of that for which one *must* contract is expanded, and the limits on that for which one *may* contract are removed; the duty to keep the contracts one has made looms larger and larger in the whole body of one's duties. The corollary of this increase of contractual relations under capitalism is, of course, that one's occupation of social roles is increasingly determined by decision rather than ascription. And a natural if not inevitable consequence is that choosing a social role is understood less and less as taking onto oneself a specific range of duties, and more and more as choosing a way of acting that promises to satisfy one's private goals. Even such a social bond as marriage is increasingly understood not as a complex of rights and duties into which one enters by commitment or ascription but as a contractual arrangement to provide benefits for benefits received.

The pervasive marketing of land and labor in capitalist economies also makes a mobility of population possible, and sometimes necessary, of proportions unknown in earlier societies except in times of great social upheaval. This too contributes to the shift of which we have been taking note, for when large and rapid shifts of population occur, then the disciplinary effect of social expectations on the performance of duties is drastically weakened, and loyalties to persons and institutions are diminished.

One more feature of a capitalist economy is worth noting, namely, the increasing differentiation, or sectoring, of social roles. In particular, the occupations of persons, their "work," are increasingly differentiated from their other social roles. Given the other features of the system, persons are invited to choose and practice their occupations not by reference to intrinsic satisfactions or social benefits but solely by reference to whether or not those occupations serve their private goals of a large paycheck, a conspicuous career, or whatever.

What then shapes life outside of work? It turns out that the regimented, bureaucratized, differentiated, competitive character of work in an economy of industrial capitalism leaves fundamental sides of a person's nature unsatisfied and unfulfilled. And that, combined with the diminishing presence of ethically infused social roles, yields the phenomenon to which many sociologists have called our attention, namely, that in the core areas of our world economy, persons outside the workplace tend to look for love and intimacy and pleasure and self-expression in family, in sports, in religion, in art, in shopping, in sex. A pervasive privatism, heavily colored with hedonism, begins to characterize the lives of people outside of work. Here is how Bellah and his associates describe the situation:

The most distinctive aspect of twentieth-century American society is the division of life into a number of separate functional sectors: home and workplace, work and leisure, white collar and blue collar, public and private. . . . Particularly powerful in modeling our contemporary sense of things has been the division between the various "tracks" to achievement laid out in schools, corporation, government, and the professions, on the one hand, and the balancing life-sectors of home, personal ties, and "leisure" on the other. . . . Domesticity, love, and intimacy increasingly become "havens" against the competitive culture of work.[6]

Educating for the Role of Citizenship

What sort of educational goals would one expect a capitalist society such as ours to set for its schools? Two come to mind. First, one would expect it to ask of its schools that they teach students—most of them—the knowledge, skills, and dispositions necessary for participating in the labor force. Second, one would expect it to ask of its schools that they enable students—many of them—to satisfy their expressive desires: offering athletic programs for those who have a taste for the peculiar bodily and emotional satisfactions that come from competitive sports; offering courses in the world's religions for those who have a taste for religion; etc. This, I said, is what one would expect a society such as ours to ask of its schools, and that is what it does ask. The *Harper's* symposiasts see our schools as oriented toward job preparation. I agree, with the qualification cited earlier, but I would add that they are also oriented toward equipping students to find personal satisfaction in those sectors of their lives outside of job and career.

It is for a society such as ours and schools such as these that the *Harper's* symposiasts propose that the schools inculcate the ethic of the citizen. In addition to the questions posed earlier about this proposal, the question we are led to ask by the reflections we have just followed is this: Is there any likelihood whatsoever that this proposal, or any other proposal concerning the ethic of common day-school education, will be generally adopted? Who are the teachers who staff and the board members who govern the public schools of our land? They are members of this very public from which the ethically infused role of citizen has virtually disappeared in reality and consciousness; not even our elected officials put the public good ahead of private careers. Teachers and board members do not constitute, for the most part, some countercultural sub-community within our society; on the average, they think and act like the average.

But suppose that somehow, someway, somewhere this proposal is embraced by the board and staff of a public educational institution. What that school will then have to do, before anything else, is explain to its students what this ethically infused role of citizen is. Students do not come knowing what that role is. They come to school with an understanding of the role of professional baseball player, for they have seen people playing this role. They have not seen many old-fashioned citizens, nor have they often seen those who do not play the role of citizen suffering under social disapproval. Militating against success in this explanatory project is the fact that the concept of an ethically infused social role in general, no matter of what specific sort, has less and less application in our society and is less and less recognized as applicable where in fact it is.

But perhaps the necessary explanations can be given, with the aid of history and fiction. Then what the schools would have to try to do is produce in students the disposition to play this role: to perform these actions and embrace this ethic, including the principle that one ought to place considerations of the common good ahead of personal interests. Obviously, what militates against success in this project is the fact that students live in a society pervasively structured so as to invite them to give pride of place in their choice and practice of roles to purely private ends. We must, indeed, restrain ourselves from thinking that this is entirely true in our society. Patriotism and its close relative nationalism lead people away from private interests to larger concerns, and it is evident that they have by no means disappeared from the contemporary scene. So too the natural affections present in families and among friends lead us out of our shells. But the ethic of the citizen is not grounded in familial affection nor in feelings of patriotism or nationalism. Indeed, these feelings of loyalty and affection all tend to collide at crucial points with what is called for by the ethic of the republican citizen.

I can imagine someone replying to these last points, with a despairing tone, by saying that of course it will be difficult to go against the grain of society and both communicate to students the concept of this ethically infused role of citizen and produce in them the disposition to embrace it. When modeling and discipline are missing, then two of the main dynamics for the cultivation of dispositions are absent. But there remains the possibility of the schools giving students *reasons* for taking up this role—and perhaps supplementing those reasons with inspiring examples culled from history and fiction.

What might those reasons be? Given the ethically infused nature of this role, the obvious answer is that playing the role of citizen is one of the *responsibilities* of adults in our society. It is their *duty* to play the role of citizen.

I myself believe that we adults in our society have a duty to play the role of citizen; I hold it to be one of our responsibilities. Thus, I believe that this is a right and correct thing for the schools to say to their students. But I also believe that there are reasons for thinking that, in the climate of our society, the schools will find this reason to be distressingly unpersuasive. Already we have had some indication of why that is so, but let us now expand the picture by adding to the social factor we have been discussing a certain cultural factor, taking note of one facet of the characteristic ideology of our society, for that complex of practices, laws, and institutions that constitute capitalism do not operate independently of the *ideas* that members of society have as to the nature of reality, humanity, and the good. The ideas influence the practices, laws, and institutions—just as the latter influence the former. Ideas and practices *interact*. Idealism and materialism are equally mistaken.

I think Bellah and his associates, along with a great many other observers of the contemporary scene, are correct in their suggestion that the ideology most prominent in American society since the latter part of the nineteenth century has been what they—and of course many others—call "individualism." I think they are also right in distinguishing two versions, or two applications, of this ideology: *utilitarian* individualism and *expressive* individualism. Benjamin Franklin, they suggest:

> gave classic expression to what many felt in the eighteenth century—and many have felt ever since—to be the most important thing about America: the chance for the individual to get ahead on his own initiative. Franklin expressed it very clearly in his advice to Europeans considering immigration to America: "If they are poor, they begin first as Servants of journeymen; and if they are sober, industrious, and frugal, they soon become Masters, establish themselves in Business, marry, raise Families, and become respectable Citizens."[7]

Just as Franklin is the classic spokesman for utilitarian individualism, so Walt Whitman is the classic spokesman for expressive individualism. "For Whitman, success had little to do with material acquisition. A life rich in experience, open to all kinds of people luxuriating in the sensual as well as the intellectual, above all a life of strong feeling, was what he perceived as a successful life."[8]

What has eventually emerged, of course, is that the contemporary American thinks of work in terms of utilitarian individualism and thinks of his or her life after work in terms of expressive individualism—with the former enabling the latter. "The split between public and private life correlates with a split between utilitarian individualism, appropriate in the economic and occupational spheres, and expressive individualism, appropriate in private life."[9]

Bellah and his associates discuss the ideology of individualism purely in the context of American society, inviting in their readers the thought that individualism is an American peculiarity. But to think thus would be profoundly mistaken. Our American ideology of individualism must be seen within the context of a vast change of mentality throughout the West that began around the time of the late Renaissance. Historically, human beings have thought of the world as being inherently meaningful and the point of human existence as being found in discerning and responding to that meaning. The people of traditional tribes saw the world and the rhythms of life as the product of the foundational acts of the gods, and they saw themselves in their work and rituals as imitating and thereby even renewing those foundational acts. Plato saw the world as mirroring the transcendent structured world of the forms and regarded true happiness as consisting of contemplating and imitating that transcendent world. And the ancient Jews saw the structure of the world and the course of history as the result of God's will and the path to shalom as learning and following that same will—walking in the path of the Torah.

In the opening chapter of his well-known book *Hegel*, Charles Taylor suggests that the essential difference between that older view of things and the modern view that came about in the seventeenth century is that

> the modern subject is self-defining, where on previous views the subject is defined in relation to a cosmic order. . . . The view of the subject that came down from the dominant tradition of the ancients, was that man came most fully to himself when he was in touch with a cosmic order. . . . The situation is now reversed: full self-possession requires that we free ourselves from the projection of meaning onto things.[10]

Taylor adds that

> the modern shift to a self-defining subject was bound up with a sense of control over the world—at first intellectual and then technological. That is, the modern certainty that the world was not to be seen as a text or an embodiment of meaning was not founded on a sense of its baffling impenetrability. On the contrary, it grew with the mapping of the regularities in things, by transparent mathematical reasoning, and with the consequent increase of manipulative control.[11]

Later, of course, the idea arose that the subject defines itself not only by its control of a world shorn of intrinsic meaning but by one or another form of expressive activity.

In the traditional picture of humanity in the world, moral requirements were seen as something required of us by God, or by the gods, or by the Good. To the question "Who requires this of me?" or "What requires this of me?" there was an answer. But what place can this notion of requirement have in our modern mentality, where the subject is regarded as self-defining through its actions of domination and expression? At best what can be said is that our own nature somehow or other requires of us that we act morally—which is exactly what the later Enlightenment philosophers attempted to show as well as perhaps the Romantic philosophers with their ideology of nationalism. But I reveal no secret when I tell you that most philosophers today judge that attempt of their Enlightenment predecessors to be a failure. And in any case, our society in general has scarcely been persuaded that the answer to the question, "Who requires this of me?" is, "Your own nature requires it."

So to the students who arrive at school or university with little or no disposition to engage in the practices and to embrace the ethic of republican citizenship, a teacher can indeed speak of their duty to do so. But will that answer prove persuasive? Are the social and cultural conditions for the success of such a moral appeal satisfied? The notion of duty is the notion of requirement. But if the student asks, "Who or what requires of me that I take up this role of citizen?" what is the school to say? The traditional answer in the West was "God." The answer that Jefferson and his associates gave when they formulated the ideal of American republican citizenship in the eighteenth century was both "God" and "human nature." But large numbers of our students no longer believe in a god or in anything else transcendent that requires things of them. And in any case, our public schools are not permitted to affirm that God requires of us the duties of citizenship. We can each speculate as to the long-range effectiveness of a school's insistence to its students that the role of citizen is required of them, when many or most of those students do not believe that there is anything transcendent requiring this of them and when the school cannot affirm that there is. My own speculation is that as our modern ideology of the self-defining subject settles ever more firmly into our consciousness, in its characteristic American forms of utilitarian and expressive individualism, moral appeals will prove less and less effective. They will find less and less to attach themselves to.

But perhaps our situation is even worse. Perhaps the demise of the conviction that someone or something requires certain things of us not only threatens the persuasiveness of appeals to moral requirement but also threatens our grasp of the very concept of a moral requirement. So argues Alasdair MacIntyre in his book *After Virtue*.[12] MacIntyre argues that, given our characteristic modern framework of beliefs, moral precepts have lost their function. It is their function to instruct us on what to do so as to move from how we happen to be to how transcendent reality and our own true end *(telos)* require us to be. But if the belief in an inherent meaning of the world and an intrinsic end of our existence disappears, then, though we may continue for some time to think in terms of duty and ought and right and responsibility, the whole point of such thinking will have been lost. And if the point of such thinking is lost, then we must expect that eventually, though the words *duty* and *ought* and *right* and *responsibility* may remain in our vocabulary, they will no longer be used to express moral requirement. That, says MacIntyre, is already becoming our situation. More and more these words are used simply to evince attitudes and to influence others.

What may be added to MacIntyre's analysis is that, under the impact of individualism, more and more it is the case that, in reflecting on the choices facing them, members of our society do not even use the vocabulary of morality. They speak instead of what would make them "feel comfortable," of what would make them "feel good," of what would advance "Number One," etc. The concept of a causal requirement for the achievement of one's goals is obviously alive and well among us. The concept of a moral requirement appears sick unto death. Of course, our society does still proffer an

order of life, with character ideals, images of the good life, and methods of attaining it. Yet it is an understanding of life generally hostile to older ideas of moral order. Its center is the autonomous individual, presumed able to choose the roles he will play and the commitments he will make, not on the basis of higher truths but according to the criterion of life-effectiveness as the individual judges it. . . . The expressive culture, now deeply allied with the utilitarian, reveals its difference from earlier patterns in its readiness to treat normative commitments as so many alternative strategies of self-fulfillment. What has dropped out are the old normative expectations of what makes life worth living.[13]

But if the ungroundedness of moral thinking in our society not only eats away at the effectiveness of moral reasons for action but also eats away at our very grasp of moral concepts, then of course the endeavor of the school to produce in students the disposition to play the ethically infused role of citizen by offering them moral reasons for doing so will prove increasingly ineffective. The conditions for success in this enterprise will be missing. Where capitalism alters society so that its basic ethic becomes the ethic of contract, individualism alters our understanding of reality so that honoring the ethic of contract recedes from view in favor of calculating the conditions for personal satisfaction. Moral education cannot succeed in the common public schools of an amoral society.

It must be noticed that it does not follow straightforwardly from this that the schools cannot give their students effective reasons of any sort whatsoever for performing the actions of citizenship. In principle, they might offer them persuasive prudential reasons for doing so. Offering such reasons is what Richard Rorty recommends—persuaded as he is that our convictions cannot be grounded in anything transcendent and ahistorical. Identifying himself as a "postmodernist bourgeois liberal," he suggests "how such liberals might convince our society that loyalty to itself is morality enough, and that such loyalty no longer needs an ahistorical backup." "I think," he says, that "they should try to clear themselves of charges of irresponsibility by convincing our society that it need be responsible only to its own traditions, and not to the moral law as well."[14] But if the school confines itself to offering purely prudential reasons to its students, then, as Rorty would readily acknowledge, the role of citizen will have to be conceived differently from how we have described it—not as an ethically infused way of acting but simply as a way of acting. And if the school offers merely prudential reasons for acting in the manner of the citizen, then it is not moral character that it develops but prudential alertness, not ethical sensitivity but pragmatic shrewdness. It does not teach the student how to appraise actions with moral concepts; neither does it teach the student moral principles for action, nor how to discover such principles.

And what, we may also ask, might such persuasive prudential reasons be? One might, as Rorty suggests, display the dignity of our society as compared to others of which we are aware. One might further, as he also suggests, construct a historical scenario as to the sad consequences for this society of ours if its adults cease to engage in the actions of citizenship. But what is the school to say to the student who grants all this but wishes to be a freeloader? And what is it to say to the millions who see themselves as deprived of most of the benefits of this society? Rorty speaks of "loyalty" to our society and of "identifying" ourselves with our society. Our century does teach us that there are ways of stirring up the loyalties and the identities of patriotism. The painful truth, however, is that the most effective ways of stirring up such loyalties and identities are at the very same time effectively destructive of the actions of citizenship.

What Shapes Our Society Shapes Our Schools

I have suggested that our socioeconomic system of capitalism and our cultural ideology of individualism have not only shaped our society but have also powerfully contributed to making our common public day-schools what they are; in particular, they have in various ways made it almost impossible for these common schools to inculcate an ethic—a way of living that is of ethical import. Let me now carry on with this already gloomy analysis by pointing to another social factor that powerfully shapes the American common public school and places before it intractable dilemmas whenever it proposes to teach its students how they should live. Or strictly, what I shall be calling to your attention is a pair of social dynamics coupled with a strong traditional preference for a particular way of structuring society in response to those dynamics. Let me speak first of the dynamics and then of the preferred structure.

I have in mind here the dynamic of increasing religious diversity in our society coupled with the somewhat halting and erratic, though nonetheless powerful, dynamic toward granting the representatives of that diversity equal freedom to exercise their religion. Typical of traditional societies was the presence of just one religion within the society; to be a member of the society was to be a participant in the religion. Such religious monolithicism was ruptured in Greco-Roman society of middle and late antiquity; it was, however, in good measure recovered by the "Constantinianism" of medieval European and Near Eastern society. But then it was ruptured again, and as we now know, destroyed for good in the West by the Protestant Reformation. Since the Reformation, the various states of the West have all had to cope with an ever increasing diversity of religions among their citizenry. They have experimented with a variety of strategies for coping with such diversity. But it is clear, in retrospect, that in all of them there has been a powerful dynamic toward giving equal legal standing to an increasingly large range of religious groups and religious convictions—and indeed, to an increasingly large range of antireligious groups and irreligious convictions.

A good many features of modern Western society are the consequence of this phenomenon of increasing religious diversity, coupled with the pressure toward giving the various representatives of this diversity equal freedom. One consequence is that religious groups, especially in America, see themselves as working in a marketplace competing for clients. Another consequence is that religious persons, confronted with alternatives to their own religious convictions, regularly feel it necessary either to explain and justify themselves or to turn in the direction of subjectivism. Yet another consequence is that we have had to adopt other strategies for achieving social consensus and have had to appeal to dynamics other than shared religious convictions for securing social loyalty. It is especially at this point that nationalism and patriotism enter the picture. Still another consequence is that what we each care most deeply about is increasingly removed from public discussion as being irrelevant to the goals of the discussion. Another consequence is that religion is increasingly removed from public life to one's private life after work—a result, as we have seen, also provoked by the dynamics of capitalism. And, to end our list, a final consequence is that ecclesiastical and other religious bodies enjoy less and less by way of legally sanctioned privilege and voice, thus yielding an increasingly secularized society in the strict sense of that term. In my own view, it is not primarily the cultural phenomenon of secular humanism but rather the social phenomenon of religious diversity that has led to the removal of officially sanctioned prayers and other forms of religious activity from the American public schools. (I do not deny that secular humanism, heavily concentrated in the intellectual elite of modern American society, may not only continue to have a voice in American culture out of proportion to its representation in the populace but may also begin to have an influence on the structure of American society out of proportion to its representation.) As Peter Berger puts it:

> While the presence of religion within modern political institutions is, typically, a matter of ideological rhetorics, this cannot be said about the opposite "pole." In the sphere of the family and of social relationships closely linked to it, religion continues to have considerable "reality" potential, that is, continues to be relevant in terms of the motives and self-interpretations of people in the sphere of everyday social activity. . . . Such private religiosity, however "real" it may be to the individuals who adopt it, cannot any longer fulfill the classical task of religion, that of constructing a common world within which all of social life receives ultimate meaning binding on everybody. Instead, this religiosity is limited to specific enclaves of social life that may be effectively segregated from the secularized sectors of modern society. The values pertaining to private religiosity are, typically, irrelevant to institutional contexts other than the private sphere. For example, a businessman or politician may faithfully adhere to the religiously legitimated norms of family life, while at the same time conducting his activities in the public sphere without any reference to religious values of any kind. . . .
>
> The overall effect of the afore-mentioned "polarization" is very curious. Religion manifests itself as public rhetoric and private virtue.[15]

Incidentally, I think it is appropriate to see the social and political liberalism espoused by John Stuart Mill as a generalization of the way that English and American society had developed for coping with religious diversity. Live and let live was the emerging practice when it came to religion. Mill generalized this by proposing that no matter what vision of the good a person set for himself or herself, be it religious or not, and no matter what goals he or she adopted, we should adopt a policy of live and let live. There is a line of influence from the plea of the Puritans for toleration to the liberalism espoused by Mill.

If we are fully to understand the impact on our schools of the dynamic of increasing religious diversity and of freedom for all, one more factor must be brought into the discussion. It would be entirely possible for a modern society in which these dynamics were operative to adopt toward the various religious communities in its midst a policy of *equal support if any support* when it comes to education. That is to say, the society might decide to support equally and impartially the efforts of the various religious and nonreligious communities in its midst to educate their children as they see fit. Furthermore, there is nothing in the language of the First Amendment of the U.S. Constitution to prohibit such a policy. It is not, however, the policy that we in our country have followed, nor is it the policy that the U.S. Supreme Court has enjoined. We have instead adopted and been enjoined to adopt a policy of *no public support for any religious orientation to which anyone objects,* and as our society has become more diverse religiously, that policy has come to coalesce with a policy of *no public support for any religious or antireligious orientation whatsoever.* No religious community will be supported in the education of its children into its own way of life; the education supported by the society as a whole will have to be neutral among all the religions (and irreligions) present in society.

It's not difficult to see why, historically, the United States has adopted such a policy. Among those who fled here from the religious intolerance they experienced in Europe were some who not only spoke for freedom and toleration but also insisted that here, unlike in the lands from which they fled, no one should be forced to support the endeavors of any religion with which he or she disagreed. All support of all religion was to be entirely voluntary. It was this line of thought that Jefferson captured in his famous metaphor of "a wall of separation," and the U.S. Supreme Court has always decided its cases as if the Constitution itself said that there must be a wall of separation between religion and the state—whereas in fact it says nothing of the sort.

To see the full picture, we must recognize that public school education has never entirely fit the policy of no support for any religious orientation with which anyone in society disagrees; when one reads documents from the past, one gets the impression that rhetorical flourishing of the principle often functioned more to conceal than to shape reality.

When public schools first emerged in the nineteenth century, the stated policy, at least in urban centers, was to provide a nonsectarian religious orientation in the schools. Not only would such an education supposedly be neutral among all the religious groups in society, but it would also fit nicely with the Enlightenment practice of distinguishing between natural religion and revealed religion. The schools would teach natural religion, which was supposedly rationally grounded; the churches would teach revealed religion. From the very beginning, however, Catholics protested that they did not find the schools to be nonsectarian; they found them to be Protestant. And eventually Jews spoke up and said that they found them to be Christian. Eventually, both these protests were heard, both in the schools and in the courts. By this time, however, there was a significant number of people present in American society who were not adherents to any religion at all; for them, supporting even the most vapid manifestations of theism in the common schools was a violation of conscience. This dynamic—over and over again new communities emerging who felt themselves excluded from the religious consensus then operative in the schools and speaking up to say this— has generated a long succession of court cases, and the U.S. Supreme Court, with remarkable consistency, has declared the protesters right. Of course, while some citizens have felt that the schools were too slow in rubbing out manifestations of religious commitment that they found offensive, others have been offended by that very "rubbing out." Such people have never received satisfaction before the high court.

Some of those dismayed by this "rubbing out" were simply betraying their failure to keep up with the times. I think certain Baptist groups are the best example of this. The Baptists have typically been ardently committed to the "wall of separation" principle; many, however, have found it difficult to accept that America has really become as non-Christian as it has and that the wall of separation principle, accordingly, leads to the exclusion of all manifestations of Christianity from the common public schools. The position of certain others who were dismayed has been more interesting, however, for their position confronts the American practice with a dilemma that the Court in particular and Americans in general have done all they can to resist acknowledging. Let me develop this point.

Various religious groups, as they watched the emergence and progress of the common public schools in America, began to have doubts about them that were grounded in their religion and focused not on the remnants of some form of sectarianism but on the very strategy that Americans had hit on so as to make a system of public education a fair and equitable arrangement in a religiously diverse society—the arrangement of teaching only what no one in the community disagreed with, a policy that led eventually in most areas to an education confined entirely to secular matters. Various groups—some Catholics, some Lutherans, some Calvinists, some Jews—found that this strategy violated their conscience. They believed that the education of their children should be religiously integrated, not divided up into two pieces, a secular piece and a religious piece. They believed that the study of nature, for example, should be set within a religious context. The more reflective of these protesters attacked the Enlightenment understanding of learning that they saw embodied in the public school system. Some of them worked out what we can now see to have been, in effect, a post-Enlightenment, or as some would call it, a postmodern, view of science. The enterprise of science, they said, is unavoidably shaped by values, including religious values. With these convictions in mind, they then started their own schools as a form of protest against the fundamental tenets of the public school strategy for dealing with religious diversity. However, they were not thereby released from the obligation to pay taxes for the support of the public school system.

Facing a Dilemma

By now a true dilemma is beginning to emerge. Suppose that a society contains groups of people of at least the following two sorts: One group is such that the consciences of the members require an education for their children devoid of religious expression; another group is such that the consciences of the members require an education for their children that is not only religiously committed but also integrated. Suppose further that the decision has been made to have a system of tax-supported schools. Suppose lastly that this society is bequeathed a constitutional provision, which says that the government shall do nothing to infringe on the free exercise of anyone's religion, and a provision of constitutional interpretation, which says that nobody shall be required to pay money that goes to the support of someone else's (or even his own) religion.

Here is the dilemma: If the government taxes for a school system that is enjoined to avoid all affirmation of religious conviction, it patently infringes on the free exercise of those whose conscience requires a religiously committed and integrated education for their children. Such parents, if they decide to educate their children in accord with their conscience, will have to start independent schools for which they will have to pay out of their own pockets—while nonetheless not being excused from paying the regular tax for the support of the public school system. This, to put it mildly, is an "infringing" effect of a governmental arrangement. But if the government goes in the other direction and funds all schools impartially, then somebody's tax money will go for the support of a religion with which he or she disagrees, and that will violate one of the principles of constitutional interpretation.

From this dilemma there is no escape, short of eliminating one of the components producing the dilemma: elimination of one of the two groups, elimination of our tax support for schools, elimination of the no-support reading of the Establishment Clause in favor of a no-preference reading, or elimination of the demand that religious belief and exercise shall not be infringed on. There is no way out of the dilemma other than that of giving up one of these components.

The serpentine character of the sequence of Supreme Court decisions concerning religion and the schools is in good measure due to the Court's confrontation with this dilemma. The Court has consistently decided to give up the demands of the Free Exercise Clause when it comes to the conscience of those who want religiously committed and integrated education for their children. Its squirmings are due to its wish to minimize the impact of those decisions.

To me it seems clear that overall the best way to escape from the dilemma is to give up the no-support reading of the Establishment Clause in favor of a no-preference reading. Why has the Court not chosen that option? For two reasons, so far as I can tell. One we have already considered: The Court has embraced that strand of thought that goes back to the days of colonial America and that was formulated in the Virginia Statute in the words, "No man shall be compelled to . . . support any religious worship, place, or ministry whatsoever." Though the First Amendment of our federal Constitution says nothing about tax moneys not supporting religion, the Court has always read the Establishment Clause as if it were only another way of stating the provision from the Virginia Statute.

But there is a second reason. A good many citizens—including members of the Court—have felt it to be a matter of great social importance that most of our students attend a common school system that inculcates the values of the American system. Justice Frankfurter, for example, emphatically insisted that this was indispensable to our unity as a people. This then is an accommodationist argument. When it comes to chaplains in the armed forces, we accommodate the demand of no establishment to the preservation of our tradition as a religious people; when it comes to religion and the schools, we accommodate the demand of free exercise to the social good of having most students attend a common school inculcating the American way. Of course, there is great irony in the offering of this argument. A society founded on the principle of liberalism, that everybody shall be allowed to pursue his or her own vision of the good, thinks its continuance depends on pressuring parents into sending their children to schools where something other than their vision of the good is taught.

Let me summarize my argument. My general thesis has been that the fundamental features of public school education in the United States are a reflection of deep features in American society and culture, and that complaints about, and proposals for the improvement of, such education regularly border on the silly in their assumption that the schools can be changed without changing those features of society and culture that have made the schools what they are. More specifically, I have argued that the proposal that the schools inculcate the ethic of the citizen, minimalist though it be, fails to take into account why the schools are not doing that and the deep difficulties in their trying to do so—not to mention the obstacles to their success. More specifically yet, I have argued that the present system imposes a severe infringement on the free exercise of those who believe that the day-school education of their children should occur in a religious context. The present system profoundly favors the secularist, along with the person who sees no special difficulty in dividing life into secular and sacred components.

This having been my argument, you will now expect me to offer solutions to the ills of American education. I have pointed to capitalism as a phenomenon that has profoundly shaped American society and thereby our schools. I do not expect the disappearance of capitalism in the foreseeable future; neither I nor anybody else knows of any serious alternative. As to the ideology of individualism, philosophers and intellectuals can, of course, develop alternatives; in my view they *should* develop alternatives. But capitalism lends to individualism such enormous social plausibility that I do not expect these alternative ideologies to win the day. Third, I do not expect the phenomenon of religious diversity to disappear in Western societies, and while I believe that some elements in this diversity are treated unjustly, I sincerely hope that the various elements of that diversity can continue to live in such peace and harmony as we enjoy here in the United States. If I have to choose, give me the United States rather than Iran or Lebanon!

By contrast, it seems to me that the hope of moving from a *no support* policy to an *equal support* policy when it comes to religion and the schools is a realistic hope. I am well aware of the strength of the traditional conviction that no one should be taxed to support anyone else's religion, and I know the power of precedent in the law. Yet it seems to me possible to persuade the American people that the present system is unjust, unfair, and inequitable and to get the Court to see that its interpretation of the First Amendment as enjoining *no support* has over and over forced them into infringing on the free exercise of the religion of a large number of people in our society.

The United States has been an Enlightenment experiment. Let us, we have said, get down to what we all share in common, to what reason tells us to be true, and base our life together on that; let us then, in our private lives and our subcommunities, add whatever peculiarities we wish to that commonality of reason. More and more it is recognized that the Enlightenment vision was an illusion. We cannot base our life together on what reason tells all of us to be the case. But fortunately, it is not necessary for living and talking together that we set all our distinct traditions and all our distinct visions of meaning on the shelf and base our discussion solely on that which we all agree on. As persons with different traditions and different visions of meaning, we can talk together, and in that very encounter we can find out where we agree and where we do not. Within our distinct communities we can pass on the traditions of that community; within our commonwealth we can encounter each other across our diverse communities and traditions. We do not have to be a melting pot. We can be a nation of nations. And we can have a school system that expresses that alternative image for our common life.

Let us not be naive. Capitalism eats away at all traditions and all subcommunities. It powerfully pushes all of us toward the melting pot. Yet there do remain within American society, so it seems to me, distinct subcommunities in which the conditions are still present for cultivating ethical sensitivity and developing moral character on an institutional basis. Here, moral categories continue to be used. Here, reflection on moral principles remains alive. Here, moral reasons still energize action. Here, an answer can still be given to the question, "Who requires this of me?"—an answer that many students will accept. Here, social expectations remain effective.

Part 4

Educating for Shalom

chapter fourteen

Task and Invitation

By the early 1990s, Christian schools similar to those belonging to the North American Christian Schools International organization existed in many countries, including Australia, England, New Zealand, the Netherlands, and South Africa. Leaders of the different school organizations agreed to hold an international conference every four years. CSI organized the first one and invited Wolterstorff to be a keynote speaker for the 1992 Toronto conference.

I begin with three stories. They're all true; I'm not capable of inventing such stories.

A few years back, when I was teaching at the Free University of Amsterdam, my wife and I were visiting in the home of one of my colleagues. Present, along with us, was an obstetrician who taught in the university medical school. Somehow the conversation led to someone asking this professor of obstetrics what advice he gave his students, future doctors

253

and nurses, for treating mothers lying in the hospital whose babies had been stillborn. "I tell them," he said, "that they need two eyes. One eye is not enough; they need two eyes. With one, they have to check the I.V., with the other they have to weep."

The second story was told to me by Max de Pree, formerly chief executive officer of the Herman Miller Furniture Company. For a good many years now, the Herman Miller Company has been structured so that it is very much a worker-participation company; all sorts of meetings are held in which workers offer their counsel about a wide range of matters concerning the operation of the company. Max told me about a woman from the assembly line who came to his office one day and asked to be excused from attending the meetings. Max was taken aback; he was very proud of his worker-participation schemes, and now one of his workers was asking to be excused from them. "You see," said the woman, "I have a mentally impaired child at home; for me, that is so emotionally draining that what I need at work is peace and not big discussions. You see, Mr. de Pree, work for me is a healing experience." A bit stunned and perplexed, Max mulled the conversation over for a while after the woman left, and then, as he told it to me, the thought suddenly came to mind: Work should be a healing experience for everybody! How can I make work at Herman Miller a healing experience for everybody who works here?

My last story is this: In the fall of 1986, I was asked by my friend Allan Boesak, a black church leader in South Africa, to come to South Africa to testify as a character witness at a hearing on his appeal for release from house arrest. For security purposes, the trial was moved from Cape Town to Malmesbury, a rather small village some miles from Cape Town. The hearing was held in the local courthouse. Adjoining the courtroom was a courtyard, open to the sun in the middle but surrounded by an arcade. Whenever the hearing was recessed—which was rather often— the audience poured out of the courtroom into the courtyard, all seventy or so of us, about sixty-seven blacks and three whites. Suddenly, during one of these recesses, a contrast struck me: There in the hot sun of the courtyard were the blacks, slapping each other on the back, telling stories, laughing; under the arcade in the shade, about thirty white soldiers dressed in gray stood stiffly upright, rifles at the ready, watchfully surveying the scene, silent, grim, not a smile crossing their faces.

I intend these stories to function as parables. I'm not going to interpret them for you now; I'll do that at the end of my talk. In the meantime, I want them to echo in the chambers of your heart. Offering you the interpretation now will, I fear, stop the echoing.

My talk today will not be linear in structure but kaleidoscopic. Our word *kaleidoscopic* comes from three Greek words—the word *kalos*, meaning "beautiful"; the word *eidos*, meaning "form"; and the word *sko-*

pos, meaning "view." Thus, putting them all together we get "view of a beautiful form." In the kaleidoscopes with which we are familiar, we change the arrangement of the objects we are looking at by spinning the mirrored box containing those objects, all the while keeping our eyes fixed. The diversity of "beautiful forms" that I will be describing for you today will be gotten in just the opposite way: While keeping the object at which we are looking fixed, I will every now and then change the angle from which we are looking at it. Since this is not the normal way of constructing a talk, I'll help you follow by telling you when I spin the wheel that moves the viewing platform.

The objects that I propose looking at are the goals of Christian education. I will be looking at these goals from a historical angle, a biblical angle, a societal angle, and so forth—even from an autobiographical angle. The assigned topic for this session is, I well know, curriculum. But I have long been convinced that intelligent and responsible decisions concerning a school's curriculum can be made only in the light of the desired outcome of the schooling process. Only when we are clear about the aim of the process can we make good decisions concerning the content.

When determining the aim of the schooling process, we must allow a number of factors to enter the picture. Central should be philosophical, religious, and ethical considerations. But those will not be sufficient; psychological considerations must also be brought into the picture. One may desire intensely to achieve something in the schooling process that, given the psychological makeup of students or teachers, is in fact unattainable. In turn, considerations of feasibility are not limited to psychology; economic considerations, for example, also enter the picture, as does constituency support. While not at all wishing to downplay the importance of such feasibility considerations, I will be focusing on the religious and philosophical aspects of the goal of Christian education. I do so in part because this is what I am best equipped to talk about, but I do so also because it is these considerations, fundamental though they be, that educators and public alike shy away from, whether in Christian education or public. We all say we want vision, but our actions belie the sincerity of the claim. Today, it's vision I will be discussing.

Step Up on the Viewing Platform

When we talk about Christian education, prominent in our speech is the word *task*. We speak of the task of the Christian school teacher, of the task of the Christian school board member, of the task of parents, of the task of students; we speak of the schooling process as aimed at equipping students to fulfill their tasks in life. These tasks, we say, come to us from God by way of the community. Sometimes we vary the language, though not the thought, and speak of *callings* and *responsibilities;* on occasion we use the word *office* in a somewhat obsolescent sense and speak of the office of the teacher, the office of the student, and so forth.

It is good that we speak thus, for to speak of tasks, callings, responsibilities, offices is to give expression to the reality that we human beings have obligations, that obligations are deeply involved at many points in schooling, and that in the last resort it is God who obligates us. On this occasion, though, I want to suggest that such talk and thought, though profoundly important, is nonetheless one-dimensional and hence incomplete.

Often, when we call one or another of our fellow human beings, we call them to ask them to do something. "Jacob, Miriam, would you carry in the groceries?" But sometimes we call someone not to ask him or her to do something but to issue an invitation. "Jacob, Miriam, would you join me for dinner?"

One invites someone to what one hopes or expects will give the invitee delight—that, at least, is the paradigmatic form of invitation. I grant that the hangman might say to the condemned man, "I invite you to put your head into the noose," but that would be to use the word ironically. And sometimes those who issue invitations to weddings fear and even expect the whole thing to be rather grim. But such cases, though not infrequent, are nonetheless aberrant; weddings are meant to be joyous.

I suggest that when thinking about Christian education we need not only the category of *task* but the category of *invitation*. We ought to school our children not only to enable them to perform their tasks in life but also to open up to them joys and delights and satisfactions that otherwise would be unavailable. The classroom itself, for students and teachers alike, should be a place not only where tasks are performed but where delight is experienced.

I Spin the Wheel That Moves the Platform

You all know the sentence from Isaiah 43:1: "Fear not, for I have redeemed you; I have called you by name, you are mine." We are each, in baptism, given the name whereby God calls us. When you think of God calling you—"Miriam," "Jacob"—what do you think of as the *content* of the call? My guess is that all of us think of God as calling us to do things. Divine calling is automatically, unthinkingly taken as God calling us to do something, as God laying responsibilities on us. We think of divine calling as coming in the imperative mood. Its paradigmatic form is God's calling of Jeremiah: "Go now to those to whom I send you" (Jer. 1:7, paraphrased).

Much of God's call to you and me is indeed in the imperative mood, but is that the whole of it? Are we not thinking in severely reductionist fashion when we think that God calls us by name only to ask us to do things? Does God not also call us to issue invitations? "Miriam, Jacob, I invite you to join me in the fun I'm having watching Leviathan play around in the water." That's only one example.

I Spin the Wheel

The invitation to me to give this address has led me to reflect on the fact that I have been giving speeches to Christian school conventions for almost thirty years now. I notice a change in what I have said over the years; I think it is a progression. At first, I said the things I had been taught to say. I said that we human beings have a cultural mandate given to us by God at creation in the words, "Be fruitful and multiply, and fill the earth . . . and have dominion" (Gen. 1:28). In those days I did not distinguish, as I would now, between culture and society; in retrospect, I see that I took the mandate as a mandate concerning both culture and society. It might be said that I took it as a *development* mandate. Develop culture, develop society, bring forth their potentials, embrace the differentiations that development requires and yields. I argued that Christian education, properly conceived, is based on this development mandate—along with the recognition that the development as practiced by the Christian community must be guided by Scripture. Christian education, I said, has to be grounded in a doctrine of creation.

Then some things happened to me. I met some blacks from South Africa; their cry of pain has haunted my imagination ever since. I met some Palestinians; their cry of pain has also never ceased to haunt my imagination. And before either of these things happened to me, there was that deeply unsettling experience of my country at war with Vietnam. The thoughts and words that I had been bequeathed and that I had repeated seemed to me irrelevant to what I had to come to terms with; they were not mistaken but inadequate, incomplete. The blacks in South Africa, the Palestinians in the Middle East, the Vietnamese in Southeast Asia were not crying out in despair over the lack of social and cultural development in their countries; they were crying out in despair over the reign of death in their countries. The source of their pain was injustice, not lack of development, the pressure of the oppressor's boot on their neck, not the lack of a builder's trowel in their hand.

God's people, I knew, could not look away from such pain and remain God's people. And if Christian education is meant to equip God's people for their work in the world, it too could not look away. So I began to say that Christian education cannot teach only for development; it must also teach for healing and reconciliation—and must do so in a way that is healing and reconciling. Christian education must be education that teaches for justice and peace while *exhibiting* justice and peace. These conclusions led me to look into moral education—or more broadly, into the ways in which schools can, as I called it, educate for responsible action. I wanted to know how schools can contribute not just to the shaping of minds but to the shaping of lives—specifically, to the shaping of lives that do justice and seek mercy in our broken world.

But I still thought in terms of task, calling, responsibility. The task, I insisted, had to be broadened beyond development to include healing; we are called not only to develop an underdeveloped world but to heal and reconcile and comfort a wounded and hostile and weeping world. But calling I still understood as calling *to do;* calling, I still assumed, was *task*.

Now, I wonder, or to speak with more candor, now, I doubt. God calls you and me by name—"Miriam," "Jacob"—not just to command but to invite. Not all of what God says when God calls is in the imperative mood; some is invitatory in mood.

I Spin the Wheel Again

Could it be that where the tradition I had imbibed thought it saw mandate we should instead have seen invitation? On the fifth day of creation, says the writer of Genesis 1, God, after bringing into being the creatures of sky and sea, stood back, saw that it was good, and blessed all these creatures with the words, "Be fruitful and multiply and fill the waters in the seas, and let birds multiply on the earth" (v. 22). The sentence in our English translation is in the imperative mood; it seems obvious, though, that it is not to be read as a command to do something but as an invitation to flourish. Its mood is more nearly the optative: "May you flourish."

With the sound still in your ears of the blessing spoken to the sea and sky creatures, listen once again to what God said to God's human creatures: "And God blessed them, and God said to them, 'Be fruitful and multiply, and fill the earth . . . and have dominion'" (Gen. 1:28). It's a blessing, not a mandate. It's an invitation to flourish that God speaks over humanity. It's an invocation of flourishing, not a command.

The question I am raising, from different angles, is this: How can the God who blesses receive recognition in Christian education, along with the God who commands?

I Spin the Wheel Again

The most prominent image of God in the tradition of Dutch neo-Calvinism—the tradition that has done more than any other to form the schools belonging to Christian Schools International—is the image of God as lawgiver. So much is this the case that "law" added to "word" in the phrase "God's Law Word" is redundant; the phrase "God's Law Word" is used as a pleonasm. No divine word is recognized other than *law*. Correspondingly, the most fundamental relation that we human beings are seen as having in regard to God is that of *obedience*.

John Calvin himself saw things differently. Let me adapt the way Brian Gerrish, theologian-historian from the University of Chicago, put Calvin's view: To be human is to be that point in the cosmos where God's majesty and goodness are meant to receive their answer in awe and gratitude. It was Calvin's view that obedience is then one of the ways in which awe and gratitude are expressed. We do not feel awe and gratitude because we are commanded to do so; we give expression to our awe and gratitude by acting obediently. Awe and gratitude are deeper than obedience. "Let us not be ashamed," said Calvin, "to take pious delight in the works of God open and manifest in this most beautiful theater . . . and so bestir ourselves to trust, invoke, praise, and love him."[1]

Calvin was, of course, well aware of the long Augustinian tradition that held that the things of this world are to be used, not enjoyed; we are to find our joy in God and God alone, Augustine had insisted. "There were," says Calvin, "some otherwise good and holy men who when they saw intemperance and wantonness . . . desired to correct this dangerous evil. This one plan occurred to them: they allowed man to use physical goods insofar as necessity required. A godly counsel indeed, but they were far too severe. For they would fetter consciences more tightly than does the Word of the Lord—a very dangerous thing."[2] Calvin then developed his point as follows:

> Let this be our principle: that the use of God's gifts is not wrongly directed when it is referred to that end to which the Author himself created and destined them for us, since he created them for our good, not for our ruin. Accordingly, no one will hold to a straighter path than he who diligently

looks to this end. Now if we ponder to what end God created food, we shall find that he meant not only to provide for necessity but also for delight and good cheer. Thus, the purpose of clothing, apart from necessity, was comeliness and decency. In grasses, trees, and fruits, apart from their various uses, there is beauty of appearance and pleasantness of odor. For if this were not true, the prophet would not have reckoned them among the benefits of God, "that wine gladdens the heart of man, that oil makes his face shine." Scripture would not have reminded us repeatedly, in commending his kindness, that he gave all such things to men. And the natural qualities themselves of things demonstrate sufficiently to what end and extent we may enjoy them. Has the Lord clothed the flowers with the great beauty that greets our eyes, the sweetness of smell that is wafted upon our nostrils, and yet will it be unlawful for our eyes to be affected by that beauty, or our sense of smell by the sweetness of that odor? What? Did he not so distinguish colors as to make some more lovely than others? What? Did he not endow gold and silver, ivory and marble, with a loveliness that tenders them more precious than other metals or stones? Did he not, in short, render many things attractive to us, apart from their necessary use?[3]

I Spin the Wheel Again

Four fundamental approaches to education, by no means equal in strength, are battling it out on the American scene today. The most prominent is the *socialization* view, according to which the fundamental goal of school education is to enable and dispose the student to occupy effectively some combination of approved social roles. Among the socialization theorists, some place their emphasis on roles in the economy, while others, such as Robert Bellah and his associates, emphasize roles in the polity.

A competitor of the socialization view is the *acculturation* view, espoused by Allan Bloom, E. D. Hirsch Jr., and so on. These theorists, while not denying that students will in fact have to occupy certain social roles, nonetheless insist that the fundamental aim of school education should be to transmit and enlarge the cultural inheritance. Those who hold this view customarily assume that immersing the student in the cultural heritage will imbue him or her with certain fundamental values. Nowadays, as you are all aware, a hot dispute is taking place concerning the canon of the cultural heritage that is to be transmitted: Should the canon be exclusively Western or broader than that, should it reflect the interests of white Western males or of others as well, and so forth?

Third, ever since the days of nineteenth-century Romanticism, the *individualization* view has been present on the American scene, waxing and waning in prominence, according to which the proper goal of education is the development of the individual. The root idea is that there is a "growth" pattern unique to each individual, and that the goal of education is to provide to each student certain of the nutriments necessary for his or her growth while avoiding, and contributing to the undoing of, inhibitions to that growth.

It is my impression that the American public in general asks of its schools that they combine, in a certain way, the socialization approach with the individualization approach: They expect the schools to teach the knowledge, abilities, and dispositions necessary for holding down a productive job during working hours, and they expect the schools in addition to teach the knowledge, abilities, and dispositions necessary for each of us to develop our own individual selves after working hours. This, I say, is what the public expects—but with one important exception. We do not expect our inner-city predominantly black schools to do this. The American public is not disturbed by the knowledge that a large proportion of black students emerge from the inner-city public schools lacking the knowledge, abilities, and dispositions necessary to occupy worthwhile roles in the economy and polity.

The least prominent theory of education on the American scene today, though to my mind the most interesting, is the *social criticism* view, represented by such people as Paulo Freire, David Purpel, and Michael Apple. According to this view, a fundamental goal of school education should be to teach the student to be a critic of society at those points where it fails to measure up to the requirements of love, justice, compassion, peace, and democracy. Purpel is of the view that this cannot be done without imparting to the student a religious vision of meaning; in the course of his discussion, it eventually becomes clear that this religious vision of meaning is identical with the highest ideals of the people.

Christian education, properly understood, is not a species of any of these. That is so for a fundamental reason. The vision of the human good that underlies the Christian story and proclamation is not only an essentially relational vision; the relations in question are pluriform. Consider, by contrast, the story that Freud tells of the human good; it is a story of ordering the internal dynamics of the self in such a way that one is happy—though it should be added that Freud thought no one could ever be fully successful in this attempt; at most we can alleviate some of the pain. Freud's vision is a tragic vision. The Christian vision, by contrast, sees the human good as achieved only by the right ordering of our relationships—with God, with society, with nature, with the legacy of human culture, and yes, with oneself. Seen from this standpoint, the views now battling it out on the American scene all look one-dimensional. One emphasizes the relation of the self to society, another, the relation of the self to culture, another, the relation of the self to self—little is said about the relation of the self to nature, nothing is said about the relation of the self to God, and none of them keeps all these relationships in view. Christian education is inspired by the vision of development, healing, and delight in all these relationships.

I Spin the Wheel Again

Education is ultimately always shaped by a vision of the nature and possibility of human flourishing; that's another way of getting at what I have been saying. The vision of human flourishing that underlies the biblical narrative and proclamation is what the biblical writers call shalom. Shalom is harmony and delight in all one's relationships—with God, with other human beings, with culture, with nature, with oneself. The picture, to say it once again, is an essentially relational picture— and then, a multi-relational picture. Of course, those nice words, "harmony and delight in all one's relationships," don't give us much clue as to the character of the relationships involved in shalom. To get further, one has to steep oneself in the Bible; there one discovers the shalom vision of human flourishing spelled out in rich detail. I have myself, in some of my writings over the last decade, emphasized the role of justice in shalom; insofar as there is injustice present in a community, that community is lacking in shalom. What must immediately be added, however, is that in the biblical writings one finds a unique picture of the contours of justice—very different from the contours of the just society as described by Plato, by John Locke, and so on. Pointing out the indispensability of justice to shalom is, however, the merest beginning of a description of the shape of shalom.

Christian education is education that strives both to exhibit shalom and equip for shalom. That is what gives it its shape.

I Spin the Wheel Again

What do I have in mind when I say that Christian education strives to equip for shalom? Shalom is the ideal; suppose we grant that. But how are you and I to relate to that ideal? And for what relationship, accordingly, are we to educate?

We *work* for shalom; that's one mode of relationship. And that work— to repeat a point I have already made several times—takes the form both of working to develop creation's potentials and of working to heal the dysfunctions in our relationships.

Second, we *pray to God* for the coming of shalom, for though we are indeed agents of shalom, all of us together are fragile, ineffective agents. Though the coming of the reign of realized shalom requires our efforts, our efforts do not bring it about. Christian life requires a dimension of prayerful waiting.

Third, we *celebrate* such shalom as comes our way; we enjoy it. This, of course, has been the main burden of my remarks today.

And last, we *lament* the absence of shalom wherever we find it absent. To speak of lament is to introduce a note that so far has not been heard in my discussion but that I think is indispensable. Christian education must exhibit and teach for lament. The cry, "This should not be," so far from being smothered, as all too often it is, must be allowed, even encouraged. Why is that? For one thing, the struggle for the healing of broken and distorted relationships can be genuine only if it emerges from a heart-felt lament. But second, to teach our students to love the earth, to love God, to love culture, to love each other, to love oneself, is, as all of us know who have loved, to court the possibility, indeed, the certainty, of grief and sorrow. The loved dog dies, the loved friend changes, the loved God is hidden by the dark night of the soul, the loved painting is ripped.

I Spin the Wheel Again

Does this really have anything to do with curriculum, some of you are asking. No doubt, it has relevance for the *tone and attitude* of the classroom; there will be more reverence, more honoring, more savoring, more amazement. But joy and delight—that just happens, doesn't it? One can't teach for it. There's no curriculum for joy and delight.

No, one can teach for it. Some of you are acquainted with Alasdair MacIntyre's notion of a social practice. A social practice, such as farming or violin playing, is an activity that one doesn't just grow up being able to perform but that one has to learn, and learning it consists of being inducted into a tradition. These traditions typically encompass disputes concerning proper goals for the practice, better and worse ways of conducting the practice, etc. Nonetheless, the activity that is a social practice is an ongoing activity with a history, and the novice who enters becomes a participant in that history, a participant also in the disputes. Furthermore—and this is the point that MacIntyre especially emphasizes—for every coherent social practice, there is a good internal to that practice, in the sense that that good can be attained only by becoming a more or less skilled participant in that practice or in a practice very much like it. Thus, fame and fortune, though they may be goods, are not goods internal to a practice; people gain fame and fortune in a wide variety of different ways. By contrast, that peculiar delight that comes from playing chess well can be experienced only by those who learn to play chess well—or perhaps, though this will be disputed, also by those who play checkers well!

Very much of what goes on in schooling consists, or should consist, of inducting students into social practices, thus understood. And if that is true, then very much of what goes on in schooling consists of making available to students delights and satisfactions that otherwise would not be available. The roads may be long, arduous, boring, and even painful, but at the ends of the roads lie the delights of mathematics, of musical performance, of playing basketball, of knowing God, of loving another human being. Schooling, well conducted, expands the range and depth of delight available to a human being.

I Spin the Wheel for the Last Time

Each educational vision tells its stories, for imitation and inspiration. Those socialization theorists who emphasize the economy tell about Horatio Alger, Andrew Carnegie, and Ronald Reagan. Those who emphasize the polity tell about Thomas Jefferson and Abraham Lincoln. Acculturation theorists tell the stories of Shakespeare, Galileo, and Einstein. Individualization theorists offer us novels in which the hero "finds" himself or herself after a long search. The social criticism theorists tell us about Socrates, Ghandi, and King—and yes, about Jesus.

What stories do we tell in Christian education, for imitation and inspiration? Or don't we tell stories? Education without stories doesn't take.

I close by returning to my opening stories. I promised to interpret them, but I suspect that you all by now pretty much see their point. To say much by way of interpretation would be to insult your intelligence.

"You need two eyes." The task of Christian education has two dimensions: The task of development and the task of healing. We need them both. And the task of healing must be energized by lament. Indeed, so must be the task of development.

"You see, work is for me a healing experience." School is to be a healing experience for students and teachers alike. What we as teachers must sadly admit is that, for many children, school is less a healing experience than what they need healing from.

Lastly, we who are Christian school teachers, who are we? Are we the ones standing in the shadows of the arcade, or are we the ones in the open sun? Those in the sun are beyond task to invitation; they are enjoying themselves. Mysteriously, they are also the weeping ones. Perhaps only those who weep can laugh.

chapter fifteen

Teaching for Gratitude

In 1980, Wolterstorff published *Educating for Responsible Action,* a book that examined what it is to teach in ways that shape specific tendencies in students. In this keynote address given in Vancouver, B.C., in the early 1990s to the teachers of the Northwest Christian Teachers Association, Wolterstorff suggests that it might be wrong to think that faithfully carrying out one's obligations is basic in the Christian life and that joy and gratitude are things we are obligated to feel. Perhaps Christian teachers should teach in ways that show that gratitude is basic and that obedience is the proper expression of gratitude, rather than the other way around.

Everything I have to say today is contained, in kernel, in an episode that occurred some fifteen years ago now, when I was speaking at Rehoboth Christian High School in New Mexico. It happened in the discussion period after my last speech. I have no recollection whatsoever as to the

265

theme of my talks, nor do I remember, more specifically, what it was I said that led one of the Native Americans teaching in the school, a Navajo, to stand up and say what he said.

Always, he said, he had felt himself something of an outsider in the school—even though the school had been established to offer Christian education to the Navajos. He felt that his Navajo background was held against him. Accordingly, he had never felt free to talk with his fellow teachers about how he tried to integrate the best of his Navajo background with how he taught in the school. He wanted to take this occasion to do so.

His speech was quite long—and incredibly intense. No one stirred. What I remember especially was this: When he was a child, he said, he used to go hunting for small game and gathering reeds for baskets with older people in the tribe. Always, before they set out, they prayed to God, or the gods—I don't remember what he said—asking that God or the gods provide them with the game and reeds that they needed and promising not to take more than needed. Then, before returning home after a successful hunt and search, they again prayed to God or the gods, giving thanks for the game and the reeds and promising to use them faithfully.

"And this," said Elmer—Elmer is in fact his name—"is how I use what I learned from my elders in my teaching here." Elmer is an art teacher. Before they start art class, he asks the students to take out all their materials and lay them on their tables, and then, before they begin working, they offer a prayer to God—no doubt in my mind now that it was *God* to whom the prayer was offered—thanking God for the wax of the crayons, the wood and graphite of the pencils, the paper, the trees from which the paper came, the paints, the chalk, and they promise to use them with care and to God's glory. Then at the end of the class, before they put their materials away, they thank God for the use of their materials.

Gratitude as Context and Act

On this occasion, I want to set off to the side the important question this episode raises about the relation of Christianity to other religions. Likewise, I want to set off to the side the ecological attitude that here comes to expression. What I want to emphasize is that hunting, gathering, and school education are here all set within the context of gratitude. Maybe it's appropriate to go a step further and say that hunting, gathering, and school education are not only set within the *context* of gratitude but are themselves understood as *acts* of gratitude.

Some of you will know that the Greek word for thanksgiving is *eucharistia*. In many Christian traditions, the Lord's Supper is called the Eucharist because it traditionally opens with a prayer of thanksgiving. Hunting, gathering, and school education were understood by Elmer as eucharistic activities. He had learned to regard them thus from his Navajo elders.

In 1980, I published a book on education called *Educating for Responsible Action*. Commissioned by Christian Schools International, my project was to offer a taxonomy of educational goals that was an alternative to the many such taxonomies then floating around and to inquire especially into the dynamics of what I there called "dispositional learning." I wanted to get some understanding of how the school can shape the way its students are disposed to act—both within the school and without. Specifically, I wanted an understanding of those dynamics that was faithful to the Christian understanding of the self.

I recently had occasion to reread the book and found myself still agreeing with almost everything in it. In fact, I found myself thinking it was better than I thought it was at the time! However, one rather troubling question kept insistently arising: Why had I called it educating for *responsible* action? Of course, we do want to educate for responsible action. But that's not the whole of what we want to educate for. We also want to educate for joyful and delighted action—and for grateful action. (I assume that when I told the story about Elmer, you all said to yourself, "Yes, how right to set learning within the context of gratitude!")

Within the book, I discussed how dispositions in general are shaped. But then, when I titled it, I called it educating for *responsible* action. Why did I do that? Could it be, I said to myself, that I was thinking that faithfully carrying out one's obligations is basic in the Christian life, and that joy and gratitude are to be seen as obligatory? If so, is that right? Is it right to think that gratitude and joy enter the picture as things we are obligated to feel? If that was indeed how I was thinking, there's an interpretation of the text you have chosen for your convention that could be cited as evidence for the propriety of this way of thinking: "And be thankful," said Paul. The grammatical mood appears to be that of the imperative; the thought appears to be that his readers *ought to be* thankful.

Whether or not that was the way I was thinking back then, that is how the Dutch neo-Calvinist tradition in which I was reared and that inspired the movement of Christian day-schools represented by Christian Schools International has customarily understood the relationship between obligation and gratitude. The fundamental relationship between God and the world is law. God sets the law *to*, or *for*, the world. In the case of nonhuman beings, this law is the law of their functioning. In the case of human beings, it is both the law *of* our functioning and the law *for* our functioning—the latter being then the laws of obligation. God is fundamentally lawgiver.

Which brings me back to Elmer. For Elmer, with his Navajo background, the relationship between gratitude and obligation was exactly the reverse of that which has characterized the Dutch neo-Calvinist tradition. It was within the context of gratitude that the Navajos expressed their resolve to act responsibly. Gratitude was basic. Obedience was an act of gratitude rather than, the other way round, gratitude being an act of obedience.

What I want to suggest today is that Elmer and his Navajo forebears got it right and that we have gotten it wrong. Gratitude is basic, and obedience is properly the expression of gratitude. Christian schools, at bottom, should be schools where gratitude is expressed and cultivated rather than schools where, at bottom, students are schooled in obedience. Don't get me wrong; I'm not speaking up for irresponsibility. What I want to argue is that the fundamental ethos of the Christian school—that which the perceptive visitor picks up as the most fundamental character of the place—should be gratitude.

I could develop the point in several different ways. I could develop it purely systematically and ahistorically, ignoring the tradition out of which these schools came and the influence of that tradition on these schools. I have decided not to do it that way but instead to confront directly the habit in this tradition of making obedience basic and gratitude secondary by arguing that this habit of ours is unfaithful to the patriarch of the tradition, John Calvin. Only thus, so I judge, is there any chance of the habit being broken.

Let me first observe that at important points in Scripture, where we in the tradition have thought we saw divine commandment, close scrutiny reveals something else. I can examine only one example, but it's perhaps the most important. Regularly in the history of the Christian school movement it has been said that at creation God gave humanity what has come to be called "the cultural mandate"—that is, the mandate, the command, to develop culture. This is our answer to the pietists who see the Christian life as focused entirely on salvation. The basis for the claim has been the following passage from Genesis 1:

> And God blessed them [i.e., the human beings], and God said to them, "Be fruitful and multiply, and fill the earth and subdue it; and have dominion over the fish of the sea and over the birds of the air and over every living thing that moves upon the earth."

> verse 28

Is this initial speech of God to humankind to be understood as a command? I submit that it is much more plausibly understood as a blessing. The words are to be heard thus: "May you be fruitful and multiply, may you fill the earth and subdue it, may you have dominion over the animals."

The speech is, for one thing, introduced with the words, "And God blessed them." The traditional interpretation would have it that after these words, we are not then offered the content of the blessing but are instead offered the content of a command, without anything at all being said about a command. Very odd! Words announcing a blessing, but then no content to the blessing. Instead, content to a command, but no words announcing a command. The traditional interpretation construes the words we have as if they were instead the following: "God blessed them; and then God also commanded them, saying . . ." Is it not much more plausible to read all the introductory words together as amounting to, "And God blessed them, saying . . ."?

Second, we must not overlook the remarkable parallelism between God's address to humankind, which I quoted, and God's earlier address to the creatures of sea and air after they had been created. This is what we read: "And God saw that it was good. And God blessed them, saying, 'Be fruitful and multiply and fill the waters in the seas, and let birds multiply on the earth'" (Gen. 1:21–22). Being spoken to animals, this obviously has to be a blessing; it cannot be a command. But then, given the parallelism, isn't it compelling to regard the speech to humankind as also a blessing—especially so when we add the fact, already mentioned, that nothing is said about a command but only about a blessing?

The Historical Appreciation of Gratitude

Let me now move on to the historical reflections that I promised. What I wish to show is that the tradition that gave rise to these schools is unfaithful to its own founder, John Calvin, when it places obedience deeper than gratitude in the Christian life. Of course, it's possible to argue that Calvin was mistaken on this matter. But when I have finished setting before you the pattern of his thought, I would guess that you will feel intuitively that there is something deeply biblical in his thought pattern.

Before I set out, let me say that my understanding of Calvin on this point has been decisively shaped by a remark that a Calvin scholar at the University of Chicago, Brian Gerrish, makes in his book *The Old Protestantism and the New*. Gerrish is talking about the overall structure of Calvin's thought. This is the remark: "Man is defined as the point of creation at which the sheer goodness of God is reflected or imaged in an act of filial piety or thankful love."[1]

A good place to begin is with a remarkable passage in which Calvin argues that we should appreciate grasses, trees, and fruits not just for their utility in keeping us nourished and warm but for their "comeliness"; we should appreciate wine and oil not only because they are useful but because wine gladdens the heart and oil makes the face shine. He concludes the passage by asking whether God did "not, in short, render many things attractive to us, apart from their necessary use?" The question is, of course, rhetorical. Let this, he says, "be our principle; that the use of God's *gifts* is not wrongly directed when it is referred to that end to which the Author himself created and destined them for us, since he created them for our good, not for our ruin."[2]

The underlying point is that we are to see the things of this world not only as the *works* of God for which we are to give God praise but also as the *gifts* of God for which we are to give God thanks—and then, gifts not only for utility but for delight. "This life, however crammed with infinite miseries it may be, is still rightly to be counted among those blessings of God which are not to be spurned. Therefore, if we recognize in it no divine benefit, we are already guilty of grave ingratitude toward God himself." "Away then with that inhuman philosophy that, while conceding only a necessary use of creatures, not only malignantly deprives us of the lawful fruit of God's beneficence but cannot be practiced unless it rob a man of all his senses and degrades him to a block."[3]

Calvin was clear on the fact that the counterpart of gratitude to God for the good things that come our way is lament to God for the bad things that come our way. "Among the Christians," he says, "there are also new Stoics, who count it depraved not only to groan and weep but also to be sad and care ridden." On this, says Calvin, they are quite wrong. We ought "not to be utterly stupefied and to be deprived of all feeling of pain. Our ideal is not that of what the Stoics of old foolishly described as 'the great-souled man'; who, having cast off all human qualities, was affected equally by adversity and prosperity, by sad times and happy ones—nay, who like a stone was not affected at all." The Stoic ideas paint "a likeness of forebearance that has never been found among men, and can never be realized," for it is contrary to our created nature. "Thus afflicted by disease, we shall both groan and be uneasy and pant after health; thus pressed by poverty we shall be pricked by the arrows of care and sorrow; thus we shall be smitten by the pain of disgrace, contempt, injustice; thus at the funerals of our dead ones we shall weep the tears that are owed to our nature."[4]

I find it impossible not to read the passage I cited above, in which Calvin says that the good things that come our way from the hand of

God are not just the things of use but also the things of delight, as an implicit criticism of a famous formula of Augustine in his *On Christian Doctrine*. Admittedly, Calvin does not say that he is criticizing Augustine; his veneration for Augustine was so deep that when he did feel compelled to criticize his great predecessor, he much preferred just doing so without saying that he was doing so. But in the first book of *On Christian Doctrine*, Augustine said that we are to use the things of the world, not to enjoy them; God alone is to be enjoyed. In Latin, the formula has an almost hypnotic ring: *uti, non frui;* to use, not to enjoy.

Obviously, this is not the occasion to engage in the niceties of Augustine scholarship. But if Calvin was indeed implicitly criticizing Augustine in the way suggested, I feel compelled to say that he was, in my judgment, misinterpreting Augustine. I grant that Augustine has regularly been misinterpreted in just that way; his words invite the misinterpretation. But I think that when one looks closely at the context of the famous *uti/frui* formula, Augustine is not saying that we are only to use the things of the world, not to enjoy them. What he is saying is that we are not to experience in them the kind of delight that comes from loving something, investing oneself in it, attaching oneself to it, and finding one's love satisfied. God alone is to be loved (as an end in itself), not the things of this world; accordingly, in God alone are we to find the delight of satisfied love. As to the things of the world, we are allowed not only to use the useful things but also to delight in the delightful things, giving God thanks and praise for them. What we are not to do— to say it again—is pursue them, love them, desire them, attach ourselves to them, invest ourselves in them. In short, Calvin and Augustine are united in the view that God's gifts to us are not only for our use but also for our delight.

Where they differ is over Augustine's insistence that we are not to *love* any of these things—not to attach ourselves to them in such a way that we grieve when they change or die on us. What lies behind Calvin's claim that it is appropriate to grieve at funerals is that it is appropriate to love our relatives and friends. When Augustine reflected on his former life, what struck him was not only the disobedient licentiousness of it but the unhappiness of it and his emotional vulnerability. He had attached his love to all sorts of things and persons that changed on him, died, turned away from him; grief ensued. It was to prevent that unhappiness and emotional vulnerability that he urged love for God alone. What is striking about Calvin, by contrast, is that he enjoins us to emotional vulnerability. Gratitude and lament belong together as intrinsic components in the Calvinist way of responding to experience and living in the world.

What's especially important for my argument is the next step. As Calvin sees it, recognition of the goodness of God, and the practice of gratitude that goes with that recognition, is what evokes and sustains faith. Faith does not arise out of the recognition of the sheer power of God. Neither does faith arise out of the fear of eternal punishment. Faith arises out of a perception of God's goodness, received with gratitude. "Briefly, he alone is truly a believer who, convinced by a firm conviction that God is a kindly and well-disposed Father toward him, promises himself all things on the basis of his generosity; who, relying upon the promises of divine benevolence toward him, lays hold on an undoubted expectation of salvation."[5] And so, says Calvin:

> let all readers know that they have with truth apprehended what it is for God to be Creator of heaven and earth, if they first of all follow the universal rule, not to pass over in ungrateful thoughtlessness or forgetfulness those conspicuous powers which God shows forth in his creatures, and then learn so to apply it to themselves that their very hearts are touched. The first part of the rule is exemplified when we reflect on the greatness of the Artificer who stationed, arranged, and fitted together the starry host of heaven in such wonderful order. . . .
>
> There remains the second part of the rule, more closely related to faith. It is to recognize that God has destined all things for our good and salvation but at the same time to feel his power and grace in ourselves and in the great benefits he has conferred upon us, and so bestir ourselves to trust, invoke, praise, and love him.[6]

The point is clear. The fundamental response on our part to God's good gifts is gratitude, grounding even faith itself. Gratitude lies at the foundation of Christian existence. From this, everything flows. If the Christian school is to educate for Christian life, it must educate for gratitude.

Modeling Gratitude

How is that to be done? In my *Educating for Responsible Action*, I argued that the three fundamental ways of shaping dispositions to action are discipline, reasoning, and modeling. In the case before us, what strikes me as central is modeling. Discipline—punishing and rewarding—seem to me out of place. And reasoning? Well, yes, one can offer students reasons for feeling gratitude toward God. But above all, I think, it will be modeling that is effective here. We teachers must ourselves exhibit gratitude. Our schools must breathe the spirit of gratitude.

For one thing—difficult as it surely is in the modern world—we must cultivate a sort of meditative reflection on God's wisdom and goodness as exhibited in God's works. Allow me to quote a lovely passage from Calvin:

> There is no doubt that the Lord would have us uninterruptedly occupied in this holy meditation; that, while we contemplate in all creatures, as in mirrors, those immense riches of his wisdom, justice, goodness, and power, we should not merely run over them cursorily, and so to speak, with a fleeting glance; but we should ponder them at length.[7]

To which he interestingly adds something eminently relevant to you and me: People "who have either quaffed or even tasted the liberal arts penetrate with their aid far more deeply into the secrets of the divine wisdom."[8]

Second, I am persuaded that we must cultivate that context of devotional gratitude that Elmer had established in his classroom. It is my clear impression that this is something we have traditionally shied away from.

"And be thankful," says Paul. "Sing psalms and hymns and spiritual songs with *thankfulness* in your hearts to God. And whatever you do, in word or deed, do everything in the name of the Lord Jesus, giving *thanks* to God the Father through him" (Col. 4:15–17, emphasis added).

Was Paul laying on us an obligation? Was he casting gratitude as one among other obligations that God lays on us—who knows why? I doubt it. I think he was reminding us of what is deepest in our Christian and human existence. Reminding us that if we are true to what we are, we will be eucharistic beings who break out into song and then go forth to perform works of obedience as acts of gratitude.

chapter sixteen

Teaching for Justice

In 1999, Wolterstorff was invited to Calvin College to give the
first of the Beversluis Lectures, named for Henry Beversluis,
who had been a faculty member in Calvin's education department. In this lecture, Wolterstorff reflects on his earlier writings
and speeches in which he stated that the goals of education are
responsible action and that students will learn to live with gratitude. He now adds to that a third dimension of the life for which
we teach and the life that we exhibit in our teaching—the concept of justice.

There's an uproar across the country today concerning competence in
elementary and high school education. It's being charged that our
schools are not producing students with the knowledge and skills that
we have a right to expect. This past Saturday on the front page of the
New York Times a story appeared with the headline "Most 8th Graders
in New York City Fail State Tests." Whether this alarmist headline has

274

a solid basis in fact I have no way of judging, since I have not looked at the tests. But for what it's worth, in my forty-two years of teaching at Calvin College and Yale University, I have never noted any significant drop in the ability of the students I deal with to write competent academic papers.

Be that as it may, however, no one would dispute that one of the aims of elementary and secondary education is indeed to produce competence in certain areas. Without knowledge in certain areas and without certain skills, a person simply cannot function productively, responsibly, or happily in society.

Everyone here would acknowledge that there's more to education than factual knowledge and competence, however. Education is also for shaping how students will live their lives—nervous as that acknowledgment makes a great many educators. Education is for inculcating virtues, as your new curriculum report here at Calvin eloquently emphasizes. I realize that some of those who identify themselves with the liberal tradition of political thought espouse the view that education should confine itself to putting all the realistic life options in front of students and then, with no coercion, urging and inviting them to function as autonomous choosers and adopt whichever catches their fancy. Whatever one may think about the moral and religious acceptability of this view, it strikes me at least as sheer fantasy to suppose that education could be set up this way or that society could long endure if it were. To which may be added the point that such a mode of education would scarcely be neutral, as it is often advertised as being, but would in fact be the expression of one highly distinctive comprehensive perspective from among the multitude of available perspectives.

I say all this to make the point that today I want to talk about the "values" side of Christian education. I don't like the word *values* when used for this purpose, but I know of none better. Specifically, I want to discuss the appropriate role of the concept of *justice* when reflecting on the values side of Christian education.

More than Responsibility

Let me begin autobiographically. In 1980, I published a book called *Educating for Responsible Action*. My thought was that one of the goals of any education, and certainly of Christian education, is to educate for responsible action: to educate persons who will act responsibly and carry out their obligations. The bulk of the book was devoted not to arguing that thesis but to asking how, in the light of whatever evidence is available, the school can most effectively do this.

What led me to ask the question was, frankly, the fact that I was in the process of recovering from a piece of naivete in some of my own earlier writings. When I was chair of the Curriculum Revision Committee at Calvin, in the early 1960s, I argued that Christian education was for Christian life and proposed a curriculum that would impart to students the knowledge and inculcate in them the skills necessary for living such a life. Shortly after publishing the proposed curriculum and getting it approved by the faculty, I began to think that proposing that curriculum for that goal was naive. Of course, living the Christian life does require knowledge and skills; the naivete was not located at that point. The naivete lay in supposing that that was anywhere near sufficient. I became convinced that one had to take the next step of considering how to enable and encourage students to cross the bridge from theory and skill to action. That, as I say, was what motivated the inquiry I undertook in *Educating for Responsible Action*.

Shortly after publishing *Educating for Responsible Action*, I began to feel a certain dissatisfaction with it as well. I began to regret the heavy and exclusive emphasis on *responsible* action. Not that I think schools should not do what they can to produce responsible persons. But there's more to life than responsibility. There's also delight, enjoyment, flourishing, shalom. In some of my own writings on art, I had emphasized the legitimacy—I mean the *Christian* legitimacy—of delight in art, in the world, and so forth. Yet in *Educating for Responsible Action*, there was scarcely a hint of that. It all sounded pretty stern and thus did not fully reflect my own view.

I have never written a book, or even an essay, to correct that impression. All I have done thus far is give a speech at a Christian school teachers convention in Vancouver, about five years ago, in which I talked about what I called "Teaching for Gratitude." I got the distinct impression that the audience did not much like what I had to say—whether the cause was something in the topic itself or in how I presented it, I don't know. I argued that though in the Calvinist tradition it has become typical to think of God first of all as lawgiver, in John Calvin's thought there was clearly something deeper than that. Calvin saw obedience as grounded in gratitude; gratitude is what's deeper. I quoted a wonderful sentence from Calvin scholar Brian Gerrish to the effect that at the very core of Calvin's perspective was the conviction that to be human is to be that point in the cosmos where God's goodness is meant to find its response in gratitude. And I pointed to those passages in Calvin's writings where he says that we should appreciate grasses, trees, and fruits not just for their utility in keeping us nourished and warm but for what he calls their "comeliness," and that we should appreciate wine and oil not only because they are useful but because wine gladdens the heart and oil makes the face shine.

What Is Justice?

Today I want to talk with you briefly about yet a third dimension of the life *for* which we teach and the life that we exhibit *in* our teaching— third in addition to teaching for responsible action and teaching for delight and gratitude. I want to talk about the place of the concept of justice in the theory and practice of Christian education.

You may think that this was in effect already discussed in my earlier discussions about responsibility. Maybe at the time of writing I myself thought that; I don't remember. But not so; justice is not a special case of responsibility. It was because I came to see that gratitude in the Christian life ultimately grounds obligation, rather than gratitude being one of the things we are obligated to feel, that I came to the view that my approach in *Educating for Responsible Action* was inadequate. So, too, it is because I have come to see that justice is a distinct dimension of the moral life, separate from obligation and responsibility, that I have come to the view that my approach was, in a second way, inadequate.

What I have to do first, obviously, is discuss, all too briefly, what I take justice to be. I would guess that for most of us the word *justice* has a cold, impersonal ring to it; what comes to mind are court proceedings, legal arrangements, prisons, and so forth. On one occasion when I wrote about justice, a friend of mine, Stanley Hauerwas, responded, "Nick, friendship, not justice; what's important is friendship."

But let's set the connotations of the word off to the side and talk a bit about the matter itself. Justice has to do with rights; a society is fully just when everybody enjoys his or her rights. Aristotle said that justice consists in receiving what's due one, that is to say, what one has a right to; I think he was correct about that.

Of course, the language of "rights" sounds at least as cold and impersonal to most people as the language of justice; what comes to the mind of many are people standing up for their rights, affiliates of the U.N. publishing lists of rights, and so forth. Further, I discover that in many Christians, talk about rights produces a strong reaction to the effect that it's responsibilities, not rights, that we ought to be talking about. What's destroying our society, so they say, is that ours is a rights society with everybody claiming their rights. Some go so far as to say that there are no rights; there are only responsibilities.

But let's think about the matter a bit more deeply for just a moment. Most of us when we hear talk about rights are inclined to start at the top, as it were, and think about big elevated things such as natural human rights. I suggest that we start instead at the bottom, with the fine texture of human existence. Since a good many of you here are students, let me start with an example that will have special relevance for you. When you write a top-notch paper for a course, you have a right to an A. My giving you an A, if I am the teacher for the course, is not an act of charity or largesse on my part; it's giving you what you have a right to, what is due you. Another example: If you win the local half marathon, you have a right to the prize that has been designated for the winner. Those who sponsor the race may not like you; they may not like your color, your ethnicity, your religion, your attitude. They may very much wish that someone else had won. No matter; if you won the race fair and square, you have a right to the prize.

Do you see from these examples what I mean when I say that rights and the recognition of rights belong to the fine texture of human existence? Yes, there are those lofty rights that are natural human rights, but we must overcome our exclusive fixation on those so as to recognize that rights pervade the fine texture of ordinary human life.

Can I say what a right is? A right, as I see it, consists of being entitled to some good—in having legitimate title to some good. There are goods of many different sorts. Many of them a given person has no legitimate title to. I think it would be a great thing to be able to live with a Rembrandt painting on my living room wall, but I don't have a legitimate claim to that good. By contrast, for each of us there are some goods to which we do have a legitimate title. Those are the things to which one has a right.

A way to understand the importance of rights is to ask yourself what life would be like if there were no rights—or if rights existed but they went unrecognized. What would your life be like and how would you act if, upon writing a top-notch paper, you had no right to an A from me, your professor? It's likely that you would beg me for an A, plead with me for it, and while doing so, you would take care to be very nice to me. You would, proverbially, polish the apple. Or maybe not; maybe you would instead be exceedingly annoying so that I would give you an A just to get you off my back. In terms of what you know of my character, you would have to calculate whether being really nice to me would be effective or whether being really annoying would be.

I think you can see that life in a world empty of rights would be demeaning. It's no accident that those in authority in oppressive situations do what they can to stop the oppressed from thinking in terms of justice and rights; they much prefer to have them think in terms of charity. When it is charity that is at stake, then there is some plausibility in the demand of the oppressors that the oppressed be really good if they want charity to be forthcoming. If you have no right to some good that is at my disposal, then in my decision as to whether or not to grant it to you I can take into account such a factor as whether or not I find you a likable person. If you have a *right* to it, however, it makes no difference whether I find you likable.

I think it will also help to get a feel for the difference between rights and justice, on the one hand, and responsibility and obligation, on the other, if we look at the dark side of each. The dark side of responsibility and obligation is guilt; if you fail to do what you ought to do, you are guilty. If there were no obligations, there would be no guilt. Now ask, similarly, what is the dark side of rights? If you fail to enjoy your rights, you are *wronged*. If there were no rights, no one would ever be wronged. If you don't have a right to an A for the paper, then you're not wronged if I don't give it to you. If you do have a right, then you are wronged.

I hope you are now beginning to see in what way there is more to the moral domain than responsibility. There's more because, in addition to guilt, there's the phenomenon of being morally wronged, and being morally wronged is a violation of rights, not of duties. There are, of course, close connections between responsibilities and rights, between duty and justice, but they're not the same. It's true that if I don't give you an A when you have written a top-notch paper, I am guilty. My point has been that, in addition, you are wronged. My being guilty is not to be identified with your being wronged.

And notice this: Without the phenomenon of being wronged, there is no such thing as forgiveness. I cannot forgive you for your being guilty; what I can forgive you for is your having wronged me. The centrality of forgiveness in Christian ethics presupposes the centrality of being wronged. Since to be wronged is to have one's rights violated, that in turn presupposes rights. The African American spiritual has it just right; there are both wounds and sins.

> There is a balm in Gilead,
>   to make the wounded whole;
> There is a balm in Gilead,
>   to heal the sin-sick soul.

Justice in Scripture

I can imagine some of you reacting to what I have said thus far by saying that this is all entirely secular. Instead of looking at those lofty things that are natural human rights, I urged that we look at the place of rights in what I called the "fine texture of human existence." Fair

enough. But what I had to say about this fine texture was entirely secular. Doesn't the Bible have something to say about this whole business
of rights? Doesn't it place question marks around standing up for one's
rights, claiming one's rights, and all that? If rights belong to the fine texture of human existence, then the Bible places question marks around
this part of the fine texture of human existence, does it not?

If what I have said about the connection between rights, being
wronged, and forgiveness is correct, then one can see at once that this
objection cannot be right. What I have argued is that if there were no
rights, there could be no forgiveness, but forgiveness is central to the
biblical picture. The truth is that the Bible is a book about justice. I don't
have time on this occasion to develop this claim in any detail; I'll have
to assume that you already have a relatively rich knowledge of the Bible
and content myself with offering a few reminders.

Recall that the Pentateuch and the books of the prophets in the Old
Testament are filled with calls by God for justice among God's people.
Recall, for example, the famous passage in Amos in which the prophet
says that God wants nothing to do with sacrifices and wheedling rituals but instead wants his people to "let justice roll down like waters"
(5:24).

Let me also remind you that when the Old Testament speaks about
justice, those regularly mentioned are the widows, the orphans, the
aliens, and the poor. What this has to mean is that a rule of thumb for
determining whether there is justice in a society is whether justice is
being rendered to such people; what justice requires is that such marginal people as these have standing in the community and a fair share
in its goods. What emerges from such reflection is that what one might
call the "contours" of justice as understood by the prophets was considerably different from the contours of justice as customarily understood in post-Enlightenment Western liberal societies. In such societies,
to find out whether a society is just, one doesn't look first to see what is
happening to its marginal ones; rather, one looks first to see whether
contracts are honored and whether the citizenry is adequately policed
against assault and battery.

I find that a good many Christians are under the impression that
though what I have said may be true for the Old Testament, it is not true
for the New Testament; between the two Testaments a fundamental
change took place so that justice is no longer a central concern of God.
I think that's mistaken. How else are we to understand Jesus' consistent
practice of bringing the outsiders in than as his practice of Old Testament justice? It's further worth mentioning that a good many of the passages in our English translations of the New Testament that speak of
"righteousness" are in fact translating the Greek word *dikaiosunē*, a word

that, in translations of Greek literature generally, is translated "justice."
The Beatitudes as recorded in Matthew 5, for example, say, "Blessed are
those who hunger and thirst for *dikaiosunē*, for they shall be satisfied"
(v. 6). The passage is translated in the Revised Standard Version as,
"Blessed are those who hunger and thirst for righteousness." Note how
different it sounds when it is rendered as, "Blessed are those who hunger
and thirst for justice."

I submit that the standard practice of translating *dikaiosunē* in the
New Testament as "righteousness" rather than as "justice" obscures from
us the deep connection between what Jesus was saying and the prophetic
witness of the Old Testament. The impression left in the mind of many
readers is that, in contrast to the Old Testament, the New Testament is
all about duties and charity, not about rights. In fact, the New Testament is like the Old Testament in being about justice, *dikaiosunē*, and
if about justice, it is perforce about rights.

Justice in Christian Education

Suppose I have succeeded in making it seem at least plausible to you
that justice and rights constitute a dimension of the moral realm distinct from that of responsibilities and duties; the question before us then
is whether justice is a concept we should use in thinking about Christian education, in addition to that of responsibility. Do we educate for
justice in addition to educating for responsibility—and for gratitude?
And must the educative community itself be just, in addition to being
responsible and grateful?

How could it be otherwise, if what I have said is correct? Let me begin
with the educative community itself. I submit that we as educators generally, and as Christian educators in particular, have been too little attentive to the rights of students—or if, in spite of all I have said, that way
of putting it still evokes the wrong connotations, too little attentive to
the ways in which students are *wronged*.

School as we know it is a hierarchical arrangement; I am not for
breaking that down and turning school into a pure democracy. Teachers have authority. But hierarchical arrangements are always rife with
the potential for wronging those lower in the hierarchy—rife with potential for not recognizing their worth. And though I haven't had time to
make a point of it today, rights and justice have to do with the recognition of *worth*; if I have wronged you, then I have in some way failed to
recognize your worth.

There are elements in the present-day Christian community that are
doing all they can to promote even more hierarchy than we already have:

Wives are told to obey husbands, children are told to obey parents, students are told to obey teachers, everybody is told to obey the government (at least when Republicans are in power), and so forth. I find this pagan. It turns a deaf ear to the dimension of justice in the Bible, that is, to the dimension of rights—to the possibility not just of failing to do one's duty but to the possibility of being wronged. Or more precisely, what it does is content itself with noting that the person above one in the hierarchy is wronged if he or she is not obeyed while paying no attention to the multiple ways in which the person below one in the hierarchy can be wronged. What we find in the New Testament "household codes," in Colossians and Ephesians, is never this one-sided hierarchy but always a mutuality of obligations and rights.

Not only is the Christian school called to *exhibit* justice in its educative practice and structure, but it is also called to teach *for* justice. If I am right that the moral life has two distinct but interlocking dimensions, a dimension of duties and a dimension of rights, a dimension of responsibilities and a dimension of justice, then we must teach for justice as well as for responsibility. We must teach our students to recognize injustice when they see it—to say, "This must not be"—and we must encourage them to contribute to rectifying injustice when the possibility of such rectification opens up before them.

How can we do this? How can we teach for justice? At this point my book *Educating for Responsible Action* becomes relevant. My topic there was how, in light of the best research and the wisdom of the ages, we can (responsibly) shape how students will tend to act; the conclusions to which I came are as relevant to teaching for justice as they are to teaching for responsibility.

What I emphasized was the interaction of three strategies: discipline, modeling, and reasoning. If one wants to encourage students to act a certain way, it helps to employ an appropriate form of discipline, it helps to present appropriate models, and it helps to give reasons for acting in ways that appeal to premises they will accept. When it comes to teaching for justice, I would supplement these three with a fourth strategy, namely, *evoking empathy*. I now think it is a serious defect in the book, and in the research on which the book was based, that empathy was never brought into the picture. If people are to be energized to struggle to undo injustice, it is important that they listen to the voices and see the faces of the victims so that empathy can be evoked. If my line of thought has been correct, then always when there is injustice there will be victims, that is, those who have been wronged.

Though I do not personally know of any relevant research, my own experience has been that reading books about injustice is, for most people, including myself, far less effective in energizing them to action than actually listening to the voices and actually seeing the faces of victims. Such acts evoke empathy, whereas reading black marks on white pages does not for most people. The struggle for justice requires attentive listening and looking—not ceaseless talking but, rather, listening with empathetic care to someone's description of being wronged. I as an empathetic listener do not have to take, and in fact should not take, everything said at face value; critical discernment is in order. But unless my own experience completely deceives me, the attentive listening and looking are indispensable.

I think it is especially at this point that we must keep in mind what I said about justice and injustice pervading the fine texture of our human existence. If the teacher talks only about lofty natural human rights and their violations, the student can easily be immobilized by the thought that it is all too big for anybody to make a difference. Best then to begin with the injustice on one's doorstep, or in the classroom. The voices and the faces of victims may well be present right there in the classroom, in the person of some of the students.

Does the concept of justice have a role to play in the theory and practice of Christian education? Its role there is indispensable!

Notes

Preface

1. Nicholas Wolterstorff, "Education or Indoctrination," *Chimes* 96, 4 April 1952, 2.
2. Nicholas Wolterstorff, "The Grace That Shaped My Life," in *Philosophers Who Believe: The Spiritual Journey of Eleven Leading Thinkers,* ed. Kelly James Clark (Downers Grove, Ill.: InterVarsity Press, 1993), 266.
3. Ibid., 263–64.
4. Ibid., 267–68.
5. Ibid., 268–69.
6. Ibid., 272–73.
7. Ibid., 275.

Chapter 5: Beyond 1984 in Philosophy of Christian Education

1. William Harry Jellema, "Calvinism and Higher Education," in *God-Centered Living,* Calvinistic Action Committee (Grand Rapids: Baker, 1951), 120.
2. Ibid., 122.
3. Ibid., 121.
4. Ibid.
5. "Created anew, made a new mankind by the regenerating and forgiving power of God, they who are by faith united with Christ are adopted as citizens of the Kingdom of God, of the Kingdom which the Father has given to the Son. The elect are elect to the Kingdom. They are saved not simply as individuals but as citizens of the Kingdom, and

285

for citizenship. And, therefore, salvation can be and is salvation not of part of man, but of the whole; salvation of man as he was created man; salvation of soul and body; salvation of man as cultural will; salvation of man as a creature intended for progressive deepening in knowledge and love of the God of all glory, but continuously dedicating himself and his world to Him. Nothing human is lost" (ibid., 119–20).

6. Ibid.

7. Ibid., 117.

8. Ibid., 125.

9. "Since the choice is choice of a *civitas*, the choice is continuous, is one which is dynamic, which is always rooting itself in all the activities of the chosen city; it is choice of a living comprehensive citizenship" (ibid., 121).

10. Formal education then is to be understood as one of those expressive activities of a kingdom that serve to form persons into adopting the mind of the kingdom.

11. Jellema, "Calvinism and Higher Education," 119.

12. "All formal education, like all cultural activity, is both expression of and education in religious decision or religious faith; a faith objectified in a kingdom. Education is by a kingdom and for citizenship in that kingdom" (ibid., 122).

13. Ibid., 112.

14. Ibid., 127.

15. William Harry Jellema, *The Curriculum in a Liberal Arts College* (Grand Rapids: Calvin College, 1958), 24.

16. Jellema thought that any *civitas*, not just the Christian, would have as its primary aim to get students to grasp and be committed to the mind of that *civitas*—once again, a mind good for all citizens of that *civitas* for all seasons. I take it that this is what he has in mind when he says, for example: "Stated as briefly and traditionally as possible, liberal education aims at the *man* in each individual; at the man, intellectual and moral. . . . Hence liberal education is not overwhelmingly concerned, curricularly, with 'individual differences,' or with transient individual student 'interests.' . . . Liberal education aims at man intellectual and moral; ultimately, at the intellectual for the sake of the moral" (ibid., 16). To understand Jellema here we must remember that in his view, what ultimately shapes how people exercise their intellectual and moral capacities is the character of their religious commitment—how they identify God.

17. "The cultural product at any given time is a complex resultant. There is that in it which is inescapable for any *civitas*, and there is that in it which embodies the genius of each of the several kingdoms" (Jellema, "Calvinism and Higher Education," 125).

18. Jellema, *The Curriculum in a Liberal Arts College*, 24. "Christian education falls short . . . as Christian education to the extent that the distinctiveness of Christianity in its antithesis to paganism, to modernity, and to the errors of medieval and Reformation culture is not made capable of concrete application. The Christian mind as the mind with which we think and evaluate and choose and believe and hope is more important than isolated opinions that we think or learn. But how is one to know it? By learning Christian ideas and principles with a mind that is modern? Or by reading perhaps Aeschylus with a mind that is modern, here and there adding a detached Christian homily? 'But surely we Christians ought to be up to date.'—For that I am pleading; we must know that modern mind also; and to know it we must know the others as well. 'But Christianity means antithesis.'— Again, for that I am pleading; to make the 'antithesis' articulate, to make it concrete, to make it more than merely verbal, to make it mean more than simply insisting on our occupying a separate suite in the same mansions of modernity, we must know the objective minds of paganism and of modernity" (ibid., 25–26). "The citizen of the kingdom of God, his selfhood tied in with the existing culture, if in his daily living he is to express his faith, must learn how in terms of the historical cultural product of his day to distinguish the *civ-*

itas dei from the other kingdoms. In other words, in order meaningfully and concretely to articulate the *civitas dei*, its citizen must learn to distinguish it from the other kingdoms as they, too, are culturally articulated; he must learn in and by means of the cultural product as this has come down to the present to discriminate between the kingdom of God and the worldly kingdoms" (Jellema, "Calvinism and Higher Education," 126–27).

19. Jellema, "Calvinism and Higher Education," 128.

20. Abraham Kuyper, *Lectures on Calvinism* (Tarrytown, N.Y.: Revell, n.d.), 89.

21. Brian Gerrish, *The Old Protestantism and the New* (Chicago: University of Chicago Press, 1982), 5.

Chapter 7: Teaching for Tomorrow Today

1. Alexander Schmemann, *For the Life of the World* (Crestwood, N.Y.: St. Vladimir's Seminary Press, 1973), 120.

2. John Calvin, *Institutes of the Christian Religion*, trans. Ford Lewis Battles (Philadelphia: Westminster Press, 1967), III, X, 2.

3. Abraham Kuyper, *Principles of Sacred Theology*, trans. J. Hendrik de Vries (Grand Rapids: Baker, 1980), 109.

4. Ibid., 111.

Chapter 11: Religion and the Schools

1. I discuss the concept of impartiality more fully in "Neutrality and Impartiality," in *Religion and Public Education*, ed. Theodore Sizer (Boston: Houghton Mifflin, 1967).

2. Compare the following passage from Justice William J. Brennan's opinion in the *Schempp* case: "It is implicit in the history and character of American public education that the public schools serve a uniquely public function: the training of American citizens in an atmosphere free of parochial, divisive, or separatist influences of any sort—an atmosphere in which children may assimilate a heritage common to all American groups and religions. . . . This is a heritage neither theistic nor atheistic, but simply civic and patriotic" (*Schempp v. School Dist. of Abington*, 374 U.S. 241–42 [1963]).

3. As to the desirability and feasibility of teaching about religion in a school system committed to affirmative impartiality, see "Neutrality and Impartiality."

4. Compare Brennan's concurring opinion in *Schempp:* "Nothing in the Establishment Clause forbids the application of legislation having purely secular ends in such a way as to alleviate burdens upon the free exercise of an individual's religious beliefs" (374 U.S. 295).

5. In addition to *Schempp*, see also these:

Court in *McCollum:* "To hold that a state cannot consistently with the First and Fourteenth Amendments utilize its public school system to aid any or all religious faiths or sects in the dissemination of their doctrines and ideals does not . . . manifest a governmental hostility to religion or religious teachings. A manifestation of such hostility would be at war with our national tradition as embodied in the First Amendments guaranty of the free exercise of religion" (*McCollum v. Board of Education*, 333 U.S. 211–12 [1948]).

Court in *Engel:* "It has been argued that to apply the Constitution in such a way as to prohibit state laws respecting an establishment of religious services in public schools is to indicate a hostility toward religion or toward prayer. Nothing, of course, could be more wrong. . . . It is neither sacrilegious nor anti-religious to say that each separate government in this country should stay out of the business of writing or sanctioning official prayers" (*Engel v. Vitale*, 370 U.S. 433–35 [1962]).

Chapter 12: Human Rights in Education: The Rights of Parents

1. G. Stanley Hall, "The Ideal School Based on Child Study," *The Forum* 32 (1901): 24.

2. The matter of the rights of groups and institutions is extremely complex, and here I shall forego saying anything on the matter other than my comments about the state.

3. Or that is how it *would* be if we fully respected the rights of parents. The truth is that in American society the public school teacher has a captive audience. He is not, like other professionals in our society, one who makes his services available to those who desire it, in competition with others offering similar services.

Chapter 13: The Schools We Deserve

1. "How Not to Fix the Schools," *Harper's* 272 (February 1986): 39–51.

2. Ibid., 43.

3. Ibid., 44.

4. Robert N. Bellah et al., *Habits of the Heart* (Berkeley: University of California Press, 1985).

5. Ibid., 38–40.

6. Ibid., 43. Compare this passage in ibid., 45: "Like the entrepreneur, the manager also has another life, divided among spouse, children, friends, community, and religious and other nonoccupational involvements. Here, in contrast to the manipulative, achievement-oriented practices of the workplace, another kind of personality is actualized, often within a social pattern that shows recognizable continuity with earlier American forms of family and community. But it is an outstanding feature of industrial life that these sectors have become radically discontinuous in the kinds of traits emphasized and the moral understanding that guides individuals within them. 'Public' and 'private' roles contrast sharply."

7. Ibid., 33.

8. Ibid., 34.

9. Ibid., 45–46.

10. Charles Taylor, *Hegel* (Cambridge: Cambridge University Press, 1975), 6–7.

11. Ibid., 7.

12. Alasdair MacIntyre, *After Virtue* (Notre Dame: University of Notre Dame Press, 1982).

13. Bellah et al., *Habits of the Heart*, 47–48.

14. Richard Rorty, "Postmodernist Bourgeois Liberalism," in *Hermeneutics and Praxis*, ed. R. Hollinger (Notre Dame: University of Notre Dame Press, 1985), 216–17.

15. Peter Berger, *The Sacred Canopy: Elements of a Sociological Theory of Religion* (Garden City, N.Y.: Doubleday, 1967), 132–33.

Chapter 14: Task and Invitation

1. Gerrish, *The Old Protestantism and the New;* Calvin, *Institutes of the Christian Religion*, I, XIV, 20, 22.

2. Ibid., III, X, 1.

3. Ibid., III, X, 2.

Chapter 15: Teaching for Gratitude

1. Gerrish, *The Old Protestantism and the New*, 200.

2. Calvin, *Institutes of the Christian Religion*, III, X, 2.

3. Ibid., III, 37.

4. Ibid., III, 38.

5. Ibid., III, II, 16.

6. Ibid., I, XIV, 21–22.

7. Ibid., I, XIV, 21.

8. Ibid., I, V, 2.

Bibliography

Audi, R., and N. P. Wolterstorff. *Religion in the Public Square: The Place of Religious Conviction in Political Debate*. Lanman, Md.: Rowman & Littlefield, 1997.

Hart, H., J. Van Der Hoeven, and N. P. Wolterstorff, eds. *Rationality in the Calvinian Tradition*. Lanham, Md.: University Press of America, 1983.

Plantinga, A., and N. P. Wolterstorff, eds. *Faith and Rationality: Reason and Belief in God*. Notre Dame: University of Notre Dame Press, 1983.

Wolterstorff, N. P. *Art in Action*. Grand Rapids: Eerdmans, 1980.

———. "Christian Higher Education in Reformed Perspective." *Lutheran Education* 134, no. 3 (1999): 129–40.

———. "Christianity and Social Justice." *Christian Scholars Review* 16, no. 3 (1987): 211–28.

———. *Divine Discourse*. Cambridge: Cambridge University Press, 1995.

———. *Educating for Responsible Action*. Grand Rapids: Eerdmans, 1980.

———. "Hearing the Cry." In *Women, Authority, and the Bible*, edited by A. Mickelson. Downers Grove, Ill.: InterVarsity Press, 1986.

———. "The Grace That Shaped My Life." In *Philosophers Who Believe: The Spiritual Journey of Eleven Leading Thinkers*, edited by Kelly James Clark. Downers Grove, Ill.: InterVarsity Press, 1993.

———. "Integration of Faith and Science—The Very Idea." *Journal of Psychology and Christianity* 3, no. 2 (1985): 12–19.

———. *John Locke and the Ethics of Belief*. Cambridge: Cambridge University Press, 1996.

289

————. *Keeping Faith: Talks for New Faculty*. Grand Rapids: Occasional Papers from Calvin College, 1989.

————. *Lament for a Son*. Grand Rapids: Eerdmans, 1987.

————. "Neutrality and Impartiality." In *Religion and Public Education*, edited by T. Sizer. Boston: Houghton Mifflin, 1967.

————. "On Christian Learning." In *Stained Glass*, edited by P. Marshall, S. Griffioen, and R. Mouw. Lanham, Md.: University Press of America, 1989.

————. "On the Idea of a Psychological Model of the Person Which Is Biblically Faithful." In *Christian Approaches to Learning Theory*. Vol. 2, *The Nature of the Learner*, edited by N. De Jong. Lanham, Md.: University Press of America, 1985.

————. *On Universals*. Chicago: University of Chicago Press, 1970.

————. *The Project of a Christian University in a Post-Modern Society*. Amsterdam: VU Boekhandel/Uitgeverij, 1988.

————. "Public Theology or Christian Learning." In *A Passion for God's Reign*, edited by M. Volf. Grand Rapids: Eerdmans, 1998.

————. *Reason within the Bounds of Religion*. Grand Rapids: Eerdmans, 1976.

————. "Should the Work of Our Hands Have Standing in the Christian College?" In *Keeping Faith: Embracing the Tensions in Christian Higher Education*, edited by R. A. Wells. Grand Rapids: Eerdmans, 1996.

————. "Teaching for Justice." In *Making Higher Education Christian: The History and Mission of Evangelical Colleges in America*, edited by J. Carpenter and K. Shipps. Grand Rapids: Eerdmans, 1987.

————. *Until Justice and Peace Embrace*. Grand Rapids: Eerdmans, 1983.

————. "Why Care about Justice?" In *Evangelicalism: Surviving Its Success*, vol. 2., edited by D. A. Fraser. St. Davids, Pa.: Eastern College Press, 1987.

————. *Works and Worlds of Art*. Oxford: Oxford University Press, 1980.

Index

291

Gloria Goris Stronks (Ed.D., Northern Illinois University) is an educational consultant and former professor of education at Calvin College in Grand Rapids, Michigan. She has authored or coauthored several books including *The Christian Middle School: An Ethos of Caring; A Vision with a Task: Christian Schooling for Responsive Discipleship; Assessment in Christian Higher Education: Rhetoric and Reality; Christian Teachers in Public Schools;* and *Reaching and Teaching Young Adolescents: Succeeding in Deeper Waters.*

Clarence W. Joldersma (Ph.D., University of Toronto) is associate professor of education at Calvin College in Grand Rapids, Michigan, where he teaches philosophy of education. He has written articles on topics that include social justice, pedagogy, public theology, and the nature of the mind.